THE DAILY STUDY BIBLE SERIES
REVISED EDITION

THE LETTERS TO THE
CORINTHIANS

THE LETTERS TO THE
CORINTHIANS

REVISED EDITION

Translated
with an Introduction and Interpretation
by
WILLIAM BARCLAY

WESTMINSTER JOHN KNOX PRESS
LOUISVILLE, KENTUCKY

Revised Edition
Copyright © 1975 William Barclay

First published by The Saint Andrew Press
Edinburgh, Scotland

First Edition, May, 1954

Second Edition, September, 1956

Published by Westminster John Knox Press
Louisville, Kentucky

PRINTED IN THE UNITED STATES OF AMERICA

19 20 21 22 23 24

Library of Congress Cataloging in Publication Data

Bible. N.T. Corinthians. English. Barclay. 1975.
The letters to the Corinthians.

(The Daily study Bible series. — Rev. ed.)
1. Bible. N.T. Corinthians — Commentaries. I. Barclay,
William, lecturer in the University of Glasgow.
II. Title. III. Series.
BS2673.B37   1975   227'.2'077   75-26563
ISBN 0-664-21308-1

GENERAL INTRODUCTION

The Daily Study Bible series has always had one aim—to convey the results of scholarship to the ordinary reader. A. S. Peake delighted in the saying that he was a "theological middleman", and I would be happy if the same could be said of me in regard to these volumes. And yet the primary aim of the series has never been academic. It could be summed up in the famous words of Richard of Chichester's prayer—to enable men and women "to know Jesus Christ more clearly, to love him more dearly, and to follow him more nearly".

It is all of twenty years since the first volume of *The Daily Study Bible* was published. The series was the brain-child of the late Rev. Andrew McCosh, M.A., S.T.M., the then Secretary and Manager of the Committee on Publications of the Church of Scotland, and of the late Rev. R. G. Macdonald, O.B.E., M.A., D.D., its Convener.

It is a great joy to me to know that all through the years *The Daily Study Bible* has been used at home and abroad, by minister, by missionary, by student and by layman, and that it has been translated into many different languages. Now, after so many printings, it has become necessary to renew the printer's type and the opportunity has been taken to restyle the books, to correct some errors in the text and to remove some references which have become outdated. At the same time, the Biblical quotations within the text have been changed to use the Revised Standard Version, but my own original translation of the New Testament passages has been retained at the beginning of each daily section.

There is one debt which I would be sadly lacking in courtesy if I did not acknowledge. The work of revision and correction has been done entirely by the Rev. James Martin, M.A., B.D., minister of High Carntyne Church, Glasgow. Had it not been for him this task would never have been undertaken, and it is impossible for me to thank him enough for the selfless toil he has put into the revision of these books.

It is my prayer that God may continue to use *The Daily Study Bible* to enable men better to understand His word.

Glasgow   WILLIAM BARCLAY

CONTENTS

CONTENTS

2 CORINTHIANS

A GENERAL INTRODUCTION
TO THE LETTERS OF PAUL

THE LETTERS OF PAUL

There is no more interesting body of documents in the New Testament than the letters of Paul. That is because of all forms of literature a letter is most personal. Demetrius, one of the old Greek literary critics, once wrote, "Every one reveals his own soul in his letters. In every other form of composition it is possible to discern the writer's character, but in none so clearly as the epistolary." (Demetrius, *On Style,* 227). It is just because he left us so many letters that we feel we know Paul so well. In them he opened his mind and heart to the folk he loved so much; and in them, to this day, we can see that great mind grappling with the problems of the early church, and feel that great heart throbbing with love for men, even when they were misguided and mistaken.

THE DIFFICULTY OF LETTERS

At the same time, there is often nothing so difficult to understand as a letter. Demetrius (*On Style,* 223) quotes a saying of Artemon, who edited the letters of Aristotle. Artemon said that a letter ought to be written in the same manner as a dialogue, because it was one of the two sides of a dialogue. In other words, to read a letter is like listening to one side of a telephone conversation. So when we read the letters of Paul we are often in a difficulty. We do not possess the letter which he was answering; we do not fully know the circumstances with which he was dealing; it is only from the letter itself that we can deduce the situation which prompted it. Before we can hope to understand fully any letter Paul wrote, we must try to reconstruct the situation which produced it.

THE ANCIENT LETTERS

It is a great pity that Paul's letters were ever called *epistles.* They are in the most literal sense *letters.* One of the great lights shed on the interpretation of the New Testament has been the discovery and the publication of the *papyri*. In the ancient world, *papyrus* was the substance on which most documents were written. It was composed of strips of the pith of a certain bulrush that grew on the banks of the Nile. These strips were laid one on top of the other to form a substance very like brown paper. The sands of the Egyptian desert were ideal for preservation, for papyrus, although very brittle, will last forever so long as moisture does not get at it. As a result, from the Egyptian rubbish heaps, archaeologists have rescued hundreds of documents, marriage contracts, legal agreements, government forms, and, most interesting of all, private letters. When we read these private letters we find that there was a pattern to which nearly all conformed; and we find that Paul's letters reproduce exactly that pattern. Here is one of these ancient letters. It is from a soldier, called Apion, to his father Epimachus. He is writing from Misenum to tell his father that he has arrived safely after a stormy passage.

"Apion sends heartiest greetings to his father and lord Epimachus. I pray above all that you are well and fit; and that things are going well with you and my sister and her daughter and my brother. I thank my Lord Serapis [his god] that he kept me safe when I was in peril on the sea. As soon as I got to Misenum I got my journey money from Caesar—three gold pieces. And things are going fine with me. So I beg you, my dear father, send me a line, first to let me know how you are, and then about my brothers, and thirdly, that I may kiss your hand, because you brought me up well, and because of that I hope, God willing, soon to be promoted. Give Capito my heartiest greetings, and my brothers and Serenilla and my friends. I sent you a little picture of myself painted by Euctemon. My military name is Antonius Maximus. I pray for your good health. Serenus sends good wishes, Agathos Daimon's boy, and Turbo, Gallonius's son." (G. Milligan, *Selections from the Greek Papyri,* 36).

Little did Apion think that we would be reading his letter to his father 1800 years after he had written it. It shows how little human nature changes. The lad is hoping for promotion quickly. Who will Serenilla be but the girl he left behind him? He sends the ancient equivalent of a photograph to the folk at home. Now that letter falls into certain sections. (i) There is a greeting. (ii) There is a prayer for the health of the recipients. (iii) There is a thanksgiving to the gods. (iv) There are the special contents. (v) Finally, there are the special salutations and the personal greetings. Practically every one of Paul's letters shows exactly the same sections, as we now demonstrate.

(i) *The Greeting: Romans* 1: 1; 1 *Corinthians* 1: 1; 2 *Corinthians* 1: 1; *Galatians* 1: 1; *Ephesians* 1: 1; *Philippians* 1: 1; *Colossians* 1: 1, 2; 1 *Thessalonians* 1: 1; 2 *Thessalonians* 1: 1.

(ii) *The Prayer:* in every case Paul prays for the grace of God on the people to whom he writes: *Romans* 1: 7; 1 *Corinthians* 1: 3; 2 *Corinthians* 1: 2; *Galatians* 1: 3; *Ephesians* 1: 2; *Philippians* 1: 3; *Colossians* 1: 2; 1 *Thessalonians* 1: 1; 2 *Thessalonians* 1: 2.

(iii) *The Thanksgiving: Romans* 1: 8; 1 *Corinthians* 1: 4; 2 *Corinthians* 1: 3; *Ephesians* 1: 3; *Philippians* 1: 3; 1 *Thessalonians* 1: 3; 2 *Thessalonians* 1: 3.

(iv) *The Special Contents:* the main body of the letters.

(v) *Special Salutations and Personal Greetings: Romans* 16; 1 *Corinthians* 16: 19; 2 *Corinthians* 13: 13; *Philippians* 4: 21, 22; *Colossians* 4: 12–15; 1 *Thessalonians* 5: 26.

When Paul wrote letters, he wrote them on the pattern which everyone used. Deissmann says of them, "They differ from the messages of the homely papyrus leaves of Egypt, not as letters but only as the letters of Paul." When we read Paul's letters we are not reading things which were meant to be academic exercises and theological treatises, but human documents written by a friend to his friends.

THE IMMEDIATE SITUATION

With a very few exceptions, all Paul's letters were written to meet an immediate situation and not treatises which he sat down to write in the peace and silence of his study. There was some threatening situation in Corinth, or Galatia, or Philippi, or Thessalonica, and he wrote a letter to meet it. He was not in the least thinking of us when he wrote, but solely of the people to whom he was writing. Deissmann writes, "Paul had no thought of adding a few fresh compositions to the already extant Jewish epistles; still less of enriching the sacred literature of his nation. . . . He had no presentiment of the place his words would occupy in universal history; not so much that they would be in existence in the next generation, far less that one day people would look at them as Holy Scripture." We must always remember that a thing need not be transient because it was written to meet an immediate situation. All the great love songs of the world were written for one person, but they live on for the whole of mankind. It is just because Paul's letters were written to meet a threatening danger or a clamant need that they still throb with life. And it is because human need and the human situation do not change that God speaks to us through them today.

THE SPOKEN WORD

One other thing we must note about these letters. Paul did what most people did in his day. He did not normally pen his own letters but dictated them to a secretary, and then added his own authenticating signature. (We actually know the name of one of the people who did the writing for him. In *Romans* 16: 22 Tertius, the secretary, slips in his own greeting before the letter draws to an end). In 1 *Corinthians* 16: 21 Paul says, "This is my own signature, my autograph, so that you can be sure this letter comes from me." (cp. *Colossians* 4: 18; 2 *Thessalonians* 3: 17.)

This explains a great deal. Sometimes Paul is hard to understand, because his sentences begin and never finish; his grammar breaks down and the construction becomes involved. We must not think of him sitting quietly at a desk, carefully polishing each sentence as he writes. We must think of him striding up and down some little room, pouring out a torrent of words, while his secretary races to get them down. When Paul composed his letters, he had in his mind's eye a vision of the folk to whom he was writing, and he was pouring out his heart to them in words that fell over each other in his eagerness to help.

INTRODUCTION TO THE LETTERS TO
THE CORINTHIANS

THE GREATNESS OF CORINTH

A glance at the map will show that Corinth was made for greatness. The southern part of Greece is very nearly an island. On the west the Corinthian Gulf deeply indents the land and on the east the Saronic Gulf. All that is left to join the two parts of Greece together is a little isthmus only four miles across. On that narrow neck of land Corinth stands. Such a position made it inevitable that it should be one of the greatest trading and commercial centres of the ancient world. All traffic from Athens and the north of Greece to Sparta and the Peloponnese had to be routed through Corinth, because it stood on the little neck of land that connected the two.

Not only did the north to south traffic of Greece pass through Corinth of necessity, by far the greater part of the east to west traffic of the Mediterranean passed through her from choice. The extreme southern tip of Greece was known as Cape Malea (now called Cape Matapan). It was dangerous, and to round Cape Malea had much the same sound as to round Cape Horn had in later times. The Greeks had two sayings which showed what they thought of it—"Let him who sails round Malea forget his home," and, "Let him who sails round Malea first make his will."

The consequence was that mariners followed one of two courses. They sailed up the Saronic Gulf, and, if their ships were small enough, dragged them out of the water, set them on rollers, hauled them across the isthmus, and re-launched them on the other side. The isthmus was actually called the *Diolkos,* the place of dragging across. The idea is the same as that which is contained in the Scottish place name *Tarbert*, which means a place where the land is so narrow that a boat can be dragged from loch to loch. If that course was not possible because the ship was too large, the cargo was disembarked, carried by porters across the isthmus, and re-embarked on another ship at the other side. This four mile journey across the isthmus, where the Corinth Canal now runs, saved a journey of two hundred and two miles round Cape Malea, the most dangerous cape in the Mediterranean.

It is easy to see how great a commercial city Corinth must have been. The north to south traffic of Greece had no alternative but to pass through her; by far the greater part of the east to west trade of the Mediterranean world chose to pass through her. Round Corinth there clustered three other towns, Lechaeum at the west end of the isthmus, Cenchrea at the east end and Schoenus just a short distance away. Farrar writes, "Objects of luxury soon found their way to the markets which were visited by every nation in the civilized world— Arabian balsam, Phoenician dates, Libyan ivory, Babylonian carpets, Cilician goats' hair, Lycaonian wool, Phrygian slaves."

Corinth, as Farrar calls her, was the Vanity Fair of the ancient world. Men called her The Bridge of Greece; one called her The Lounge of Greece. It has been said that if a man stands long enough in Piccadilly Circus he will in the end meet everyone in the country. Corinth was the Piccadilly Circus of the Mediterranean. To add to the concourse which came to it, Corinth was the place where the Isthmian Games were held, which were second only to the Olympics. Corinth was a rich and populous city with one of the greatest commercial trades in the ancient world.

THE WICKEDNESS OF CORINTH

There was another side to Corinth. She had a reputation for commercial prosperity, but she was also a byword for evil living. The very word *korinthiazesthai*, to live like a Corinthian, had become a part of the Greek language, and meant to live with drunken and immoral debauchery. The word actually penetrated to the English language, and, in Regency times, a Corinthian was one of the wealthy young bucks who lived in reckless and riotous living. Aelian, the late Greek writer, tells us that if ever a Corinthian was shown upon the stage in a

Greek play he was shown drunk. The very name Corinth was synonymous with debauchery and there was one source of evil in the city which was known all over the civilized world. Above the isthmus towered the hill of the Acropolis, and on it stood the great temple of Aphrodite, the goddess of love. To that temple there were attached one thousand priestesses who were sacred prostitutes, and in the evenings they descended from the Acropolis and plied their trade upon the streets of Corinth, until it became a Greek proverb, "It is not every man who can afford a journey to Corinth." In addition to these cruder sins, there flourished far more recondite vices, which had come in with the traders and the sailors from the ends of the earth, until Corinth became not only a synonym for wealth and luxury, drunkenness and debauchery, but also for filth.

THE HISTORY OF CORINTH

The history of Corinth falls into two parts. She was a very ancient city. Thucydides, the Greek historian, claims that it was in Corinth that the first triremes, the Greek battleships, were built. Legend has it that it was in Corinth that the *Argo* was built, the ship in which Jason sailed the seas, searching for the golden fleece. But in 146 B.C. disaster befell her. The Romans were engaged in conquering the world. When they sought to reduce Greece, Corinth was the leader of the opposition. But the Greeks could not stand against the disciplined Romans, and in 146 B.C. Lucius Mummius, the Roman general, captured Corinth and left her a desolate heap of ruins.

But any place with the geographical situation of Corinth could not remain a devastation. Almost exactly one hundred years later, in 46 B.C. Julius Caesar rebuilt her and she arose from her ruins. Now she became a Roman colony. More, she became a capital city, the metropolis of the Roman province of Achaea, which included practically all Greece.

In those days, which were the days of Paul, her population was very mixed. (i) There were the Roman veterans whom

Julius Caesar had settled there. When a Roman soldier had served his time, he was granted the citizenship and was then sent out to some newly-founded city and given a grant of land so that he might become a settler there. These Roman colonies were planted all over the world, and always the backbone of them was the contingent of veteran regular soldiers whose faithful service had won them the citizenship. (ii) When Corinth was rebuilt the merchants came back, for her situation still gave her commercial supremacy. (iii) There were many Jews among the population. The rebuilt city offered them commercial opportunities which they were not slow to take. (iv) There was a sprinkling of Phoenicians and Phrygians and people from the east, with their exotic customs and their hysterical ways. Farrar speaks of "this mongrel and heterogeneous population of Greek adventurers and Roman bourgeois, with a tainting infusion of Phoenicians; this mass of Jews, ex-soldiers, philosophers, merchants, sailors, freedmen, slaves, trades-people, hucksters and agents of every form of vice." He characterizes her as a colony "without aristocracy, without traditions and without well-established citizens."

Remember the background of Corinth, remember its name for wealth and luxury, for drunkenness and immorality and vice, and then read 1 *Corinthians* 6: 9, 10.

> Are you not aware that the unrighteous will not inherit the Kingdom of God? Make no mistake—neither fornicators, nor idolaters, nor adulterers, nor sensualists, nor homosexuals, nor thieves, nor rapacious men, nor drunkards, nor slanderers, nor robbers shall inherit the Kingdom of God—*and such were some of you.*

In this hotbed of vice, in the most unlikely place in all the Greek world, some of Paul's greatest work was done, and some of the mightiest triumphs of Christianity were won.

PAUL IN CORINTH

Paul stayed longer in Corinth than in any other city, with the single exception of Ephesus. He had left Macedonia with his life in peril and had crossed over to Athens. There he had had little success and had gone on to Corinth, and he remained there for eighteen months. We realize how little we really know of his work when we see that the whole story of that eighteen months is compressed by Luke into 17 verses (*Acts* 18: 1–17).

When Paul arrived in Corinth he took up residence with Aquila and Prisca. He preached in the synagogue with great success. With the arrival of Timothy and Silas from Macedonia, he redoubled his efforts, but the Jews were so stubbornly hostile that he had to leave the synagogue. He took up his residence with one Justus who lived next door to the synagogue. His most notable convert was Crispus, who was actually the ruler of the synagogue, and amongst the general public he had good success.

In the year A.D. 52 there came to Corinth as its new governor a Roman called Gallio. He was famous for his charm and gentleness. The Jews tried to take advantage of his newness and good nature and brought Paul to trial before him on a charge of teaching contrary to their law. But Gallio, with impartial Roman justice, refused to have anything to do with the case or to take any action. So Paul completed his work in Corinth and moved on to Syria.

THE CORRESPONDENCE WITH CORINTH

It was when he was in Ephesus in the year A.D. 55 that Paul, learning that things were not all well in Corinth, wrote to the church there. There is every possibility that the Corinthian correspondence as we have it is out of order. We must remember that it was not until A.D. 90 or thereby that Paul's correspondence was collected. In many churches it must have existed only on scraps of papyrus and the putting it together would be a problem: and it seems that, when the Corinthian letters were collected, they were not all discovered and were not arranged in the right order. Let us see if we can reconstruct what happened.

(i) There was a letter which preceded 1 *Corinthians*. In 1 *Corinthians* 5: 9 Paul writes, "I wrote you a letter not to associate with immoral men." This obviously refers to some previous letter. Some scholars believe that letter is lost without trace. Others think it is contained in 2 *Corinthians* 6: 14—7: 1. Certainly that passage suits what Paul said he wrote about. It occurs rather awkwardly in its context, and, if we take it out and read straight on from 2 *Corinthians* 6: 13 to 7: 2, we get excellent sense and connection. Scholars call this letter *The Previous Letter*. (In the original letters there were no chapter or verse divisions. The chapters were not divided up until the thirteenth century and the verses not till the sixteenth, and because of that the arranging of the collection of letters would be much more difficult).

(ii) News came to Paul from various sources of trouble at Corinth. (*a*) News came from those who were of the household of Chloe (1 *Corinthians* 1: 11). They brought news of the contentions with which the church was torn. (*b*) News came with the visit of Stephanas, Fortunatus and Achaicus to Ephesus. (1 *Corinthians* 16: 17). By personal contact they were able to fill up the gaps in Paul's information. (*c*) News came in a letter in which the Corinthian Church had asked Paul's guidance on various problems. In 1 *Corinthians* 7: 1 Paul begins, "Concerning the matters about which you wrote. . . ." In answer to all this information Paul wrote 1 *Corinthians* and despatched it to Corinth apparently by the hand of Timothy (1 *Corinthians* 4: 17).

(iii) The result of the letter was that things became worse than ever, and, although we have no direct record of it, we can deduce that Paul paid a personal visit to Corinth. In 2 *Corinthians* 12: 14 he writes, "The *third* time I am ready to come to you." In 2 *Corinthians* 13: 1, 2, he says again that he is coming to them for the *third* time. Now, if there was a *third* time, there must have been a *second* time. We have the record of only one visit, whose story is told in *Acts* 18: 1–17. We have no record at all of the second, but Corinth was only two or three days' sailing from Ephesus.

(iv) The visit did no good at all. Matters were only exacerbated and the result was an exceedingly severe letter.

We learn about that letter from certain passages in 2 *Corinthians*. In 2 *Corinthians* 2: 4 Paul writes, "I wrote to you out of much affliction and anguish of heart and with many tears." In 2 *Corinthians* 7: 8 he writes, "For even if I made you sorry with my letter, I do not regret it though I did regret it; for I see that that letter has grieved you, though only for a while." It was a letter which was the product of anguish of mind, a letter so severe that Paul was almost sorry that he ever sent it.

Scholars call this *The Severe Letter*. Have we got it? It obviously cannot be 1 *Corinthians*, because it is not a tear-stained and anguished letter. When Paul wrote it, it is clear enough that things were under control. Now if we read through 2 *Corinthians* we find an odd circumstance. In chapters 1 to 9 everything is made up, there is complete reconciliation and all are friends again; but at chapter 10 comes the strangest break. Chapters 10 to 13 are the most heart-broken cry Paul ever wrote. They show that he has been hurt and insulted as he never was before or afterwards by any church. His appearance, his speech, his apostleship, his honesty have all been under attack.

Most scholars believe that chapters 10 to 13 are the severe letter, and that they have become misplaced when Paul's letters were put together. If we want the real chronological course of Paul's correspondence with Corinth, we really ought to read chapters 10 to 13 of 2 *Corinthians before* chapters 1 to 9. We do know that this letter was sent off with Titus. (2 *Corinthians* 2: 13; 7: 13).

(v) Paul was worried about this letter. He could not wait until Titus came back with an answer, so he set out to meet him (2 *Corinthians* 2: 13; 7: 5, 13). Somewhere in Macedonia he met him and learned that all was well, and, probably at Philippi, he sat down and wrote 2 *Corinthians* chapter 1 to 9, the letter of reconciliation.

Stalker has said that the letters of Paul take the roof off the early churches and let us see what went on inside. Of none of them is that truer than the letters to Corinth. Here we see what "the care of all the churches" must have meant to

Paul. Here we see the heart-breaks and the joys. Here we see Paul, the shepherd of his flock, bearing the sorrows and the problems of his people on his heart.

THE CORINTHIAN CORRESPONDENCE

Before we read the letters in detail let us set down the progress of the Corinthian correspondence in tabular form.

(i) *The Previous Letter,* which *may* be contained in 2 *Corinthians* 6: 14—7: 1.

(ii) The arrival of Chloe's people, of Stephanas, Fortunatus and Achaicus, and of the letter to Paul from the Corinthian Church.

(iii) 1 *Corinthians* is written in reply and is despatched with Timothy.

(iv) The situation grows worse and Paul pays a personal visit to Corinth, which is so complete a failure that it almost breaks his heart.

(v) The consequence is *The Severe Letter,* which is almost certainly contained in 2 *Corinthians* 10–13, and which was despatched with Titus.

(vi) Unable to wait for an answer, Paul sets out to meet Titus. He meets him in Macedonia, learns that all is well and, probably from Philippi, writes 2 *Corinthians* 1–9, *The Letter of Reconciliation.*

The first four chapters of 1 *Corinthians* deal with the divided state of the Church of God at Corinth. Instead of being a unity in Christ it was split into sects and parties, who had attached themselves to the names of various leaders and teachers. It is Paul's teaching that these divisions had emerged because the Corinthians thought too much about human wisdom and knowledge and too little about the sheer grace of God. In fact, for all their so-called wisdom, they are really in a state of immaturity. They think that they are wise men, but really they are no better than babies.

1 CORINTHIANS

AN APOSTOLIC INTRODUCTION

1 *Corinthians* 1 : 1–3

> Paul, called by the will of God to be an apostle of Jesus Christ,
> and Sosthenes, our brother, write this letter to the Church of God
> which is at Corinth, to those who have been consecrated in Christ
> Jesus, to those who have been called to be God's dedicated people
> in the company of those who in every place call upon the name of
> our Lord Jesus—their Lord and ours. Grace be to you and peace
> from God, our Father, and from the Lord Jesus Christ.

IN the first ten verses of Paul's First Letter to the Corinthians
the name of Jesus Christ occurs no fewer than ten times. This
was going to be a difficult letter for it was going to deal with
a difficult situation, and in such a situation Paul's first and
repeated thought was of Jesus Christ. Sometimes in the Church
we try to deal with a difficult situation by means of a book
of laws and in the spirit of human justice; sometimes in our
own affairs we try to deal with a difficult situation in our
own mental and spiritual power. Paul did none of these things;
to his difficult situation he took Jesus Christ, and it was in the
light of the Cross of Christ and the love of Christ that he
sought to deal with it.

This introduction tells us about two things.

(i) It tells us something about the Church. Paul speaks of
The Church of God which is at Corinth. It was not the Church
of Corinth; it was the Church of God. To Paul, wherever
an individual congregation might be, it was a part of the one
Church of God. He would not have spoken of the Church of
Scotland or the Church of England; he would not have given
the Church a local designation; still less would he have
identified the congregation by the particular communion or
sect to which it belonged. To him the Church was the
Church of God. If we thought of the Church in that
way we might well remember more of the reality which unites
us and less of the local differences which divide us.

(ii) This passage tells us something about the individual Christian. Paul says three things about him.

(*a*) He is *consecrated in Jesus Christ.* The verb *to consecrate* (*hagiazo*) means to set a place apart for God, to make it holy, by the offering of a sacrifice upon it. The Christian has been consecrated to God by the sacrifice of Jesus Christ. To be a Christian is to be one for whom Christ died and to know it, and to realize that that sacrifice in a very special way makes us belong to God.

(*b*) He describes the Christians as *those who have been called to be God's dedicated people.* We have translated one single Greek word by this whole phrase. The word is *hagios,* which the Authorised Version translates *saints.* Nowadays that does not paint the right picture to us. *Hagios* describes a thing or a person that has been devoted to the possession and the service of God. It is the word by which to describe a temple or a sacrifice which has been marked out for God. Now, if a person has been marked out as specially belonging to God, he must show himself to be fit in life and in character for that service. That is how *hagios* comes to mean *holy, saintly.*

But the root idea of the word is *separation.* A person who is *hagios* is *different* from others because he has been separated from the ordinary run in order specially to belong to God. This was the adjective by which the Jews described themselves; they were the *hagios laos*, the holy people, the nation which was quite different from other peoples because they in a special way belonged to God and were set apart for his service. When Paul calls the Christian *hagios* he means that he is different from other men because he specially belongs to God and to God's service. And that difference is not to be marked by withdrawal from ordinary life, but by showing there a quality which will mark him out.

(*c*) Paul addresses his letter to those who have been called *in the company of those who in every place call upon the name of the Lord.* The Christian is called into a community whose boundaries include all earth and all heaven. It would be greatly to our good if sometimes we lifted our eyes beyond our own little circle and thought of ourselves as part of the Church of God which is as wide as the world.

(iii) This passage tells us something about Jesus Christ. Paul speaks of our Lord Jesus Christ, and then, as it were, he corrects himself and adds *their Lord and ours.* No man, no Church, has exclusive possession of Jesus Christ. He is our Lord but he is also the Lord of all men. It is the amazing wonder of Christianity that all men possess all the love of Jesus Christ, that "God loves each one of us as if there was only one of us to love."

THE NECESSITY OF THANKSGIVING

1 *Corinthians* 1 : 4-9

> Always I thank my God for you, for the grace of God which has been given to you in Christ Jesus. I have good reason to do so, because in him you have been enriched in everything, in every form of speech and in every form of knowledge, inasmuch as what we promised you that Christ could do for his people has been proved to be true in you. The result is that there is no spiritual gift in which you lag behind, while you eagerly wait for the appearing of our Lord Jesus Christ, who will keep you secure right to the end so that no one will be able to impeach you in the Day of our Lord Jesus Christ. You can rely on God, by whom you were called to share the fellowship of his Son, Jesus Christ our Lord.

In this passage of thanksgiving three things stand out.

(i) There is the promise which came true. When Paul preached Christianity to the Corinthians he told them that Christ could do certain things for them, and now he proudly claims that all that he pledged that Christ could do has come true. A missionary told one of the ancient Pictish kings, "If you will accept Christ, you will find wonder upon wonder—and every one of them true." In the last analysis we cannot argue a man into Christianity; we can only say to him, "Try it and see what happens," in the certainty that, if he does, the claims we make for it will all come true.

(ii) There is the gift which has been given. Paul here uses a favourite word of his. It is *charisma*, which means a gift freely given to a man, a gift which he did not deserve and which he could never by himself have earned. This gift of God, as Paul saw it, comes in two ways.

(*a*) Salvation is the *charisma* of God. To enter into a right relationship with God is something which a man could never achieve himself. It is an unearned gift, coming from the sheer generosity of the love of God. (cp. *Romans* 6: 23).

(*b*) It gives a man whatever special gifts he may possess and whatever special equipment he may have for life. (1 *Corinthians* 12: 4–10; 1 *Timothy* 4: 14; 1 *Peter* 4: 10). If a man has the gift of speech or the gift of healing, if he has the gift of music or of any art, if he has a craftsman's gifts upon his hands, all these are gifts from God. If we fully realized that, it would bring a new atmosphere and character into life. Such skills as we possess are not our own achievement, they are gifts from God, and, therefore, they are held in trust. They are not to be used as *we* want to use them but as *God* wants us to use them; not for our profit or prestige but for the glory of God and the good of men.

(iii) There is the ultimate end. In the Old Testament the phrase, *The Day of the Lord*, keeps recurring. It was the day when the Jews expected God to break directly into history, the day when the old world would be wiped out and the new world born, the day when all men would be judged. The Christians took over this idea, only they took *The Day of the Lord* in the sense of *The Day of the Lord Jesus*, and regarded it as the day on which Jesus would come back in all his power and glory.

That indeed would be a day of judgment. Cædmon, the old English poet, drew a picture in one of his poems about the day of judgment. He imagined the Cross set in the midst of the world; and from the Cross there streamed a strange light which had a penetrating X-ray quality about it and stripped the disguises from things and showed them as they were. It is Paul's belief that when the ultimate judgment comes the man who is in Christ can meet even it unafraid because he will be clothed not in his own merits but in the merits of Christ so that none will be able to impeach him.

A DIVIDED CHURCH

1 *Corinthians* 1: 10–17

> Brothers, I urge you through the name of our Lord Jesus Christ that you should make up your differences and that you should see to it that there may be no divisions among you, but that you should be knit together in the same mind and the same opinion. Brothers, it has become all too clear to me, from information that I have received from members of Chloe's household, that there are outbreaks of strife amongst you. What I mean is this—each of you is saying, "I belong to Paul; I belong to Apollos; I belong to Cephas; I belong to Christ." Has Christ been partitioned up? Was it Paul's name into which you were baptized? As things have turned out, I thank God that I baptized none of you, except Crispus and Gaius, so that no one can say you were baptized into my name. Now that I think of it, I baptized the household of Stephanas too. For the rest, I do not know if I baptized anyone else, for Christ did not send me to baptize but to proclaim the good news, and that not with wisdom of speech, lest the Cross of Christ should be emptied of its effectiveness.

PAUL begins the task of mending the situation which had arisen in the Church at Corinth. He was writing from Ephesus. Christian slaves who belonged to the establishment of a lady called Chloe had had occasion to visit Corinth and they had come back with a sorry tale of dissension and disunity.

Twice Paul addresses the Corinthians as *brothers*. As Beza, the old commentator said, "In that word too there lies hidden an argument." By the very use of the word Paul does two things. First, he softens the rebuke which is given, not as from a schoolmaster with a rod, but as from one who has no other emotion than love. Second, it should have shown them how wrong their dissensions and divisions were. They were brothers and they should have lived in brotherly love.

In trying to bring them together Paul uses two interesting phrases. He bids them *to make up their differences*. The phrase he uses is the regular one used of two hostile parties reaching agreement. He wishes them to be *knit together*, a medical word used of knitting together bones that have been fractured or joining together a joint that has been dislocated. The disunion is unnatural and must be cured for the sake of the health and efficiency of the body of the Church.

Paul identifies four parties in the Church at Corinth. They have not broken away from the Church; the divisions are as yet within it. The word he uses to describe them is *schismata*, which is the word for *rents in a garment*. The Corinthian Church is in danger of becoming as unsightly as a torn garment. It is to be noted that the great figures of the Church who are named, Paul and Cephas and Apollos, had nothing to do with these divisions. There were no dissensions between them. Without their knowledge and without their consent their names had been appropriated by these Corinthian factions. It not infrequently happens that a man's so-called supporters are a bigger problem than his open enemies. Let us look at these parties and see if we can find out what they were standing for.

(i) There were those who claimed to belong to *Paul*. No doubt this was mainly a Gentile party. Paul had always preached the gospel of Christian freedom and the end of the law. It is most likely that this party were attempting to turn liberty into licence and using their new found Christianity as an excuse to do as they liked. Bultmann has said that the Christian indicative always brings the Christian imperative. They had forgotten that the indicative of the good news brought the imperative of the Christian ethic. They had forgotten that they were saved, not to be free to sin, but to be free not to sin.

(ii) There was the party who claimed to belong to *Apollos*. There is a brief character sketch of Apollos in *Acts* 18: 24. He was a Jew from Alexandria, an eloquent man and well versed in the scriptures. Alexandria was the centre of intellectual activity. It was there that scholars had made a science of allegorizing the scriptures and finding the most recondite meanings in the simplest passages. Here is an example of the kind of thing they did. The Epistle of Barnabas, an Alexandrian work, argues from a comparison of *Genesis* 14:14 and 18:23 that Abraham had a household of 318 people whom he circumcised. The Greek for 18—the Greeks used letters as symbols for numbers—is *iota* followed by *eta*, which are the first two letters of the name *Jesus*; and the Greek for 300 is the letter *tau*, which is the shape of the Cross; therefore this old incident is a foretelling of the crucifixion of Jesus on his Cross! Alexandrian learning was full of that kind of thing. Further, the Alexandrians were enthusiasts for literary graces. They were in fact the people who *intellectualized* Christianity. Those who claimed to belong to Apollos were, no doubt, the intellectuals who were fast turning Christianity into a philosophy rather than a religion.

(iii) There were those who claimed to belong to *Cephas*. Cephas is the Jewish form of Peter's name. These were most likely Jews; and they sought to teach that a man must still observe the Jewish law. They were legalists who exalted law, and, by so doing, belittled grace.

(iv) There were those who claimed to belong to *Christ*. This may be one of two things. (*a*) There was absolutely no punctuation in Greek manuscripts and no space whatever between the words. This may well not describe a party at all. It may be the comment of Paul himself. Perhaps we ought to punctuate like this: "I am of Paul; I am of Apollos; I am of Cephas—but *I* belong to Christ." It may well be that this is Paul's own comment on the whole wretched situation. (*b*) If that is not so and this does describe a party, they must have been a small and rigid sect who claimed that they were the only true Christians in Corinth. Their real fault was not in saying that they belonged to Christ, but in acting as if Christ belonged to them. It may well describe a little, intolerant, self-righteous group.

It is not to be thought that Paul is belittling baptism. The people he did baptize were very special converts. Stephanas was probably the first convert of all (1 *Corinthians* 16: 15); Crispus had once been no less than the ruler of the Jewish synagogue at Corinth (*Acts* 18: 8); Gaius had probably been Paul's host (*Romans* 16: 23). The point is this—baptism was *into the name of Jesus*.

That phrase in Greek implies the closest possible connection. To give money into a man's name was to pay it into his account. To sell a slave into a man's name was to give that slave into his undisputed possession. A soldier swore loyalty into the name of Caesar; he belonged absolutely to the Emperor. *Into the name of* implied utter possession. In Christianity it implied even more; it implied that the Christian was not only possessed by Christ but was in some strange way identified with him. All that Paul is saying is, "I am glad that I was so busy preaching, because if I had baptized it would have given some of you the excuse to say that you were baptized into my possession instead of into Christ's." He is not making little of baptism; he is simply glad that no act of his could be misconstrued as annexing men for himself and not for Christ.

It was Paul's claim that he set before men the Cross of Christ in its simplest terms. To decorate the story of the Cross with rhetoric and cleverness would have been to make men think more of the language than of the facts, more of the speaker than of the message. It was Paul's aim to set before men, not himself, but Christ in all his lonely grandeur.

A STUMBLING-BLOCK TO THE JEWS AND FOOLISHNESS TO THE GREEKS

1 *Corinthians* 1: 18–25

For the story of the Cross is foolishness to those who are on the way to destruction, but it is the power of God to those who are on the way to salvation. For it stands written, "I will wipe out the wisdom of the wise and I will bring to nothing the cleverness of the clever." Where is the wise? Where is the expert in the law? Where is the man who debates about this world's wisdom? Did not God render foolish the wisdom of this world? For when, in God's wisdom, the world for all its wisdom did not know God, it pleased God to save those who believe by, what men would call, the foolishness of the Christian message. For the Jews ask for signs and the Greeks search for wisdom, but we proclaim Christ upon his Cross; to the Jews a stumbling-block, to the Greeks a thing of foolishness; but to those who have been called, both Jews and Greeks, Christ the power of God and the wisdom of God, for the foolishness of God is wiser than men, and the weakness of God is stronger than men.

BOTH to the cultured Greek and to the pious Jew the story that Christianity had to tell sounded like the sheerest folly. Paul begins by making free use of two quotations from Isaiah (*Isaiah* 29: 14; 33: 18) to show how mere human wisdom is bound to fail. He cites the undeniable fact that for all its wisdom the world had never found God and was still blindly and gropingly seeking him. That very search was designed by God to show men their own helplessness and so to prepare the way for the acceptance of him who is the one true way.

What then was this Christian message? If we study the four great sermons in the Book of Acts (*Acts* 2: 14–39; 3: 12–26; 4: 8–12; 10: 36–43) we find that there are certain constant elements in the Christian preaching. (i) There is the claim that the great promised time of God has come. (ii) There is a summary of the life, death and resurrection of Jesus. (iii) There is a claim that all this was the fulfilment of prophecy. (iv) There is the assertion that Jesus will come again. (v) There is an urgent invitation to men to repent and receive the promised gift of the Holy Spirit.

(i) To the *Jews* that message was a stumbling-block. There were two reasons.

(*a*) To them it was incredible that one who had ended life upon a cross could possibly be God's Chosen One. They pointed to their own law which unmistakably said, "He that is hanged is accursed by God." (*Deuteronomy* 21: 23). To the Jew the fact of the crucifixion, so far from proving that Jesus was the Son of God, disproved it finally. It may seem

A2

extraordinary, but even with *Isaiah* 53 before their eyes, the Jews had never dreamed of a suffering Messiah. The Cross to the Jew was and is an insuperable barrier to belief in Jesus.

(*b*) The Jew sought for signs. When the golden age of God came he looked for startling happenings. This very time during which Paul was writing produced a crop of false Messiahs, and all of them had beguiled the people into accepting them by the promise of wonders. In A.D. 45 a man called Theudas had emerged. He had persuaded thousands of the people to abandon their homes and follow him out to the Jordan, by promising that, at his word of command, the Jordan would divide and he would lead them dryshod across. In A.D. 54 a man from Egypt arrived in Jerusalem, claiming to be the Prophet. He persuaded thirty thousand people to follow him out to the Mount of Olives by promising that at his word of command the walls of Jerusalem would fall down. That was the kind of thing that the Jews were looking for. In Jesus they saw one who was meek and lowly, one who deliberately avoided the spectacular, one who served and who ended on a Cross—and it seemed to them an impossible picture of the Chosen One of God.

(ii) To the *Greeks* the message was foolishness. Again there were two reasons.

(*a*) To the Greek idea the first characteristic of God was *apatheia*. That word means more than *apathy*; it means *total inability to feel*. The Greeks argued that if God can feel joy or sorrow or anger or grief it means that some man has for that moment influenced God and is therefore greater than he. So, they went on to argue, it follows that God must be incapable of all feeling so that none may ever affect him. A God who suffered was to the Greeks a contradiction in terms.

They went further. Plutarch declared that it was an insult to God to involve him in human affairs. God of necessity was utterly detached. The very idea of *incarnation*, of God becoming a man, was revolting to the Greek mind. Augustine, who was a very great scholar long before he became a Christian, could say that in the Greek philosophers he found a parallel to almost all the teaching of Christianity; but one thing, he said, he never found, "The Word became flesh and dwelt among us." Celsus, who attacked the Christians with such vigour towards the end of the second century A.D., wrote, "God is good and beautiful and happy and is in that which is most beautiful and best. If then 'He descends to men' it involves change for him, and change from good to bad, from beautiful to ugly, from happiness to unhappiness, from what is best to what is worst. Who would choose such a change? For mortality it is only nature to alter and be changed; but for the immortal to abide the same forever. God would never accept such a change." To the thinking Greek the incarnation was a total impossibility. To people who thought like that it was incredible that one who had suffered as Jesus had suffered could possibly be the Son of God.

(*b*) The Greek sought wisdom. Originally the Greek word *sophist* meant *a wise man* in the good sense; but it came to mean a man with a clever mind and cunning tongue, a mental acrobat, a man who with glittering and persuasive rhetoric could make the worse appear the better reason. It meant a man who would spend endless hours discussing hair-splitting trifles, a man who had no real interest in solutions but who simply gloried in the stimulus of "the mental hike." Dio Chrysostom describes the Greek wise men. "They croak like frogs in a marsh; they are the most wretched of men, because, though ignorant, they think themselves wise; they are like peacocks, showing off their reputation and the number of their pupils as peacocks do their tails."

It is impossible to exaggerate the almost fantastic mastery that the silver-tongued rhetorician held in Greece. Plutarch says, "They made their voices sweet with musical cadences and modulations of tone and echoed resonances." They thought not of what they were saying, but of how they were saying it. Their thought might be poisonous so long as it was enveloped in honeyed words. Philostratus tells us that Adrian, the sophist, had such a reputation in Rome, that when his messenger appeared with a notice that he was to lecture, the senate emptied and even the people at the games abandoned them to flock to hear him.

Dio Chrysostom draws a picture of these so-called wise men and their competitions in Corinth itself at the Isthmian games. "You might hear many poor wretches of sophists, shouting and abusing each other, and their disciples, as they call them, squabbling; and many writers of books reading their stupid compositions, and many poets singing their poems, and many jugglers exhibiting their marvels, and many sooth-sayers giving the meaning of prodigies, and ten thousand rhetoricians twisting lawsuits, and no small number of traders driving their several trades." The Greeks were intoxicated with fine words; and to them the Christian preacher with his blunt message seemed a crude and uncultured figure, to be laughed at and ridiculed rather than to be listened to and respected.

It looked as if the Christian message had little chance of success against the background of Jewish or Greek life; but, as Paul said, "What looks like God's foolishness is wiser than men's wisdom; and what looks like God's weakness is stronger than men's strength."

THE GLORY OF THE SHAME

1 Corinthians 1: 26–31

Brothers, just look at the way in which you have been called. You can see at once that not many wise men—by human standards—not many powerful men, not many high-born men have been called. But God has chosen the foolish things of the world to put to shame the wise men; and God has chosen the weak things of the world to put to shame the strong things; and God has chosen the ignoble and the despised things of the world, yes, and the things which are not, to bring to nothing the things which are; and he did this so that no human being might be able to boast in the sight of God. It is through him that we are in Christ Jesus, who, for us, by God, was made wisdom and righteousness and consecration and deliverance, so that what stands written might come true in us. Let him who boasts, boast in the Lord.

PAUL glories in the fact that, for the most part, the Church was composed of the simplest and the humblest people. We must never think that the early Church was entirely composed of slaves. Even in the New Testament we see that people from the highest ranks of society were becoming Christians. There was Dionysius at Athens (*Acts* 17: 34); Sergius Paulus, the proconsul of Crete (*Acts* 13: 6–12); the noble ladies at Thessalonica and Beroea (*Acts* 17: 4, 12); Erastus, the city treasurer, probably of Corinth (*Romans* 16: 23). In the time of Nero, Pomponia Graecina, the wife of Plautius, the conqueror of Britain, was martyred for her Christianity. In the time of Domitian, in the latter half of the first century, Flavius Clemens, the cousin of the Emperor himself, was martyred as a Christian. Towards the end of the second century Pliny, the governor of Bithynia, wrote to Trajan the Emperor, saying that the Christians came from every rank in society. But it remains true that the great mass of Christians were simple and humble folk.

Somewhere about the year A.D. 178 Celsus wrote one of the bitterest attacks upon Christianity that was ever written. It was precisely this appeal of Christianity to the common people that he ridiculed. He declared that the Christian point of view was, "Let no cultured person draw near, none wise, none sensible; for all that kind of thing we count evil; but if any man is ignorant, if any is wanting in sense and culture, if any is a fool let him come boldly." Of the Christians he wrote, "We see them in their own houses, wool dressers, cobblers and fullers, the most uneducated and vulgar persons." He said that the Christians were "like a swarm of bats—or ants creeping out of their nests—or frogs holding a symposium round a swamp—or worms in conventicle in a corner of mud."

It was precisely this that was the glory of Christianity. In the Empire there were sixty million slaves. In the eyes of the law a slave was a "living tool," a thing and not a person

at all. A master could fling out an old slave as he could
fling out an old spade or hoe. He could amuse himself by
torturing his slaves; he could even kill them. For them there
was no such thing as marriage; even their children belonged
to the master, as the lambs of the fold belonged not to the
sheep but to the shepherd. Christianity made people who
were things into real men and women, more, into sons and
daughters of God; it gave those who had no respect, their
self-respect; it gave those who had no life, life eternal; it told
men that, even if they did not matter to other men, they still
mattered intensely to God. It told men who, in the eyes of
the world were worthless, that, in the eyes of God they were
worth the death of his only Son. Christianity was, and still is,
the most uplifting thing in the whole universe.

The quotation with which Paul finishes this passage is from
Jeremiah 9: 23, 24. As Bultmann put it, the one basic sin is
self-assertion, or the *desire for recognition.* It is only when we
realize that we can do nothing and that God can and will do
everything that real religion begins. It is the amazing fact of
life that it is the people who realize their own weakness and
their own lack of wisdom, who in the end are strong and wise.
It is the fact of experience that the man who thinks that he can
take on life all by himself is certain in the end to make
shipwreck.

We must note the four great things which Paul insists
Christ is for us.

(i) He is *wisdom.* It is only in following him that we walk
aright and only in listening to him that we hear the truth.
He is the expert in life.

(ii) He is *righteousness.* In the writings of Paul *righteousness*
always means *a right relationship with God.* Of our own efforts
we can never achieve that. It is ours only by realizing through
Jesus Christ that it comes not from what we can do for God,
but from what he has done for us.

(iii) He is *consecration.* It is only in the presence of Christ
that life can be what it ought to be. Epicurus used to tell his
disciples, "Live as if Epicurus always saw you." There is no

"as if" about our relationship to Christ. The Christian walks with him and only in that company can a man keep his garments unspotted from the world.

(iv) He is *deliverance*. Diogenes used to complain that men flocked to the oculist and to the dentist but never to the man (he meant the philosopher) who could cure their souls. Jesus Christ can deliver a man from past sin, from present helplessness, and from future fear. He is the emancipator from slavery to self and to sin.

THE PROCLAMATION AND THE POWER

1 *Corinthians* 2: 1–5

> So, brothers, when I came to you, I did not come announcing God's secret to you with any outstanding gifts of rhetoric or wisdom, for it was my deliberate decision to know nothing among you except Jesus Christ, and him upon his Cross. So I was with you in weakness and in diffidence and in much nervousness. My story and my proclamation were not made with persuasive words of wisdom; it was by the Spirit and by power that they were unanswerably demonstrated to be true, so that your faith should not depend on the wisdom of men, but on the power of God.

PAUL remembers back to the time when first he came to Corinth, and three things stand out.

(i) He came speaking in *simplicity*. It is worth noting that Paul had come to Corinth from Athens. It was at Athens that, for the only time in his life, as far as we know, he had attempted to reduce Christianity to philosophic terms. There, on Mars' Hill, he had met the philosophers and had tried to speak in their own language (*Acts* 17: 22–31); and it was there that he had one of his very few failures. His sermon in terms of philosophy had had very little effect (*Acts* 17: 32–34). It would almost seem that he had said to himself, "Never again! From henceforth I will tell the story of Jesus in utter simplicity. I will never again try to wrap it up in human

categories. I will know nothing but Jesus Christ, and him
upon his Cross."

It is true that the sheer unadorned story of the life of
Jesus has in it a unique power to move the hearts of men.
Dr. James Stewart quotes an example. The Christian missionaries had come to the court of Clovis, the king of the
Franks. They told the story of the Cross, and, as they did,
the hand of the old king stole to his sword hilt. "If I and my
Franks had been there," he said, "we would have stormed
Calvary and rescued him from his enemies." When we deal
with ordinary, untechnical people, a vivid, factual picture
has a power that a close knit argument lacks. For most
people, the way to the recesses of a man's inmost being
lies, not through his mind, but through his heart.

(ii) He came speaking in *fear*. Here we have to be careful
to understand. It was not fear for his own safety; still less
was it that he was ashamed of the gospel that he was
preaching. It was what has been called "the trembling anxiety
to perform a duty." The very phrase which he uses here of
himself Paul also uses of the way in which conscientious
slaves should serve and obey their masters. (*Ephesians* 6: 5).
It is not the man who approaches a great task without a
tremor who does it really well. The really great actor is he
who is wrought up before the performance; the really effective
preacher is he whose heart beats faster while he waits to
speak. The man who has no nervousness, no tension, in any
task, may give an efficient performance; but it is the man
who has this trembling anxiety who can produce an effect
which artistry alone can never achieve.

(iii) He came with results and not with words alone. The
result of Paul's preaching was that things happened. He says
that his preaching was unanswerably demonstrated to be true
by the Spirit and by power. The word he uses is the word for
the most stringent possible proof, the kind against which
there can be no argument. What was it? It was the proof
of changed lives. Something re-creating had entered into the
polluted society of Corinth.

John Hutton used to tell a story with gusto. A man who had been a reprobate and a drunkard was captured by Christ. His workmates used to try to shake him and say, "Surely a sensible man like you cannot believe in the miracles that the Bible tells about. You cannot, for instance, believe that this Jesus of yours turned water into wine." "Whether he turned water into wine or not," said the man, "I do not know; but in my own house I have seen him turn beer into furniture."

No one can argue against the proof of a changed life. It is our weakness that too often we have tried to talk men into Christianity instead of, in our own lives, showing them Christ. "A saint," as someone said, "is someone in whom Christ lives again."

THE WISDOM WHICH IS FROM GOD

1 *Corinthians* 2: 6–9

> True, we speak wisdom among those who are mature—but it is a wisdom which does not belong to this world, nor to the rulers of this world whose extinction is inevitable. But we speak the wisdom of God in a way that only he who is initiated into Christianity can understand, a wisdom which up to now has been kept hidden, a wisdom which God fore-ordained before time for our eternal glory, a wisdom which none of the leaders of this world knew; for if they had known it, they would not have crucified the Lord of glory; but as it stands written, "Things which eye has not seen, which ear has not heard and which have not entered into the heart of man, all these God has prepared for them that love him."

THIS passage introduces us to a distinction between different kinds of Christian instruction and different stages of the Christian life. In the early Church there was a quite clear distinction between two kinds of instruction. (i) There was what was called *Kerygma*. *Kerygma* means *a herald's announcement from a king;* and this was the plain announcement of the basic facts of Christianity, the announcement of the facts of the life, death and resurrection of Jesus and his coming again. (ii) There was what was called *Didache. Didache* means *teaching;* and this was the explanation of the meaning of the facts which had already been announced. Obviously it is a second stage for those who have already received *kerygma.*

That is what Paul is getting at here. So far he has been talking about Jesus Christ and him crucified; that was the basic announcement of Christianity; but, he goes on to say, we do not stop there; Christian instruction goes on to teach not only the facts but the meaning of the facts. Paul says that this is done amongst those who are *teleioi.* The Authorised Version translates that word as *perfect.* That is certainly one of its meanings; but it is not appropriate here. *Teleios* has a physical sense; it describes an animal or a person who has reached the height of his physical development. It has a mental sense. Pythagoras divided his disciples into those who were babes and those who were *teleioi.* That is to say it describes a person who is a mature student. That is the translation given in the Revised Standard version, and that is the sense in which Paul uses it here. He says, "Out in the streets, and to those who have just newly come into the Church, we talk about the basic elements of Christianity; but when people are a little more mature we give them deeper teaching about what these basic facts mean." It is not that Paul is hinting at a kind of caste distinction between Christians; it is a difference of the stages at which they are. The tragedy so often is that people are content to remain at the elementary stage when they should be going on strenuously to think things out for themselves.

Paul uses a word here which has a technical sense. The Authorised Version has it, "We speak the wisdom of God *in a mystery."* The Greek word *musterion* means something whose meaning is hidden from those who have not been initiated, but crystal clear to those who have. It would describe a ceremony carried out in some society whose meaning was quite clear to the members of the society, but unintelligible to the outsider. What Paul is saying is, "We go on to explain things which only the man who has already given his heart to Christ can understand."

He insists that this special teaching is not the product of the intellectual activity of men; it is the gift of God and it came into the world with Jesus Christ. All our discoveries are not so much what our minds have found out as what God has told us. This by no means frees us from the responsibility of human effort. Only the student who works can make himself fit to receive the real riches of the mind of a great teacher. It is so with us and God. The more we strive to understand, the more God can tell us; and there is no limit to this process, because the riches of God are unsearchable.

SPIRITUAL THINGS TO SPIRITUAL MEN

1 *Corinthians* 2: 10–16

> But God revealed it through his Spirit, for the Spirit explores all things, even the deep things of God. For what man knows the things of the man unless the spirit of the man which is in him? So no one ever knew the things of God except the Spirit of God. It is not the spirit of the world that we have received, but the Spirit which comes from God, so that we may know the things given to us by the grace of God. The things we speak we do not speak in words taught by human wisdom, but in words taught by the Spirit, interpreting spiritual things to spiritual people. A man who has no life but physical life cannot understand the things of the Spirit of God. To him they are foolishness and he cannot understand them, because it takes the Spirit to discern them. But a spiritual man exercises his judgment on the value of all things, but he himself is under no man's judgment. For who ever understood the mind of the Lord so as to be able to instruct him? But we have the mind of Christ.

THERE are certain very basic things in this passage.

(i) Paul lays down that the only person who can tell us about God is the Spirit of God. He uses a human analogy. There are feelings which are so personal, things which are so private, experiences which are so intimate that no one knows them except a man's own spirit. Paul argues that the same is true of God. There are deep and intimate things in him which only his Spirit knows; and that Spirit is the only person who can lead us into really intimate knowledge of God.

(ii) Even then it is not every man who can understand these things. Paul speaks about interpreting spiritual things to spiritual people. He distinguishes two kinds of men. (*a*) There are those who are *pneumatikoi*. *Pneuma* is the word for Spirit; and the man who is *pneumatikos* is the man who is sensitive to the Spirit and whose life is guided by the Spirit. (*b*) There is the man who is *psuchikos*. *Psuche* in Greek is often translated *soul;* but that is not its real meaning. It is the *principle of physical life*. Everything which is alive has *psuche;* a dog, a cat, any animal has *psuche,* but it has not got *pneuma*. *Psuche* is that physical life which a man shares with every living thing; but *pneuma* is that which makes a man different from the rest of creation and kin to God.

So in verse 14 Paul speaks of the man who is *psuchikos*. He is the man who lives as if there was nothing beyond physical life and there were no needs other than material needs, whose values are all physical and material. A man like that cannot understand spiritual things. A man who thinks that nothing is more important than the satisfaction of the sex urge cannot understand the meaning of chastity; a man who ranks the amassing of material things as the supreme end of life cannot understand generosity; and a man who has never a thought beyond this world cannot understand the things of God. To him they look mere foolishness. No man need be like this; but if he stifles "the immortal longings" that are in his soul he may make himself like this so that the Spirit of God will speak and he will not hear.

It is easy to become so involved in the world that there exists nothing beyond it. We must pray to have the mind of Christ, for only when he dwells within us are we safe from the encroaching invasion of the demands of material things.

THE SUPREME IMPORTANCE OF GOD

1 *Corinthians* 3: 1–9

> And I, brothers, could not talk to you as I would to spiritual men, but I had to talk to you as to those who had not yet got beyond merely human things, as to infants in Christ. I gave you milk to drink, not solid food. But now not even yet can you digest solid food, because you are still under the sway of human passions. Where there is envy and strife among you, are you not under the sway of human passions and is not your behaviour on a purely human level? For when anyone says, "I belong to Paul," and, "I belong to Apollos," are you not acting like merely human creatures? What then is Apollos? And what is Paul? They are only servants through whom you believed, and what success each of them had was the gift of God. It was I who planted; it was Apollos who watered; but it was God who made the seed grow. So that neither he who plants nor he who waters is anything; but God who made the seed grow is everything. He who plants and he who waters are in the same category. Each will receive his own reward according to his own labour. We are fellow-workers and we both belong to God; you are God's husbandry; you are God's building.

PAUL has just been talking about the difference between the man who is spiritual (*pneumatikos*), and who therefore can understand spiritual truths, and the man who is *psuchikos*, whose interests and aims do not go beyond physical life and who is therefore unable to grasp spiritual truth. He now accuses the Corinthians of being still at the physical stage. But he uses two new words to describe them.

In verse 1 he calls them *sarkinoi*. This word comes from *sarx* which means *flesh* and is so common in Paul. Now all Greek adjectives ending in *-inos* mean *made of something or other*. So Paul begins by saying that the Corinthians are made of flesh. That was not in itself a rebuke; a man just because he is a man is made of flesh, *but* he must not stay that way. The trouble was that the Corinthians were not only *sarkinoi* they were *sarkikoi*, which means not only *made of flesh* but *dominated by the flesh*. To Paul the *flesh* is much more than merely a physical thing. It means *human nature apart from God,* that part of man both mental and physical which provides a bridgehead for sin. So the fault that Paul finds with the Corinthians is not that they are made of flesh—all men are—but that they have allowed this lower side of their nature to dominate all their outlook and all their actions.

What is it about their life and conduct that makes Paul level such a rebuke at them? It is their party spirit, their strife and their factions. This is extremely significant because it means that *you can tell what a man's relations with God are by looking at his relations with his fellow men.* If he is at variance with his fellow men, if he is a quarrelsome, argumentative, trouble-making creature, he may be a diligent church attender, he may even be a church office-bearer, but he is not a man of God. But if a man is at one with his fellow men, if his relations with them are marked by love and unity and concord then he is on the way to being a man of God.

If a man loves God he will also love his fellow men. It was this truth that Leigh Hunt took from an old eastern tale and enshrined in his poem:

> Abou Ben Adhem (may his tribe increase!)
> Awoke one night from a deep dream of peace,
> And saw, within the moonlight in his room,
> Making it rich, and like a lily in bloom,
> An angel writing in a book of gold:
> Exceeding peace had made Ben Adhem bold,
> And to the presence in the room he said,
> "What writest thou?"—The vision rais'd its head,
> And with a look made of all sweet accord,
> Answer'd, "The names of those who love the Lord."
> "And is mine one?" said Abou. "Nay, not so,"
> Replied the angel. Abou spoke more low,
> But cheerly still; and said, "I pray thee then,
> Write me as one that loves his fellow men."
>
> The angel wrote, and vanish'd. The next night
> It came again with a great wakening light,

And show'd the names whom love of God had bless'd,
And lo! Ben Adhem's name led all the rest.

Paul goes on to show the essential folly of this party spirit with its glorification of human leaders. In a garden one man may plant a seed and another may water it; but neither can claim to have made the seed grow. That belongs to God and to God alone. The man who plants and the man who waters are on one level; neither can claim any precedence over the other; they are but servants working together for the one Master—God. God uses human instruments to bring to men the message of his truth and love; but it is he alone who wakes the hearts of men to new life. As he alone created the heart, so he alone can re-create it.

THE FOUNDATION AND THE BUILDERS

1 *Corinthians* 3: 10–15

According to the grace of God that was given to me, I laid the foundation like a skilled master-builder, but another builds upon it. Let each see to it how he builds upon it; for no one can lay any other foundation beside that which is already laid, which is Jesus Christ. If anyone builds upon that foundation gold, silver, costly stones, wood, straw, stubble, it will become quite clear what each man's work is. The Day will show it because it is going to be revealed by fire, and the fire itself will test what kind of work each man's work is. If the work which any man erected upon that foundation remains he will receive a reward. If the work of any man will be burned up he will lose it all. But he himself will be saved, though it be like one who has passed through fire.

IN this passage Paul is surely speaking from personal experience. He was of necessity a foundation layer and was forever on the move. True, he stayed for eighteen months in Corinth (*Acts* 18: 11) and for three years in Ephesus (*Acts* 20: 31); but in Thessalonica he can have stayed less than a month, and that was far more typical. There was so much ground waiting to be covered; there were so many men who had never heard the name of Jesus Christ; and, if a fair start was to be made with the evangelization of the world, Paul could only lay the foundations and move on. It was only when he was in prison that his restless spirit could stay in the one place.

Wherever he went, he laid the same foundation. That was the proclamation of the facts about and the offer of Jesus Christ. It was his tremendous function to introduce men to Jesus Christ because it is in him, and in him alone, that a man can find three things.

(a) He finds *forgiveness for past sins*. He finds himself in a new relationship to God and suddenly discovers that he is his friend and not his enemy. He discovers that God is like Jesus; where once he saw hatred he now sees love, and where once he saw infinite remoteness he now sees tender intimacy.

(b) He finds *strength for the present*. Through the presence and help of Jesus he finds courage to cope with life, for he is now no longer an isolated unit fighting a lonely battle with an adverse universe. He lives a life in which nothing can separate him from the love of God in Christ Jesus his Lord. He walks life's ways and fights its battles with Christ.

(c) He finds *hope for the future*. He no longer lives in a world in which he is afraid to look forward but in one where God is in control and working together all things for good. He lives in a world where death is no longer the end, but only the prelude to greater glory. Without the foundation of Christ a man can have none of these things.

But on this foundation of Christ others built. Paul is not here thinking of the building up of wrong things, but the building up of inadequate things. A man may present to his fellow men a version of Christianity which is weak and watered down; a one-sided thing which has stressed some things too much and others too little, and in which things have got out of balance; a warped thing in which even the greatest matters have emerged distorted.

The Day that Paul refers to is the Day when Christ will

come again. Then will come the final test. The wrong and the inadequate will be swept away. But, in the mercy of God, even the inadequate builder will be saved, because at least he tried to do something for Christ. At best all our versions of Christianity are inadequate; but we would be saved much inadequacy if we tested them not by our own prejudices and presuppositions, nor by agreement with this or that theologian, but set them in the light of the New Testament and, above all, in the light of the Cross. Longinus the great Greek literary critic, offers his students a test. "When you write anything," he said, "ask yourself how Homer or Demosthenes would have written it; and, still more, ask yourself how Homer and Demosthenes would have listened to it." When we speak for Christ we must speak as if Christ was listening— as indeed he is. A test like that will rescue us from many a mistake.

WISDOM AND FOOLISHNESS

1 *Corinthians* 3: 16–22

Do you not know that you are God's temple, and that the Spirit of God has his dwelling place in you? If anyone destroys the temple of God, God will destroy him; for the temple of God is holy and you are that temple.

Let no one deceive you. If any one among you thinks he is wise in this world, let him become a fool that he may become wise. For the wisdom of this world is foolishness with God, for it stands written, "He who clutches the wise in their cunning craftiness"; and again, "The Lord knows that the thoughts of their hearts are vain." So then, let no one boast in men. For all things are yours, whether Paul, or Apollos, or Cephas, or life, or death, or things present, or things to come; all are yours, but you are Christ's and Christ is God's.

To Paul the Church was the very temple of God because it was the society in which the Spirit of God dwelt. As Origen later said, "We are most of all God's temple when we prepare ourselves to receive the Holy Spirit." But, if men introduce dissension and division into the fellowship of the Church, they destroy the temple of God in a double sense.

(*a*) They make it impossible for the Spirit to operate. Immediately bitterness enters a church, love goes from it. The truth can neither be spoken nor heard rightly in that atmosphere. "Where love is, God is," but, where hatred and strife are, God stands at the door and knocks and receives no entry. The very badge of the Church is love for the brethren. He who destroys that love destroys the Church and thereby destroys the temple of God.

(*b*) They split up the Church and reduce it to a series of disconnected ruins. No building can stand firm and foursquare if sections of it are removed. The Church's greatest weakness is still its divisions. They too destroy it.

Paul goes on once again to pin down the root cause of this dissension and consequent destruction of the Church. It is the worship of intellectual, worldly wisdom. He shows the condemnation of that wisdom by two Old Testament quotations—*Job* 5: 13 and *Psalm* 94: 11. It is by this very worldly wisdom that the Corinthians assess the worth of different teachers and leaders. It is this pride in the human mind which makes them evaluate and criticize the way in which the message is delivered, the correctness of the rhetoric, the weight of the oratory, the subtleties of the arguments, rather than think only of the content of the message itself. The trouble about this intellectual pride is that it is always two things.

(*a*) It is always *disputatious*. It cannot keep silent and admire; it must talk and criticize. It cannot bear to have its opinions contradicted; it must prove that it and it alone is right. It is never humble enough to learn; it must always be laying down the law.

(*b*) Intellectual pride is characteristically *exclusive*. Its tendency is to look down on others rather than to sit down beside them. Its outlook is that all who do not agree with it are wrong. Long ago Cromwell wrote to the Scots, "I beseech you by the bowels of Christ, think it possible that you may be mistaken." That is precisely what intellectual pride cannot think. It tends to cut men off from each other rather than to unite them.

Paul urges the man who would be wise to become a fool. This is simply a vivid way of urging him to be humble enough to learn. No one can teach a man who thinks that he knows it all already. Plato said, "He is the wisest man who knows himself to be very ill-equipped for the study of wisdom." Quintilian said of certain students, "They would doubtless have become excellent scholars if they had not been so fully persuaded of their own scholarship." The old proverb laid it down, "He who knows not, and knows not that he knows not is a fool; avoid him. He who knows not, and knows that he knows not is a wise man; teach him." The only way to become wise is to realize that we are fools; the only way to knowledge is to confess our ignorance.

In verse 22, as so often happens in his letters, the march of Paul's prose suddenly takes wings and becomes a lyric of passion and poetry. The Corinthians are doing what is to Paul an inexplicable thing. They are seeking to give themselves over into the hands of some man. Paul tells them that, in point of fact, it is not they who belong to him but he who belongs to them. This identification with some party is the acceptance of slavery by those who should be kings. In fact they are masters of all things, because they belong to Christ and Christ belongs to God. The man who gives his strength and his heart to some little splinter of a party has surrendered everything to a petty thing, when he could have entered into possession of a fellowship and a love as wide as the universe. He has confined into narrow limits a life which should be limitless in its outlook.

THE THREE JUDGMENTS

1 *Corinthians* 4: 1–5

Let a man then so think of us as the servants of Christ and

stewards of the secrets which God reveals to his own people. In ordinary everyday life, that a man should be found faithful, is a quality required in stewards. To me it matters very little that I should be judged by you or by any human day. No—I do not even judge myself. For, supposing that I am conscious of no fault, yet I am not acquitted because of that. He who judges me is the Lord. So then, make a practice of passing no judgment before the proper time—until the Lord comes—for he will light up the hidden things of darkness and he will bring to light the counsels of men's hearts; and then each man will receive his praise from God.

PAUL urges the Corinthians not to think of Apollos and Cephas and himself as leaders of parties; but to think of them all as servants of Christ. The word that he uses for a *servant* is interesting; it is *huperetes* and originally meant a rower on the lower bank of a trireme, one of the slaves who pulled at the great sweeps which moved the triremes through the sea. Some commentators have wished to stress this and to make it a picture of Christ as the pilot who directs the course of the ship and Paul as the servant who accepts the pilot's orders and labours only as his Master directs.

Then Paul uses another picture. He thinks of himself and his fellow preachers as *stewards* of the secrets which God desires to reveal to his own people. The steward (*oikonomos*) was the *major domo*. He was in charge of the whole administration of the house or the estate; he controlled the staff; he issued the supplies; but, however much he controlled the household staff, he himself was still a slave where the master was concerned. Whatever be a man's position in the Church, and whatever power he may yield there or whatever prestige he may enjoy, he still remains the servant of Christ.

That brings Paul to the thought of judgment. The one thing that an *oikonomos* must be is reliable. The very fact that he enjoys so much independence and responsibility makes it all the more necessary that his master should be able to depend absolutely upon him. The Corinthians, with their sects and their appropriation of the leaders of the Church as their masters, have exercised judgments on these leaders, preferring one to the other. So Paul speaks of three judgments that every man must face.

(i) He must face the judgment of his *fellow men*. In this case Paul says that that is nothing to him. But there is a sense in which a man cannot disregard the judgment of his fellow men. The odd thing is that, in spite of its occasional radical mistakes, the judgment of our fellow men is often right. That is due to the fact that every man instinctively admires the basic qualities of honour, honesty, reliability, generosity, sacrifice and love. Antisthenes, the Cynic philosopher, used to say, "There are only two people who can tell you the truth about yourself—an enemy who has lost his temper and a friend who loves you dearly." It is quite true that we should never let the judgment of men deflect us from what we believe to be right; but it is also true that the judgment of men is often more accurate than we would like to think, because they instinctively admire the lovely things.

(ii) He must face the judgment of *himself*. Once again Paul disregards that. He knew very well that a man's judgment of himself can be clouded by self-satisfaction, by pride and by conceit. But in a very real sense every man must face his own judgment. One of the basic Greek ethical laws was, "Man, know thyself." The Cynics insisted that one of the first characteristics of a real man was "the ability to get on with himself." A man cannot get away from himself and if he loses his self-respect, life becomes an intolerable thing.

(iii) He must face the judgment of *God*. In the last analysis this is the only real judgment. For Paul, the judgment he awaited was not that of any human day but the judgment of the Day of the Lord. God's is the final judgment for two reasons. (*a*) Only God knows all the *circumstances*. He knows the struggles a man has had; he knows the secrets that a man can tell to no one; he knows what a man might have sunk to and he also knows what he might have climbed to. (*b*) Only God knows all the *motives*. "Man sees the deed but God sees the intention." Many a deed that looks noble may have been done from the most selfish and ignoble motives;

and many a deed which looks base may have been done from the highest motives. He who made the human heart alone knows it and can judge it.

We would do well to remember two things—first, even if we escape all other judgments or shut our eyes to them, we cannot escape the judgment of God; and, second, judgment belongs to God and we do well not to judge any man.

APOSTOLIC HUMILITY AND UNCHRISTIAN PRIDE

1 Corinthians 4: 6–13

> Brothers, I have transferred these things by way of illustration to myself and to Apollos, so that through us you may learn to observe the principle of not going beyond that which is written, so that none of you may speak boastfully of one teacher and disparagingly of the other.
>
> Who sees anything special in you? What do you possess that you did not receive? And, if you did receive it, why are you boasting as if you had acquired it yourself? No doubt you are already fed to the full! No doubt you are already rich! No doubt you have already come into your kingdom without any help from us! I would that you had already come into your kingdom so that we too might reign with you! For I think that God has exhibited the apostles, bringing up the rear of the procession, like men marked out to die! I think that we have become a spectacle for the world and for angels and for men! We are fools for Christ's sake, but you are wise in Christ! We are weak but you are strong! You are famous, we have no honour! Until this very hour, we are hungry, we are thirsty, we are naked, we are buffeted, we are homeless wanderers, we toil working with our own hands. When we are insulted, we bless; when we are persecuted, we bear it. When we are slandered, we gently plead. We have been treated like the scum of the earth, like the dregs of all things—and this treatment still goes on.

ALL that Paul has been saying about himself and about Apollos is true not only for them but also for the Corinthians. It is not only he and Apollos who must be kept humble by the thought that it is not the judgment of men they are facing, but the judgment of God; the Corinthians must walk in a like humility. Paul had a wonderfully courteous way of including himself in his own warnings and his own condemnations. The true preacher seldom uses the word *you* and always uses the word *we*; he does not speak down to men; he speaks as one who sits where they sit and who is a man of like passions with them. If we really wish to help and to save men our attitude must be not that of condemnation but of pleading; our accent must be not that of criticism but of compassion. It is not his own words that Paul insists the Corinthians must not go beyond; it is the word of God, which condemns all pride.

Then Paul asks them the most pertinent and basic of all questions. "What do you possess," he said, "that you did not receive?" In this single sentence Augustine saw the whole doctrine of grace. At one time Augustine had thought in terms of human achievement, but he came to say, "To solve this question we laboured hard in the cause of the freedom of man's will, but the grace of God won the day." No man could ever have known him unless God had revealed himself; no man could ever have won his own salvation; a man does not save himself, he is saved. When we think of what we have done and think of what God has done for us, pride is ruled out and only humble gratitude remains. The basic fault of the Corinthians was that they had forgotten that they owed their souls to God.

Then comes one of these winged outbursts which meet us ever and again in the letters of Paul. He turns on the Corinthians with scathing irony. He compares their pride, their self-satisfaction, their feeling of superiority with the life that an apostle lives. He chooses a vivid picture. When a Roman general won a great victory he was allowed to parade his victorious army through the streets of the city with all the trophies that he had won; the procession was called a Triumph. But at the end there came a little group of captives who were doomed to death; they were being taken to the arena to fight with the beasts and so to die. The Corinthians in their blatant pride were like the conquering general displaying the trophies of his prowess; the apostles were like the little group of captives doomed to die. To the Corinthians the Christian life meant flaunting their privileges and reckoning up their achievement; to Paul it meant humble service and a readiness to die for Christ.

In the list of things which Paul declares that the apostles undergo there are two specially interesting words. (i) He says that they are *buffeted* (*kolaphizesthai*). That is the word used for beating a slave. Plutarch tells how a witness gave evidence that a slave belonged to a certain man because he had seen the man beating him and this is the word that is used. Paul was willing for the sake of Christ to be treated like a slave. (ii) He says, "When we are *insulted* (*loidoresthai*), we bless." We probably do not realize just how surprising a statement this would be to a pagan. Aristotle declares that the highest virtue is *megalopsuchia, great-heartedness*, the virtue of the man with the great soul; and he defines this virtue as the quality which will not endure to be insulted. To the ancient world Christian humility was a virtue altogether new. This indeed was the kind of conduct that to men looked crazily foolish although this very foolishness was the wisdom of God.

A FATHER IN THE FAITH

1 *Corinthians* 4: 14–21

It is not to shame you that I write these things, but to warn you as my beloved children. You may have thousands of tutors in Christ, but you have not many fathers; for, in Christ Jesus, through the good news, I begat you. So then, I urge you, show yourselves imitators of me. That is why I send to you Timothy, who is my beloved child and faithful in the Lord, for he will bring back to your memory my ways in Christ—exactly the same things as I teach everywhere and in every Church. There are some who have been inflated with their own importance, as though I were not coming to you. I will come to you soon, if the Lord will, and I will find out, not what these inflated people say, but what they can do; for the Kingdom of God does not exist in talking but in powerful action. What do you wish? Am I to come to you with a stick? Or am I to come in love and in the spirit of gentleness?

WITH this passage Paul brings to an end the section of the letter which deals directly with the dissensions and divisions at Corinth. It is as a father that he writes. The very word which he uses in verse 14 for *to warn* (*nouthetein*) is the word regularly used to express the admonition and advice which a father gives his children. (*Ephesians* 6: 4). He may be speaking with the accents of severity; but it is not the severity which seeks to bring an unruly slave to heel, but the severity which seeks to put back on the right rails a foolish son who has gone astray.

Paul felt that he was in a unique position as regards the Corinthian Church. The tutor (*paidagogos:* cp. *Galatians* 3: 24) was not the teacher of the child. He was an old and trusted slave who daily took the child to school, who trained him in moral matters, cared for his character and tried to make a man of him. A child might have many tutors but he had only one father; in the days to come the Corinthians might have many tutors but none of them could do what Paul had done; none of them could beget them to life in Christ Jesus.

Then Paul says an amazing thing. In effect he says, "I call upon my children to take after their father." It is so seldom that a father can say that. For the most part it is too often true that a father's hope and prayer is that a son will turn out to be all that he has never succeeded in being. Most of us who teach cannot help saying, not, "Do as I do," but, "Do as I say." But Paul, not with pride, but with complete unself-consciousness, can call upon his children in the faith to copy him.

Then he pays them a delicate compliment. He says that he will send Timothy to remind them of his ways. In effect, he says that all their errors and mistaken ways are due, not to deliberate rebellion, but to the fact that they have forgotten. That is so true of human nature. So often it is not that we rebel against Christ; it is simply that we forget him. So often it is not that we deliberately turn our backs upon him; it is simply that we forget that he is in the scheme of things at all. Most of us need one thing above all—a deliberate effort to live in the conscious realization of the presence of Jesus Christ. It is not only at the sacrament but at every moment of every day that Jesus Christ is saying to us, "Remember Me."

Paul moves on to a challenge. They need not say that because he is sending Timothy he is not coming himself. He will come if the way opens up; and then will come their test. These Corinthians can talk enough; but it is not their high-sounding words that matter; it is their deeds. Jesus never said, "By their words you shall know them," He said, "By their fruits you shall know them." The world is full of talk about Christianity, but one deed is worth a thousand words.

In the end Paul demands whether he is to come to mete out discipline or to company with them in love. The love of Paul for his children in Christ throbs through every letter he wrote; but that love was no blind, sentimental love; it was a love which knew that sometimes discipline was necessary and was prepared to exercise it. There is a love which can ruin a man by shutting its eyes to his faults; and there is a love which can mend a man because it sees him with the clarity of the eyes of Christ. Paul's love was the love which knows that sometimes it has to hurt in order to amend.

Paul has dealt with the problem of strife and divisions within the Corinthian Church, and now he goes on to deal with certain very practical questions and certain very grave situations within the Church, of which news has come to him. This section includes chapters 5 and 6. 5: 1–8 deals with a case of incest. 5: 9–13 urges discipline for the unchaste. 6: 1–8 deals with the tendency of the Corinthians to go to law with each other. 6: 9–20 stresses the need for purity.

SIN AND COMPLACENCY

1 *Corinthians* 5: 1–8

> It is actually reported that there is unchastity among you, and unchastity so monstrous that it does not even exist among the heathen, unchastity the consequence of which is that a certain man has formed a union with his father's wife; and you have regarded the matter with inflated self-complacency and you have not—as you should have—regarded it with a grief so bitter that it would take steps to see that the perpetrator of this deed should be removed from your midst. Now I, absent in the body but present in the spirit, have already come to a decision as if I were present. Regarding the man who has perpetrated this deed, it is my judgment that when you have assembled together in the name of the Lord and when my spirit is with you, backed by the power of the Lord Jesus, you should hand over this man who has acted in such a way to Satan until his sinful lusts shall be eliminated from his body so that his spirit may be saved in the day of our Lord Jesus. Your glorying is no fine thing. Do you not know that a little evil influence can corrupt a whole society? Cleanse out the old evil influence that you may make a clean fresh start, even as you are cleansed from it; for our Passover sacrifice has been made—I mean Christ; so that we feast not on the old corrupt things nor with the evil influence of wickedness but with the pure bread of sincerity and truth.

PAUL is dealing with what, for him, was an ever recurring problem. In sexual matters the heathen did not know the meaning of chastity. They took their pleasure when and where they wanted it. It was so hard for the Christian Church to escape the infection. They were like a little island surrounded on every side by a sea of paganism; they had come so newly into Christianity; it was so difficult to unlearn the practices which generations of loose-living had made part of their lives; and yet if the Church was to be kept pure they must say a final good-bye to the old heathen ways. In the Church at Corinth a specially shocking case had arisen. A man had formed an illicit association with his own step-mother, a thing which would revolt even a heathen and which was explicitly forbidden by the Jewish law (*Leviticus* 18: 8). The phrasing of the charge may suggest that this woman was already divorced from her husband. She herself must have been a heathen, for Paul does not seek to deal with her at all so that she must have been outside the jurisdiction of the Church.

Shocked as he was at the sin, Paul was even more shocked by the attitude of the Corinthian Church to the sinner. They had complacently accepted the situation and done nothing about it when they should have been grief-stricken. The word Paul uses for the grief they should have shown (*penthein*) is the word that is used for mourning for the dead. An easy-going attitude to sin is always dangerous. It has been said that our one security against sin lies in our being shocked at it. Carlyle said that men must see the infinite beauty of holiness and the infinite damnability of sin. When we cease to take a serious view of sin we are in a perilous position. It is not a question of being critical and condemnatory; it is a question of being wounded and shocked. It was sin that crucified Jesus Christ; it was to free men from sin that he died. No Christian man can take an easy-going view of it.

Paul's verdict is that the man must be dealt with. In a vivid phrase he says that he must be handed over to Satan. He means that he must be excommunicated. The world was looked upon as the domain of Satan (*John* 12: 31; 16: 11; *Acts* 26: 18; *Colossians* 1: 13) just as the Church was the domain of God. Send this man back to Satan's world to which he belongs, is Paul's verdict. But we have to note that even a punishment as serious as that was not vindictive. It was in order to humiliate the man, to bring about the taming and the eradication of his lusts so that in the end his spirit should be saved. It was discipline, not exercised solely to punish, but rather to awaken; and was a verdict to be carried out, not with cold, sadistic cruelty, but rather in sorrow as for one who had died. Always at the back of punishment and discipline in the early Church there is the conviction that they must seek not to break but to make the man who has sinned.

Paul goes on to some very practical advice. Verses 6–8 have been modernised in the translation. In the original they literally run: "Do you not know that a little leaven leavens the whole lump? Cleanse out the old leaven that you may be a new lump, even as you are unleavened. For our Passover sacrifice has been sacrificed—I mean Christ, so that we feast not with the old leaven, nor with the leaven of wickedness and evil, but on the unleavened bread of sincerity and truth." Here we have a picture expressed in Jewish terms. With very few exceptions, leaven stands in Jewish literature for an evil influence. It was dough which had been kept over from a previous baking and which, in the keeping, had fermented. The Jews identified fermentation with putrefaction; and so leaven stood for a corrupting influence.

Now the Passover bread was unleavened (*Exodus* 12: 15ff; 13: 7). More than that, on the day before the Passover Feast the law laid it down that the Jew must light a candle and search his house ceremonially for leaven, and that every last bit must be cast out (cp. the picture of God's search in *Zephaniah* 1: 12). (We may note in the bygoing that the date of this search was 14th April and that in the search has been seen the origin of spring-cleaning!). Paul takes that picture. He says our sacrifice has been sacrificed, even Christ; it is his sacrifice which has delivered us from sin, as God delivered the Israelites from Egypt. Therefore, he goes on, the last remnant of evil must be cleared out of your lives. If you let an evil influence into the Church, it can corrupt the whole society, as the leaven permeates the whole lump of dough.

Here again we have a great practical truth. Discipline has sometimes to be exercised for the sake of the Church. To shut our eyes to offences is not always a kind thing to do; it may be damaging. A poison must be eliminated before it spreads; a weed must be plucked out before it pollutes the whole ground. Here we have a whole principle of discipline. Discipline should never be exercised for the satisfaction of the person who exercises it, but always for the mending of the person who has sinned and for the sake of the Church. Discipline must never be vengeful; it must always be curative and prophylactic.

THE CHURCH AND THE WORLD

1 *Corinthians* 5: 9-13

> In my letter I wrote to you not to associate with fornicators. You cannot altogether avoid associating with the fornicators of this world, or with those who are greedy and grasping for this world's goods, or with idolaters, for, in that case, you would have to withdraw entirely from the world. But, as things now are, I write to you not to associate or to eat with anyone who bears the name of brother, if he is a fornicator, or a greedy person, or an idolater, or a slanderer, or a drunken person, or a thief. What business have I to judge those who are outside the Church? Is it not those who are within the Church that you judge, while God judges those who are outside? Put away the wicked man from among you.

IT appears that Paul had already written a letter to the Corinthians in which he had urged them to avoid the society of all evil men. He had meant that to apply only to members of the Church; he had meant that wicked men must be disciplined by being ejected from the society of the Church until they mended their ways. But some at least of the Corinthians had taken this to be an absolute prohibition, and, of course, such a prohibition could be observed only if they withdrew themselves from the world altogether. In a place like Corinth it would have been impossible to carry on a normal life at all without associating in ordinary everyday affairs with those whose lives the Church would utterly condemn.

But Paul never meant that; he would never have recommended a kind of Christianity which withdrew from the world; to him it was something that had to be lived out in the world. "God," as the old saint said to John Wesley, "knows nothing of solitary religion." And Paul would have agreed with that.

It is very interesting to see the three sins which he chooses as typical of the world; he names three classes of people.

(i) There are the *fornicators,* those guilty of lax morality. Christianity alone can guarantee purity. The root cause of sexual immorality is a wrong view of men. In the end it views men as beasts.

It declares that the passions and instincts which they share with the beasts must be shamelessly gratified and regards the other person merely as an instrument through which that gratification may be obtained. Now Christianity regards man as a child of God, and, just because of that, as a creature who lives in the world but who always looks beyond it, a person who will not dictate his life by purely physical needs and desires, one who has a body but also a spirit. If men regarded themselves and others as the sons and daughters of God, moral laxity would automatically be banished from life.

(ii) There are those who are *greedy* for this world's goods. Once again only Christianity can banish that spirit. If we judge things by purely material standards, there is no reason why we should not dedicate our lives to the task of getting. But Christianity introduces a spirit which looks outwards and not inwards. It makes love the highest value in life and service the greatest honour. When the love of God is in a man's heart, he will find his joy not in getting but in giving.

(iii) There are the *idolaters.* Ancient idolatry is paralleled in modern superstition. There can have been few ages so interested in amulets and charms and luck-bringers, in astrologers and horoscopes, as this. The reason is that it is a basic rule of life that a man must worship something. Unless he worships the true God he will worship the gods of luck. Whenever religion grows weak, superstition grows strong.

It is to be noted that these three basic sins are representative of the three directions in which a man sins.

(*a*) Fornication is a sin against *a man's own self.* By falling to it he has reduced himself to the level of an animal; he has sinned against the light that is in him and the highest that he knows. He has allowed his lower nature to defeat his higher and made himself less than a man.

(*b*) Greediness is a sin against *our neighbours and our fellow men*. It regards human beings as persons to be exploited rather than as brothers to be helped. It forgets that the only proof that we do love God must be the fact that we love our neighbours as ourselves.

(*c*) Idolatry is a sin against *God*. It allows things to usurp God's place. It is the failure to give God the first and only place in life.

It is Paul's principle that we are not to judge those outside the Church. "Those outside" was a Jewish phrase used to describe people outside the Chosen People. We must leave their judgment to God who alone knows the hearts of men. But the man within the Church has special privileges and therefore special responsibilities; he is a man who has taken an oath to Christ and can therefore be called in question for how he keeps it.

So Paul comes to an end with the definite command, "Put away the wicked man from amongst you." That is a quotation from *Deuteronomy* 17: 7 and 24: 7. There are times when a cancer must be cut out; there are times when drastic measures must be taken to avoid infection. It is not the desire to hurt or the wish to show his power that moves Paul; it is the pastor's desire to protect his infant Church from the ever-threatening infection of the world.

THE FOLLY OF THE LAW COURTS

1 *Corinthians* 6: 1–8

When any of you has a ground of complaint against his fellow, does he dare to go to law before unrighteous men, and not before God's dedicated people? Are you not aware that God's dedicated people will one day judge the world? And if the world is to be judged by you, are you unfit to deal with the smallest matters of judgment? Are you not aware that we will judge angels—let alone things which have to do with ordinary everyday life? If then you have questions of judgment which have to do with ordinary everyday life, put those who are of no consequence in the eyes of the Church in charge of them. It is to shame you that I speak. Do you go on like this because there is not a wise man among you who will be able to arbitrate between one brother and another? Must brother really go to law with brother, and that before unbelievers? If it comes to that there is a grave defect among you that you have court cases with each other at all. Why not rather submit to injury? Why not rather submit to being deprived of something? But you injure others and you deprive others of things—and brothers at that!

PAUL is dealing with a problem which specially affected the Greeks. The Jews did not ordinarily go to law in the public law courts at all; they settled things before the elders of the village or the elders of the synagogue; to them justice was far more a thing to be settled in a family spirit than in a legal spirit. In fact the Jewish law expressly forbade a Jew to go to law at all in a non-Jewish court; to do so was considered blasphemy against the divine law of God. It was far otherwise with the Greeks; they were characteristically a litigious people. The law courts were one of their chief entertainments.

When we study the details of Athenian law we see what a major part the law courts played in the life of any Athenian citizen; and the situation in Corinth would not be so very different. If there was a dispute in Athens, the first attempt to settle it was by private arbitrator. In that event one arbitrator was chosen by each party, and a third was chosen by agreement between both parties to be an impartial judge. If that failed to settle the matter, there was a court known as The Forty. The Forty referred the matter to a public arbitrator and the public arbitrators consisted of all Athenian citizens in their sixtieth year; and any man chosen as an arbitrator had to act whether he liked it or not under penalty of disfranchisement. If the matter was still not settled, it had to be referred to a jury court which consisted of two hundred and one citizens for cases involving less than about £50 and

A3

four hundred and one for cases involving more than that figure. There were indeed cases when juries could be as large as anything from one thousand to six thousand citizens. Juries were composed of Athenian citizens over thirty years of age. They were actually paid three obols a day for acting as jurymen, an obol being worth about ½p. The citizens entitled to act as jurymen assembled in the mornings and were allocated by lot to the cases on trial.

It is plain to see that in a Greek city every man was more or less a lawyer and spent a very great part of his time either deciding or listening to law cases. The Greeks were in fact famous, or notorious, for their love of going to law. Not unnaturally, certain of the Greeks had brought their litigious tendencies into the Christian Church; and Paul was shocked. His Jewish background made the whole thing seem revolting to him; and his Christian principles made it even more so. "How," he demanded, "can anyone follow the paradoxical course of looking for justice in the presence of the unjust?"

What made the matter still more fantastic to Paul was that, in the picture of the golden age to come, the Messiah was to judge the nations and the saints were to share in that judgment. *The Book of Wisdom* says, "They shall judge the nations and have dominion over the people" (3: 8). *The Book of Enoch* says, "I will bring forth those who have loved my name clad in shining light, and I will set each on the throne of his honour" (108: 12). So Paul demands, "If some day you are going to judge the world, if even the angels, the highest created beings, are going to be subject to your judgment, how, in the name of all that is reasonable, can you go and submit your cases to men and to heathen men at that?" "If you must do it," he says, "do it inside the Church, and give the task of judging to the people of whom you think least, for no man who is destined to judge the world could possibly be bothered getting himself involved in petty everyday squabbles."

Then suddenly Paul seizes on the great essential principle. To go to law at all, and especially to go to law with a

brother, is to fall far below the Christian standard of
behaviour. Long ago Plato had laid it down that the good
man will always choose to suffer wrong rather than to do
wrong. If the Christian has even the remotest tinge of the
love of Christ within his heart, he will rather suffer insult and
loss and injury than try to inflict them on someone else—still
more so, if that person is a brother. To take vengeance is
always an unchristian thing. A Christian does not order his
dealings with others by the desire for recompense and the
principles of crude justice. He orders them by the spirit of
love; and the spirit of love will insist that he live at peace
with his brother, and will forbid him to demean himself by
going to law.

SUCH WERE SOME OF YOU

1 *Corinthians* 6: 9–11

> Are you not aware that the unrighteous will not inherit the
> Kingdom of God? Make no mistake—neither fornicators, nor
> idolaters, nor adulterers, nor sensualists, nor homosexuals, nor
> thieves, nor rapacious men, nor drunkards, nor slanderers, nor
> robbers shall inherit the Kingdom of God—and such were some of
> you. But you have been washed; you have been consecrated; you
> have been put into a right relationship with God through the
> name of our Lord Jesus Christ and through the Spirit of our God.

PAUL breaks out into a terrible catalogue of sins that is a
grim commentary on the debauched civilization in which the
Corinthian Church was growing up. There are certain things
which are not pleasant to talk about, but we must look at
this catalogue to understand the environment of the early
Christian Church; and to see that human nature has not
changed very much.

There were *fornicators* and *adulterers*. We have already seen
that sexual laxity was part of the background of heathen life
and that the virtue of chastity was well-nigh unknown. The

word used for *fornicators* is specially unpleasant; it means a male prostitute. It must have been hard to be a Christian in the tainted atmosphere of Corinth.

There were *idolaters*. The greatest building in Corinth was the Temple of Aphrodite, the goddess of love, where idolatry and immorality flourished side by side. Idolatry is a grim example of what happens when we try to make religion easier. An idol did not begin by being a god; it began by being a symbol of a god; its function was to make the worship of the god easier by providing some object in which his presence was localized. But very soon men began to worship not the god behind the idol but the idol itself. It is one of the chronic dangers of life that men will come to worship the symbol rather than the reality behind it.

There were *sensualists*. The word (*malakos*) literally means those who are soft and effeminate, those who have lost their manhood and live for the luxuries of recondite pleasures. It describes what we can only call a kind of wallowing in luxury in which a man has lost all resistance to pleasure. When Ulysses and his sailors came to the island of Circe they came to the land where the lotus flower grew. He who ate of that flower forgot his home and his loved ones and wished to live forever in that land where "it was always afternoon." He had no more any of the stern joy that comes from "climbing up the climbing wave." The sensualist desires this life in which it is always afternoon.

There were *thieves* and *robbers*. The ancient world was cursed with them. Houses were easy to break into. The robbers particularly haunted two places—the public baths and the public gymnasia where they stole the clothes of those who were washing or exercising themselves. It was common to kidnap slaves who had special gifts. The state of the law shows how serious this problem was. There were three kinds of theft punishable by death: (i) Theft to the value of more than 50 drachmae, that is, about £2. (ii) Theft from the baths, the gymnasia and the ports and harbours to the value of 10 drachmae, that is about 40 pence. (iii) Theft of anything by night. The Christians lived in the middle of a pilfering population.

There were *drunkards*. The word used comes from a word (*methos*) which signifies uncontrolled drinking. Even little children in ancient Greece drank wine; the name for breakfast is *akratisma* and it consisted of bread dipped in wine. The universality of wine drinking was of course due to the inadequate water-supplies. But normally the Greeks were sober people, for their drink was three parts of wine mixed with two of water. But in luxury-loving Corinth uncontrolled drunkenness abounded.

There were *rapacious* men and *robbers*. Both words are interesting. The word used for *rapacious* is *pleonektes*. It describes, as the Greeks defined it, "the spirit which is always reaching after more and grabbing that to which it has no right." It is aggressive getting. It is not the miser's spirit, for it aimed to get in order to spend, so that it could live in more luxury and greater pleasure; and it cared not over whom it took advantage so long as it could get. The word translated *robbers* is *harpax*. It means *grasping*. It is interesting to note that it is used for a certain kind of wolf and also for the grappling irons by which ships were boarded in naval battles. It is the spirit which grasps that to which it has no right with a kind of savage ferocity.

We have left the most unnatural sin to the end —there were *homosexuals*. This sin had swept like a cancer through Greek life and from Greece, invaded Rome. We can scarcely realize how riddled the ancient world was with it. Even so great a man as Socrates practised it; Plato's dialogue *The Symposium* is always said to be one of the greatest works on love in the world, but its subject is not natural but unnatural love. Fourteen out of the first fifteen Roman Emperors practised unnatural vice. At this very time Nero was emperor. He had taken a boy called Sporus and had him castrated. He then married him with a full marriage ceremony and took him home in procession to his palace and lived with him as wife. With an incredible viciousness, Nero had himself married a man called Pythagoras and called him his husband. When Nero was eliminated and Otho came to the throne one of the first things he did was to take possession of Sporus. Much later, the Emperor Hadrian's name was associated with a Bithynian youth called Antinous. He lived with him inseparably, and, when he died, he deified him and covered the world with his statues and immortalised his sin by calling a star after him. In this particular vice, in the time of the Early Church, the world was lost to shame; and there can be little doubt that this was one of the main causes of its degeneracy and the final collapse of its civilization.

After this dreadful catalogue of vices, natural and unnatural, comes Paul's shout of triumph "and such were some of you." The proof of Christianity lay in its power. It could take the dregs of humanity and make them into men. It could take men lost to shame and make them sons of God. There were in Corinth, and all over the world, men who were living proofs of the re-creating power of Christ.

The power of Christ is still the same. No man can change himself, but Christ can change him. There is the most amazing contrast between the pagan and the Christian literature of the day. Seneca, a contemporary of Paul, cries out that what men want is "a hand let down to lift them up." "Men," he declared, "are overwhelmingly conscious of their weakness in necessary things." "Men love their vices," he said with a kind of despair, "and hate them at one and the same time." He called himself a *homo non tolerabilis,* a man not to be tolerated. Into this world, conscious of a tide of decadence that nothing could stop, there came the radiant power of Christianity, which was triumphantly able to make all things new.

BOUGHT WITH A PRICE

1 *Corinthians* 6: 12–20

True, all things are allowed to me; but all things are not good for me. All things are allowed to me, but I will not allow any thing to get control of me. Foods were made for the stomach and the stomach was made for foods; but God will obliterate both it and them. The body is not made for fornication but for the Lord, and the Lord is for the body. God raised up the Lord, and by his power he will raise us too. Are you not aware that your bodies are the limbs of Christ? Am I then to take away the limbs which belong to Christ and make them the limbs which belong to a harlot? Or, are you not aware that he who has intercourse with a harlot is one body with her? For these two, it says, will become one flesh. But he who unites himself to the Lord is of one spirit with him. Strenuously avoid fornication at all times. Every sin which a man may commit is external to his body; but the man who commits fornication sins against his own body. Or, are you not aware that your body is the temple of the Holy Spirit who is within you, the Spirit which you have received from God? So you are not your own, for you have been bought with a price. So then glorify God with your body.

In this passage Paul is up against a whole series of problems. It ends with the summons, "Glorify God with your body." This is Paul's battlecry here.

The Greeks always looked down on the body. There was a proverbial saying, "The body is a tomb." Epictetus said, "I am a poor soul shackled to a corpse." The important thing was the soul, the spirit of a man; the body was a thing that did not matter. That produced one of two attitudes. Either it issued in the most rigorous asceticism in which everything was done to subject and humiliate the desires and instincts of the body. Or—and in Corinth it was this second outlook which was prevalent—it was taken to mean that, since the body was of no importance, you could do what you liked with it; you could let it sate its appetites. What complicated this was the doctrine of Christian freedom which Paul preached. If the Christian man is the freest of all men, then is he not free to do what he likes, especially with this completely unimportant body of his?

So, the Corinthians argued, in a way that they thought very enlightened, let the body have its way. But what is the body's way? The stomach was made for food and food for the stomach, they went on. Food and the stomach naturally and inevitably go together. In precisely the same way the body is made for its instincts; it is made for the sexual act and the sexual act is made for it; therefore let the desires of the body have their way.

Paul's answer is clear. Stomach and food are passing things; the day will come when they will both pass away. But the body, the personality, the man as a whole will not pass away; he is made for union with Christ in this world and still closer union hereafter. What then happens if he commits fornication? He gives his body to a harlot, for scripture says that intercourse makes two people into one united body (*Genesis* 2: 24). That is to say, a body which rightly belongs to Christ has been prostituted to someone else.

Remember that Paul is not writing a systematic treatise; he is preaching, pleading with a heart on fire and a tongue that will use whatever arguments it can find. He says that of all sins fornication is the one that affects a man's body and insults it. That is not strictly true—drunkenness might do the same. But Paul is not writing in order to satisfy an examiner in logic, but in order to save the Corinthians in body and in soul; and so he pleads that other sins are external to a man, but in this he sins against his own body, which is destined for union with Christ.

Then he makes one last appeal. Just because God's Spirit dwells in us we have become a temple of God; and so our very bodies are sacred. And more—Christ died to save not a bit of a man, but the whole man, body and soul. Christ gave his life to give a man a redeemed soul and a pure body. Because of that a man's body is not his own to do with as he likes; it is Christ's and he must use it, not for the satisfaction of his own lusts, but for the glory of Christ.

There are two great thoughts here.

(i) It is Paul's insistence that, though he is free to do anything, he will let nothing master him. The great fact of the Christian faith is, not that it makes a man free to sin, but that it makes a man free *not* to sin. It is so easy to allow habits to master us; but the Christian strength enables us to master them. When a man really experiences the Christian power, he becomes, not the slave of his body, but its master. Often a man says, "I will do what I like," when he means that he will indulge the habit or passion which has him in its grip; it is only when a man has the strength of Christ in him that he can really say, "I will do what I like," and not, "I will satisfy the things that have me in their power."

(ii) It is Paul's insistence that we are not our own. There is no such thing in this world as a self-made man. The Christian is a man who thinks not of his rights but of his debts. He can never do what he likes, because he never belongs to himself; he must always do what Christ likes, because Christ bought him at the cost of his life.

In the section of our letter which stretches from the beginning of chapter 7 to the end of chapter 15, Paul sets himself to deal with a set of problems concerning which the Corinthian Church had written to him, asking advice. He begins the section by saying, "With regard to what you wrote to me about. . . ." In modern language, we might say, "With reference to your letter. . . ." We shall outline each problem as we come to it. Chapter 7 deals with a whole series of problems regarding *marriage*. Here is a summary of the areas in which the Corinthian Church sought and obtained advice from Paul.

Verses 1 *and* 2: Advice to those who think that Christians should not marry at all.

Verses 3–7: Advice to those who urge that even those who are married should abstain from all sexual relations with each other.

Verses 8 *and* 9: Advice to the unmarried and to widows.

Verses 10 *and* 11: Advice to those who think that married people should separate.

Verses 12–17: Advice to those who think that, if the

marriage is one in which one of the partners is a Christian and one a pagan, it should be broken up and dissolved.

Verses 18 *and* 24: Instruction to live the Christian life in whatever state they happen to be.

Verse 25 *and verses* 36–38: Advice regarding virgins.

Verses 26–35: Exhortation that nothing should interfere with concentration upon serving Christ because the time is short and he will very soon come again.

Verses 38–40: Advice to those who wish to remarry.

We must study this chapter with two facts firmly in our minds. (i) Paul is writing to Corinth which was the most immoral town in the world. Living in an environment like that, it was far better to be too strict than to be too lax. (ii) The thing which dominates every answer Paul gives is the conviction that the Second Coming of Christ was about to happen almost immediately. This expectation was not realized; but Paul was convinced that he was giving advice for a purely temporary situation. We can be quite certain that in many cases his advice would have been quite different if he had visualized a permanent, instead of a temporary, situation. Now let us turn to the chapter in detail.

COMPLETE ASCETICISM

1 *Corinthians* 7: 1, 2

> With regard to your letter and its suggestion that it would be a fine thing for a man not to have anything to do with a woman—to avoid fornication, let each man possess his own wife, and each woman her own husband.

WE have already seen that in Greek thought there was strong tendency to despise the body and the things of the body; and that that tendency could issue in a position where men said, "The body is utterly unimportant; therefore we can do what we like with it and it makes no difference if we allow its appetites to have their fullest play." But that very tendency could issue in a precisely opposite point of view. It could move a man to say, "The body is evil; therefore we must bring it into subjection; therefore we must completely obliterate, and if that is not possible, we must completely deny, all the instincts and desires which are natural to it." It is that second way of looking at things with which Paul is dealing here. The Corinthians, or at least some of them, had suggested that, if a man was going to be a Christian in the fullest sense of the term, he must have done with physical things and must refuse to marry altogether.

Paul's answer is extremely practical. In effect he says, "Remember where you are living; remember that you are living in Corinth where you cannot even walk along the street without temptation rearing its head at you. Remember your own physical constitution and the healthy instincts which nature has given you. You will be far better to marry than to fall into sin."

This sounds like a low view of marriage. It sounds as if Paul is advising marriage in order to avoid a worse fate. In point of fact he is honestly facing the facts and laying down a rule which is universally true. No man should attempt a way of life for which he is naturally unfitted; no man should set out on a pathway whereby he deliberately surrounds himself with temptations. Paul knew very well that all men are not made the same. "Examine yourself," he says, "and choose that way of life in which you can best live the Christian life, and don't attempt an unnatural standard which is impossible and even wrong for you being such as you are."

THE PARTNERSHIP OF MARRIAGE

1 *Corinthians* 7: 3–7

Let the husband give to the wife all that is due to her; and in the same way let the wife give to the husband all that is due to him. A wife is not in absolute control of her own body, but her husband is. In the same way a husband is not in absolute control of his own body, but his wife is. Do not deprive each other of each other's legitimate rights, unless it be by common agreement, and for a limited time. You could do so in order to have time for prayer and afterwards come together again; but you must come together again, so that Satan may not get the chance to tempt you because you find it impossible to control your desires. But I am giving this advice more as a concession than as a command. I wish that all men were like myself; but each man has his own gift from God, one one way, and another another.

THIS passage arises from a suggestion from Corinth that if married people are to be really Christian they must abstain from all intercourse with each other. This is another manifestation of that line of thought which looked on the body and its instincts as essentially evil. Paul declares a supremely great principle. Marriage is a partnership. The husband cannot act independently of the wife, nor the wife of the husband. They must always act together. The husband must never regard the wife simply as a means of self-gratification. The whole marriage relationship, both in its physical and spiritual sides, is something in which both are to find their gratification and the highest satisfaction of all their desires. In a time of special discipline, in a time of long and earnest prayer, it might be right to set aside all bodily things; but it must be by mutual agreement and only for a time, or it simply begets a situation which gives temptation an easy chance.

Once again Paul seems to belittle marriage. This, he suggests, is not an ideal command; it is a considerate concession to human weakness. He would prefer as an ideal that everyone was as he was. What exactly was that? We can only deduce.

We may be fairly certain that at some time Paul had been married. (i) We may be certain of that on general grounds. He was a Rabbi and it was his own claim that he had failed in none of the duties which Jewish law and tradition laid down. Now orthodox Jewish belief laid down the obligation of marriage. If a man did not marry and have children, he was said to have "slain his posterity," "to have lessened the image of God in the world." Seven were said to be excommunicated from heaven, and the list began, "A Jew who has no wife; or who has a wife but no children." God had said, "Be fruitful and multiply," and, therefore, not to marry and not to have children was to be guilty of breaking a positive commandment of God. The age for marriage was considered to be eighteen; and therefore it is in the highest degree unlikely that so devout and orthodox a Jew as Paul once was would have remained unmarried. (ii) On particular grounds there is also evidence that Paul was married. He must have been a member of the Sanhedrin for he says that he gave his vote against the Christians. (*Acts* 26: 10). It was a regulation that members of the Sanhedrin must be married men, because it was held that married men were more merciful.

It may be that Paul's wife died; it is even more likely that she left him and broke up his home when he became a Christian, so that he did indeed literally give up all things for the sake of Christ. At all events he banished that side of life once and for all and never remarried. A married man could never have lived the life of journeying which Paul lived. His desire that others ideally should be the same sprang entirely from the fact that he expected the Second Coming at once; time was so short that earthly ties and physical things must not be allowed to interfere. It is not that Paul is really disparaging marriage; it is rather that he is insisting that all a man's concentration must be on being ready for the coming of Christ.

THE BOND THAT MUST NOT BE BROKEN

1 *Corinthians* 7: 8–16

> To the unmarried and to the widows I say, it would be a fine thing if they were to remain like myself; but if they find continence impossible, let them marry; for it is better to marry than to go on being inflamed with passion. To those who are married I give this order—and the order is not mine but the Lord's—that a wife should

not separate herself from her husband; but if she does separate, let her either remain unmarried or be reconciled to her husband; and that a husband should not put his wife away. To others I say this—but I give it as my advice and not as a commandment of the Lord—if any brother has a wife who is not a believer, and she agrees to live with him, let him not put her away; and if there is any wife who has a husband who is not a believer, and he agrees to live with her, let her not put her husband away; for the unbelieving husband is consecrated by his wife and the unbelieving wife is consecrated by the husband who is a brother. If this were not so your children would not be cleansed; but as it is they are set apart for God. If the unbelieving partner wishes to separate, let him or her separate, for the Christian brother or sister in such cases is not under any slavish obligation. It is in peace that God has called us. Wife, how can you tell whether you will save your husband? Or, Husband, how can you tell whether you will save your wife?

THIS passage deals with three different sets of people.

(i) It deals with those who are unmarried or who are widows. In the circumstances of an age which, as Paul thought, was hastening to its end, they would be better to remain as they are; but once again, he warns them not to court temptation, not to attempt a situation which would be for them dangerous. If they have a nature naturally passionate, let them marry. Paul was always sure that no one could lay down one course of action for everyone. It all depended on the person involved.

(ii) It deals with those who are married. Paul forbids divorce on the ground that Jesus forbade it. (*Mark* 10: 9; *Luke* 16: 18). If there is such a separation, he forbids remarriage. This may seem a hard doctrine, but in Corinth with its characteristic laxity, it was better to keep the standards so high that no taint of loose-living could enter the Church.

(iii) It deals with the marriage of believers and unbelievers. On this Paul has to give his own judgment, because there is no definite command of Jesus to which he can refer them. The background must be that there were those in Corinth who declared that a believer must never live with an unbeliever; and that, in the event of one partner of a marriage becoming a Christian and the other remaining a heathen, separation must at once follow.

In fact one of the great heathen complaints against Christianity was exactly that Christianity did break up families and was a disruptive influence in society. "Tampering with domestic relationships" was one of the first charges brought against the Christians. (1 *Peter* 4: 15). Sometimes the Christians did in fact take a very high stand. "Of what parents are you born?" the judge asked Lucian of Antioch. "I am a Christian," Lucian answered, "and a Christian's only relatives are the saints."

Undoubtedly mixed marriages produced problems. Tertullian wrote a book about them in which he describes the heathen husband who is angry with his Christian wife because, "for the sake of visiting the brethren she goes round from street to street to other men's cottages, especially those of the poor. . . . He will not allow her to be absent all night long at nocturnal convocations and paschal solemnities . . . or suffer her to creep into prison to kiss a martyr's bonds, or even to exchange a kiss with one of the brethren." (In the early Church Christians greeted each other with the holy kiss of peace). It is indeed difficult not to sympathize with the heathen husband.

Paul dealt with this problem with supreme practical wisdom. He knew the difficulty and he refused to exacerbate it. He said that if the two could agree to live together by all means let them do so; but if they wished to separate and found living together intolerable, let them do so, because the Christian was never meant to be a slave.

Paul has two great things to say which are of permanent value.

(i) He has the lovely thought that the unbelieving partner is consecrated by the believer. They two have become one flesh and the wonder is that in such a case it is not the taint of heathenism but the grace of Christianity which wins the victory. There is an infection about Christianity which involves all those who come into contact with it. A child born into a Christian home, even into a home where only one of the partners is a Christian, is born into the family of Christ. In a partnership between a believer and an unbeliever, it is not so much that the believer is brought into contact with the realm of sin, as that the unbeliever is brought into contact with the realm of grace.

(ii) He has the equally lovely thought that this very association may be the means of saving the soul of the unbelieving partner. For Paul evangelization began at home. The unbeliever was to be looked on, not as something unclean to be avoided with repulsion, but as another son or daughter to be won for God. Paul knew that it is blessedly true that often human love has led to love of God.

SERVING GOD WHERE GOD HAS SET US

1 *Corinthians* 7: 17–24

The one thing that is necessary is that each man should walk as God has allotted to him and as God has called him. It is thus that I order things in all the Churches. Was any man called after he had been circumcised? Let him not try to efface it. Was any man called when he was not circumcised? Let him not get himself circumcised. Circumcision is of no importance and uncircumcision is of no importance, but keeping God's commandments is everything. Let each man remain in the condition in which he was when God called him. Were you called as a slave? Do not let that distress you. But if you can become free, grasp the opportunity, for he who, in the Lord, was called as a slave is the Lord's free man; and in the same way, the free man who has been called is Christ's slave. You have been bought with a price. Do not become slaves of men. Brothers, let each man remain in the sight of God in the state in which he was called.

PAUL lays down one of the first rules of Christianity, "Be a Christian where you are." It must often have happened that when a man became a Christian he would have liked to break away from his job, and from the circle in which he moved, and begin a new life. But Paul insisted that the function of

Christianity was not to give a man a new life, but to make his old life new. Let the Jew remain a Jew; let the Gentile remain a Gentile; race and the marks of race made no difference. What did make a difference was the kind of life he lived. Long ago the Cynics had insisted that a true man can never be a slave in nature although he may be a slave in status; and that a false man can never be a free man in reality but is always a slave. Paul reminds them that slave or free, a man is a slave of Christ because Christ bought him with a price.

Here there is a picture in Paul's mind. In the ancient world it was possible for a slave at a great effort to purchase his own freedom. This was how he did it. In the little spare time he had, he took odd jobs and earned a few coppers. His master had the right to claim commission even on these poor earnings. But the slave would deposit every farthing he could earn in the Temple of some god. When, it might be at the end of years, he had his complete purchase price laid up in the Temple, he would take his master there, the priest would hand over the money, and then symbolically the slave became the property of the god and therefore free of all men. That is what Paul is thinking of. The Christian man has been purchased by Christ; therefore, no matter what his human status may be, he is free of all men because he is the property of Christ.

Paul insists that Christianity does not make a man kick over the traces and become querulously discontented with things as they are; it makes him, wherever he is, carry himself as the slave of Christ. Even the meanest work is no longer done for men but for Christ. As George Herbert wrote:

> All may of thee partake;
>   Nothing can be so mean,
> Which with this tincture, "for thy sake,"
>   Will not grow bright and clean.
>
> A servant with this clause
>   Makes drudgery divine:
> Who sweeps a room, as for, thy laws,
>   Makes that and the action fine.

> This is the famous stone
>> That turneth all to gold;
> For that which God doth touch and own
>> Cannot for less be told.

WISE ADVICE ON A DIFFICULT PROBLEM

1 *Corinthians* 7: 25, 36–38

> I have no command of the Lord with regard to virgins, but I give
> you my opinion, as one who has found the mercy of God and
> who can be trusted. . . . If anyone thinks that his conduct to his
> virgin is unseemly, if he finds that his passions are too strong, and
> if he thinks that they ought to marry, let him do what he wishes.
> He does no wrong; let them marry. But if any man is fixed and
> settled in his mind, and if there is no cumpulsion on him, but if he
> has complete power to abide by his own wish, and if in his mind
> he has come to the decision to keep his own virgin, he will do well.
> The thing comes to this—he who marries his virgin acts rightly;
> and he who does not marry her will do better.

VERSES 25 to 38, while they form a paragraph, really fall into
two parts, which it is simpler to examine separately. Verses 25
and 36–38 deal with this problem concerning virgins; while
the verses between give the reason for accepting the advice
which runs through the whole chapter. This section *concerning
virgins* has always been a problem. It has been given three
different explanations.

(i) It has been regarded simply as advice to fathers as to the
marriage of their unmarried daughters; but it does not read
like that; and it is hard to see why Paul uses the word *virgin*
if he means *daughter;* and for a father to speak of *his virgin*
when he meant *his daughter* would be an odd way of speaking.

(ii) It has been regarded as dealing with a problem which
in later times became acute and which more than one Church
Council tried to deal with and forbade. Certainly later on it
was the custom for a man and woman to live together,
sharing the same house and even sharing the same bed, and
yet to have no physical relations with each other at all. The

idea was that if they could discipline themselves to share the spiritual life in such intimacy without allowing the body to enter into their relationship at all, it was a specially meritorious thing. We can understand the idea behind this, the attempt to cleanse human relationships of all passion; but it is clear how dangerous a practice it was, and how, on occasion, it must have resulted in a quite impossible situation. In such a relationship the woman was known as the man's virgin. It may well be that that custom had arisen in the Church at Corinth. If so, and we think that it was so, then Paul is saying, "If you can retain this difficult situation, if your self-discipline and your self-control are sufficient to maintain it, then it is better to do so; but, if you have tried it and have found that it is too great a strain on human nature, then abandon it and marry; and to do so will be no discredit to you."

(iii) While we think that is the correct interpretation of this passage, there is a modification of it which deserves to be noted. It is suggested that in Corinth there were men and women who had actually gone through the marriage ceremony but had decided never to consummate the marriage and to live in absolute continence so as to devote themselves entirely to the spiritual life. Having done so, it might well be that they discovered that what they planned to do placed too great a strain upon them. In that case, Paul would be saying, "If you can keep your vow, you will do supremely well; but if you cannot, frankly admit it and enter into normal relations with each other."

To us the whole relationship seems dangerous and abnormal and even wrong; and so indeed it was; and in time the Church was compelled to brand it as wrong. But given the situation, Paul's advice is full of wisdom. He really says three things.

(i) Self-discipline is an excellent thing. Any means whereby a man tames himself until he has every passion under perfect control is an excellent thing; but it is no part of Christian duty to eliminate the natural instincts of man; rather the Christian uses them to the glory of God.

(ii) Paul really says, "Don't make an unnatural thing of your religion." That, in the last analysis, is the fault of the monks and the hermits and the nuns. They regard it as necessary to eliminate the natural feelings of mankind in order to be truly religious; they regard it as necessary to separate themselves from all the normal life of men and women in order to serve God. But Christianity was never meant to abolish normal life; it was meant to glorify it.

(iii) In the end Paul is saying, "Don't make an agony of your religion." Collie Knox tells how, when he was a young man, he was apt to find religion a stress and a strain; and he tells how a well-loved chaplain once came to him and laid a hand on his shoulder and said, "Young Knox, don't make an agony of your religion." It was said of Burns that he was "haunted rather than helped by his religion." No man should be ashamed of the body God gave him, the heart God put into him, the instincts that, by God's creation, dwell within him. Christianity will teach him, not how to eliminate them, but how to use them in such a way that passion is pure and human love the most ennobling thing in all God's world.

THE TIME IS SHORT

1 *Corinthians* 7: 26–35

> I think that this is the right thing because of the present crisis—that it is the right thing for a man to remain as he is. Have you been bound to a wife? Do not seek to be released from that bond. Are you free from marriage ties? Do not seek a wife. But, if you do marry, you have committed no sin. Those who do marry will have trouble about bodily things, and I would wish to spare you this. This I do say, brothers, the time is short, so short that, for the future those who have wives must live as if they had not, those who have sorrow must live as not sorrowing, those who rejoice must live as not rejoicing, those who buy must buy as if they had no secure possession of anything, those who use this world must use it as if they had no full use of it; for the outward form of

this world is passing away. I want you to be without anxieties. The man who remains unmarried is anxious for the things of the Lord; his anxiety is how he may please the Lord. The man who marries is anxious for the things of the world; his anxiety is how he may please his wife. There is a distinct difference between the married and the unmarried woman. The unmarried woman is anxious for the things of the Lord; her aim is that she may be dedicated to God both in her body and in her spirit. The woman who has married is anxious for the things of the world; her anxiety is that she may please her husband. It is for your advantage that I am saying this. I do not want to put a halter round your neck. My aim is that you should live a lovely life and that you should serve the Lord without distractions.

It is in many ways a pity that Paul did not begin the chapter with this section because it has the heart of his whole position in it. All through this chapter we must have felt that he was belittling marriage. It looked again and again as if he was allowing marriage only as a concession to avoid fornication and adultery; as if marriage was only a second best.

We have seen that the Jews glorified marriage and considered it a sacred duty. There was only one valid reason, according to Jewish tradition, for not marrying, and that was in order to study the law. Rabbi ben Azai asked, "Why should I marry? I am in love with the Law. Let others see to the prolongation of the human race." In the Greek world, Epictetus, the stoic philosopher, never married. He said that he was doing far more for the world by being a teacher than if he had produced two or three "ugly-nosed brats." "How," he asked, "can one whose function is to teach mankind be expected to run for something in which to heat the water to give the baby its bath?" But that was not the Jewish point of view and it was certainly not the Christian point of view.

Nor was it Paul's final point of view. Years later when he wrote the letter to the Ephesians he had changed; for there he uses the relationship of man and wife as a symbol of the relationship between Christ and the Church (*Ephesians* 5: 22–26). When he wrote to the Corinthians, his outlook was dominated by the fact that he expected the Second Coming of Christ at any moment. What he is laying down is crisis legislation. "The time is short." So soon was Christ to come, he believed, that everything must be laid aside in one tremendous effort to concentrate on preparation for that coming. The most important human activity and the dearest human relationship must be abandoned if they threatened to interrupt or to slacken that concentration. A man must have no ties whatsoever to keep him when Christ bade him rise and go. He must think of pleasing no one other than Christ. Had Paul thought that he and his converts were living in a permanent situation, he would never have written as he did. By the time he wrote *Ephesians* he had realized the permanency of the human situation and regarded marriage as the most precious relationship within it, the only one which was even faintly parallel to the relationship of Christ and the Church.

For us it must always be true that home is the place which does two things for us. It is the place where we find the noblest opportunity to live the Christian life; and the pity is it is so often the place where we claim the right to be as querulous and critical and boorish as we may, and to treat those who love us as we would never dare to treat a stranger. Also it is the place from whose rest and sweetness we draw strength to live more nearly as we ought within the world.

Paul in this chapter looked on marriage as a second best because he believed that life as we know it had only days to run; but the day came when he saw it as the loveliest relationship upon earth.

MARRYING AGAIN

1 *Corinthians* 7: 39, 40

> A wife is bound for as long as her husband is alive; but, if her husband dies, she is free to marry anyone she wishes, so long as the marriage is made in the Lord. In my opinion she will be

happier if she remains as she is—and I think that I have the Spirit of God.

AGAIN Paul takes up his consistent point of view. Marriage is a relationship which can be broken only by death. A second marriage is perfectly allowable, but Paul would rather see the widow stay a widow. We know now that he was speaking only of the crisis situation in which he thought men were living.

In many ways a second marriage is the highest compliment that the one who survives can pay the one who has gone before; for it means that without him or her life was so lonely as to be insupportable; it means that with him or her the married state was so happy that it can fearlessly be entered into again. So far from being an act of disrespect it can be a mark of honour to the dead.

One condition Paul lays down—it must be a marriage in the Lord. That is, it must be a marriage between Christian folk. It is seldom that a mixed marriage can be successful. Long, long ago Plutarch laid it down, that "marriage cannot be happy unless husband and wife are of the same religion." The highest love comes when two people love each other and their love is sanctified by a common love of Christ. For then they not only live together but also pray together; and life and love combine to be one continual act of worship to God.

Chapters 8, 9 and 10 deal with a problem which may seem extremely remote to us, but was intensely real to the Christians at Corinth and demanded a solution. It was the problem of whether or not to eat meat which had been offered to idols. Before we begin to study these chapters in detail, it will be well to state the problem and the broad lines of the solutions which Paul offers in the various cases in which it impinged upon life.

Sacrifice to the gods was an integral part of ancient life. It might be of two kinds, private or public. In neither case was the whole animal consumed upon the altar. Often all that was burned was a mere token part as small as some of the hairs cut from the forehead.

In *private* sacrifice the animal, so to speak, was divided into three parts. First, a token part was burned on the altar. Second, the priests received as their rightful portion the ribs, the ham and the left side of the face. Third, the worshipper himself received the rest of the meat. With the meat he gave a banquet. This was specially the case at times like weddings. Sometimes these feasts were in the house of the host; sometimes they were even in the temple of the god to whom the sacrifice had been made. We have, for instance, a papyrus invitation to dinner which runs like this: "Antonius, son of Ptolemaeus, invites you to dine with him at the table of our Lord Serapis." Serapis was the god to whom he had sacrificed.

The problem which confronted the Christian was, "Could he take part in such a feast? Could he possibly take upon his lips meat that had been offered to an idol?" If he could not, then obviously he was going to cut himself off almost entirely from social occasions.

In *public* sacrifice, that is sacrifice offered by the state, and such sacrifices were common, after the requisite symbolic amount of the meat had been burned and after the priests had received their share, the rest of the meat fell to the magistrates and others. What they did not need, they sold to the shops and the markets; and therefore, even when meat was bought in the shops, it might well have been already offered to some idol. A man never knew when he might be eating meat that had formed part of a sacrifice to an idol.

What complicated matters still further was that this age believed strongly and fearfully in demons and devils. The air was full of them and they were always lurking to gain an entry into a man, and, if they did, they would injure his body and unhinge his mind. One of the special ways in which these spirits gained entry was through food; they settled on the food as a man ate and so got inside him. One of the ways of avoiding that was to dedicate the meat to some good god whose presence in the meat put up a barrier against the evil spirit. For that reason, nearly all animals were dedicated to a god before being slaughtered; and, if that was not done, as a defence meat was blessed in the name of a god before it was eaten.

It therefore followed that a man could hardly eat meat at all which was not in some way connected with a heathen god. Could the Christian eat it? That was the problem; and, clearly, although to us it may be a matter of merely antiquarian interest, the fact remains that, to the Christian in Corinth or any other Greek city, it was one which pervaded all life, and which had to be settled one way or another.

Paul's advice falls into different sections.

(i) In chapter 8 he lays down the principle that, however safe the strong and enlightened Christian may feel from the infection of heathen idols and even if he believes that an idol is the symbol of something which does not exist at all, he must do nothing which will hurt or bewilder a brother whose conscience is neither so enlightened nor so strong as his.

(ii) In chapter 9 he deals with those who invoke the principle of Christian freedom. He points out that there are many things that he is free to do which he abstains from doing for the sake of the Church. He is well aware of Christian freedom, but equally aware of Christian responsibility.

(iii) In chapter 10: 1–13 he deals with those who declare that their Christian knowledge and privileged position make them quite safe from any infection. He cites the example of the Israelites who had all the privileges of God's Chosen People and who yet fell into sin.

(iv) In chapter 10: 14–22 he uses the argument that any man who has sat at the table of the Lord cannot sit at the table of a heathen god, even if that god be nothing. There is something essentially wrong in taking meat offered to a false god upon lips that have eaten the body and blood of Christ.

(v) In chapter 10: 23–26 he advises against overfussiness. A man can buy what is offered in the shops and ask no questions.

(vi) In chapter 10: 27, 28 he deals with the problem of what to do in a private house. In a private house the Christian

will eat what is put before him and ask no questions; *but* if
he is deliberately informed that the meat set before him was
part of a heathen sacrifice, that is a challenge to his Christian
position and he will refuse to eat it.

(vii) Finally in chapter 10: 29—11: 1 Paul lays down the
principle that the conduct of the Christian must be so far
above reproach that it gives no possible offence either to Jew
or non-Jew. He is better to sacrifice his rights than to allow
these rights to become an offence.

Now we can proceed to deal with these chapters in detail.

ADVICE TO THE WISE

1 Corinthians 8

With reference to things offered to idols—we are well aware that
we all possess knowledge; but knowledge inflates a man, whereas
love builds him up. If anyone thinks he has reached a certain
stage of knowledge, it is not the kind of knowledge it ought to be.
If a man loves God, he is known by God. With regard to food
which consists of things offered to idols, we well know that there
is nothing in the universe for which an idol stands, and that there
is no God but one; and even if the so-called gods do exist, just
as there are gods many and lords many, as far as we are concerned,
it remains true that there is one God, the Father, from whom all
things come and to whom we go; and there is one Lord, Jesus
Christ, through whom all things came into being and through
whom we were re-created. But it is not everyone who has knowledge;
but there are some who, even up to now, have been accustomed
to regard idols as real, and who still cannot help doing so; the
consequence is that, when they eat meat offered to idols, they
regard it as eating a real sacrifice, and because their conscience is
weak, a stain is left upon it. Food will not commend us to God.
If we do not eat it we are none the worse; and if we do eat it we
are not specially better. You must take care to see to it that your
very liberty does not become a stumbling-block to those who are
weak. For if anyone sees you, who have knowledge, sitting at meat
in the temple of an idol, will the conscience of the weak man not
be encouraged to eat things which have been offered to idols,

while he still really believes in the reality of the idol and the sacrifice? And so the person who is weak will be ruined by your knowledge, the brother for whom Christ died. If you sin like that against a brother, and if you strike blows like that against his conscience in its weakness, you are sinning against Christ. Therefore, if a thing like food is going to cause my brother to stumble, I will most certainly abstain from eating flesh forever, so that I may not cause my brother to stumble.

WE have seen how it was scarcely possible to live in any Greek city and not to come daily up against the problem of what to do about eating meat that had been offered as a sacrifice to idols. There were certain of the Corinthians to whom the matter was no problem. They held that their superior knowledge had taught them that the heathen gods simply did not exist, and that therefore it was possible for a Christian to eat meat that had been offered to idols without a qualm. In reality Paul has two answers to that. One does not come until 10: 20. In that passage Paul makes it clear that, although he quite agreed that the heathen gods did not exist, he felt certain that the spirits and the demons did exist and that they were behind the idols and were using them to seduce men from the worship of the true God.

In the present passage he uses a much simpler argument. He says that in Corinth there were men who all their lives, up until now, had really believed in the heathen gods; and these men, simple souls, could not quite rid themselves of a lingering belief that an idol really was something, although it was a false something. Whenever they ate meat offered to idols, they had qualms of conscience. They could not help it; instinctively they felt that it was wrong. So Paul argues that if you say that there is absolutely no harm in eating meat offered to idols you are really hurting and bewildering the conscience of these simple souls. His final argument is that, even if a thing is harmless for you, when it hurts someone else, it must be given up, for a Christian must never do anything which causes his brother to stumble.

In this passage which deals with so remote a thing there are three great principles which are eternally valid.

(i) What is safe for one man may be quite unsafe for another. It has been said, and it is blessedly true, that God has his own secret stairway into every heart; but it is equally true that the devil has his own secret and subtle stairway into every heart. We may be strong enough to resist some temptation, but it may well be that someone else is not. Something may be no temptation whatever to us, but it may be a violent temptation to someone else. Therefore, in considering whether we will or will not do anything, we must think not only of its effect on us, but of its effect on others as well.

(ii) Nothing ought to be judged solely from the point of view of knowledge; everything ought to be judged from the point of view of love. The argument of the advanced Corinthians was that they knew better than to regard an idol as anything; their knowledge had taken them far past that. There is always a certain danger in knowledge. It tends to make a man arrogant and feel superior and look down unsympathetically on the man who is not as far advanced as himself. Knowledge which does that is not true knowledge. But the consciousness of intellectual superiority is a dangerous thing. Our conduct should always be guided not by the thought of our own superior knowledge, but by sympathetic and considerate love for our fellow man. And it may well be that for his sake we must refrain from doing and saying certain otherwise legitimate things.

(iii) This leads to the greatest truth of all. No man has any right to indulge in a pleasure or to demand a liberty which may be the ruination of someone else. He may have the strength of mind and will to keep that pleasure in its proper place; that course of action may be safe enough for him; but he has not only himself to think about, he must think of the weaker brother. An indulgence which may be the ruin of someone else is not a pleasure but a sin.

THE UNCLAIMED PRIVILEGES

1 *Corinthians* 9: 1–14

> Am I not free? Am I not an apostle? Have I not seen Jesus our
> Lord? Are you not my work in the Lord? Even if I am not an
> apostle to others, I certainly am to you; you are the seal of my
> apostleship in the Lord. This is my defence to those who are
> trying to put me on my trial. Do you mean to say that I have
> not the right to eat and drink at the cost of the Church? Do you
> mean to say that I have not the right to take a sister about with
> me as wife, as the rest of the apostles and the brothers of the Lord
> and Cephas do? Are you going to maintain that it is only I and
> Barnabas who have not the right to be set free from manual
> labour? What soldier who goes on a campaign has ever to provide
> his own rations? Who plants a vineyard and has no right to eat
> of its fruits? Who shepherds a flock and has not the right to drink
> of the milk of the flock? Don't think that this is a merely human
> point of view. Doesn't the law itself say this? For in the law of
> Moses it stands written, "You must not muzzle the ox while it is
> treading out the grain." Is it only oxen that God was thinking
> about? Or, was it not really for our sakes that he says this? It
> was for our sakes that it was written, because the ploughman
> ought to plough and the thresher ought to thresh in the expectation
> of a share of the crop. If we have sown for you things which
> nourish the spirit, is it a great boon if we reap from you things
> which nourish the body? If others share in the privileges which you
> provide, should we not even more? But we have not used our
> right to this privilege; but we have put up with all things so as
> not to put any hindrance in the way of the good news of Christ.
> Are you not aware that those who perform the Temple rites have
> a right to eat their share of the Temple offerings, that those who
> serve at the altar share things with the altar? Just so the Lord laid
> it down that those who proclaim the good news should get enough
> to live on from the good news.

At first sight this chapter seems quite disconnected from what
goes before but in fact it is not. The whole point lies in this—
the Corinthians who considered themselves mature Christians
have been claiming that they are in such a privileged position
that they are free to eat meat offered to idols if they like.

Their Christian freedom gives them—as they think—a special position in which they could do things which might not be permissible to lesser men. Paul's way of answering that argument is to set forth the many privileges which he himself had a perfect right to claim, but which he did not claim in case they should turn out to be stumbling-blocks to others and hindrances to the effectiveness of the gospel.

First, he claims to be an apostle, which immediately set him in a very special position. He uses two arguments to prove the reality of his apostleship.

(i) *He has seen the Lord.* Over and over again the Book of Acts makes it clear that the supreme test of an apostle is that he is a witness of the Resurrection. (*Acts* 1: 22; 2: 32; 3: 15; 4: 33). This is of intense importance. Faith, in the New Testament, is very seldom acquiescence in a creed; it is almost always trust in a person. Paul does not say, "I know *what* I have believed." He says, "I know *whom* I have believed." (2 *Timothy* 1: 12). When Jesus called his disciples, he did not say to them, "I have a philosophy which I would like you to examine," or, "I have an ethical system which I would like you to consider," or, "I offer you a statement of belief which I would like you to discuss." He said, "Follow me." All Christianity begins with this personal relationship with Jesus Christ. To be a Christian is to know him personally. As Carlyle once said when a minister was being chosen, "What this Church needs is someone who knows Christ other than at second-hand."

(ii) Paul's second claim is that *his ministry has been effective.* The Corinthians themselves are the proof of that. He calls them his *seal.* In ancient days the seal was extremely important. When a cargo of grain or dates or the like was being sent off, the last thing done was that the containers were sealed with a seal to show that the consignment was genuinely what it claimed to be. When a will was made it was sealed with seven seals; and it was not legally valid unless it was produced with the seven seals intact. The seal was the guarantee of genuineness. The very fact of the Corinthian

Church was the guarantee of Paul's apostleship. The final proof that a man himself knows Christ is that he can bring others to him. It is said that once a young soldier, lying in pain in a hospital, said to Florence Nightingale as she bent over to tend him, "You are Christ to me." The reality of a man's Christianity is best proved by the fact that he helps others to be Christian.

The privilege that Paul might have claimed was support from the Church. Not only could he have claimed such support for himself but also for a wife. In fact the other apostles did receive such support. The Greeks despised manual labour; no free Greek would willingly work with his hands. Aristotle declared that all men were divided into two classes— the cultured and the hewers of wood and drawers of water who existed solely to perform the menial tasks for the others, and whom it was not only mistaken but actually wrong to seek to raise and educate. The enemies of Socrates and Plato had in fact taunted them because they took no money for teaching, and had hinted that they did so because their teaching was worth nothing. It is true that every Jewish Rabbi was supposed to teach for nothing and to have a trade whereby he earned his daily bread; but these same Rabbis took very good care to inculcate the teaching that there was no more meritorious deed than to support a Rabbi. If a man wished a comfortable place in heaven he could not better assure himself of it than by supplying all a Rabbi's needs. On every ground Paul could have claimed the privilege of being supported by the Church.

He uses ordinary human analogies. No soldier has to provide his own rations. Why should the soldier of Christ have to do so? The man who plants a vineyard shares in the fruits. Why should the man who plants churches not do so? The shepherd of the flock gets his food from the flock. Why should not the Christian pastor do likewise? Even scripture says that the ox who works the threshing machine is not to be muzzled but is to be allowed to eat of the grain (*Deuteronomy* 25: 4). As any Rabbi would, Paul allegorizes that instruction and makes it apply to the Christian teacher.

The priest who serves in the Temple receives his share of the offerings. In Greek sacrifice the priest, as we have seen, received the ribs, the ham and the left side of the face. But it is worth while looking at the perquisites of the priests in the Temple at Jerusalem.

There were five main offerings. (i) *The Burnt-offering.* This alone was burnt entire except the stomach, the entrails and the sinew of the thigh (cp. *Genesis* 32: 32). But even in this the priests received the hides, and did a flourishing trade with them. (ii) *The Sin-offering.* In this case only the fat was burned on the altar and the priests received all the flesh. (iii) *The Trespass-offering.* Again the fat alone was burned and the priests received all the flesh. (iv) *The Meat-offering.* This consisted of flour and wine and oil. Only a token part was offered on the altar; by far the greater part was the perquisite of the priests. (v) *The Peace-offering.* The fat and the entrails were burned on the altar; the priest received the breast and the right shoulder; and the rest was given back to the worshipper.

The priests enjoyed still further perquisites. (i) They received *the first-fruits of the seven kinds*—wheat, barley, the vine, the fig-tree, the pomegranate, the olive and honey. (ii) *The Terumah.* This was the offering of the choicest fruits of every growing thing. The priests had the right to an average of one fiftieth of any crop. (iii) *The Tithe.* A tithe had to be given of "everything which may be used as food and is cultivated and grows out of the earth." This tithe belonged to the Levites; but the priests received a tithe of the tithe that the Levites received. (iv) *The Challah.* This was the offering of kneaded dough. If dough was made with wheat, barley, spelt, oats or rye, a private individual had to give to the priests one twenty-fourth part, a public baker one forty-eighth part.

All this is at the back of Paul's refusal to accept even the basic supplies of life from the Church. He refused for two reasons. (i) The priests were a byword. While the ordinary Jewish family ate meat at the most once a week the priests suffered from an occupational disease consequent on eating too much meat. Their privileges, the luxury of their lives, their rapacity were notorious; Paul knew all about this. He knew how they used religion as a means to grow fat; and he was determined that he would go to the other extreme and take nothing. (ii) The second reason was his sheer independence. It may well be that he carried it too far, because it seems that he hurt the Corinthians by refusing all aid. But Paul was one of those independent souls who would starve rather than be beholden to anyone.

In the last analysis one thing dominated his conduct. He would do nothing that would bring discredit on the gospel or hinder it. Men judge a message by the life and character of the man who brings it; and Paul was determined that his hands would be clean. He would allow nothing in his life to contradict the message of his lips. Someone once said to a preacher, "I cannot hear what you say for listening to what you are." No one could ever say that to Paul.

THE PRIVILEGE AND THE TASK

1 *Corinthians* 9: 15–23

> But I have claimed none of these rights. I am not writing this to claim that these privileges should be extended to me. I would rather die than let anyone make ineffective my boast that I take nothing for my work. If I preach the gospel, I have nothing to boast about in that. I do it because necessity is laid upon me. Woe is me if I do not preach the gospel! If I do this of my own choice I do deserve a reward. But if I do it whether I like it or not, it is because I have been entrusted with this task. What then is my reward? My reward is that by my preaching I make the good news free, so that I do not use the privileges that I could claim as a preacher. For, though I am free from all men, yet I make myself a slave to all men, so that I might win more. To the Jews I became as a Jew that I might win the Jews. To those under the law I became

as under the law, although I am not under the law, that I might win those under the law. To those who live without the law I became as one without the law—not without the law of God, but within the law of Christ—that I might win those who live without the law. To the weak I became weak that I might win the weak. I have become all things to all men, so that by any means I might save some. I do this because of the good news, that I may share it with all men.

In this passage there is a kind of outline of Paul's whole conception of his ministry.

(i) He regarded it as *a privilege*. The one thing he will not do is take money for working for Christ. When a certain famous American professor retired from his chair he made a speech in which he thanked his university for paying him a salary all these years for doing work which he would gladly have paid to do. This does not mean that a man must always work for nothing; there are certain obligations that he must fulfil which he cannot fulfil for nothing; but it does mean that he should never work primarily for money. He should regard his work not as a career of accumulation but as an opportunity of service. He must regard himself as a man whose primary duty is not to help himself but whose privilege is to serve others for God's sake.

(ii) He regarded it as *a duty*. Paul's point of view was that if he had chosen to be a preacher of the gospel he might quite legitimately have demanded payment for his work; but he had not chosen the work; it had chosen him; he could no more stop doing it than he could stop breathing; and there could, therefore, be no question of payment.

Ramon Lull, the great Spanish saint and mystic, tells us how he became a missionary of Christ. He had been living a careless and pleasure-loving life. Then one day, when he was alone, Christ came carrying his Cross and saying to him, "Carry this for me." But he refused. Again, when he was in the silence of a great cathedral, Christ came and asked him to carry his Cross; and again he refused. In a lonely moment Christ came a third time, and this time, said Ramon Lull,

"He took his Cross and with a look he left it lying in my hands. What could I do but take it up and carry it on?" Paul would have said, "What can I do but tell men the good news of Christ?"

(iii) In spite of the fact that he would take no payment, Paul knew that he received daily *a great reward*. He had the satisfaction of bringing the gospel freely to all men who would receive it. It is always true that the real reward of any task is not its money payment but the satisfaction of a job well done. That is why the biggest thing in life is not to choose the job with the biggest pay but the one in which we will find the greatest satisfaction.

Albert Schweitzer describes the kind of moment which brought him the greatest happiness. Someone suffering intensely is brought into his hospital. He soothes the man by telling him that he will put him to sleep and will operate on him and all will be well. After the operation he sits beside the patient waiting for him to regain consciousness. Slowly he opens his eyes and then whispers in sheer wonderment, "I have no more pain." That was it. There was no material reward there, but a satisfaction as deep as the depths of the heart itself.

To have mended one shattered life, to have restored one wanderer to the right way, to have healed one broken heart, to have brought one soul to Christ is not a thing whose reward can be measured in financial terms, but its joy is beyond all measurement.

(iv) Finally, Paul speaks about *the method of his ministry,* which was to become all things to all men. This is not a case of being hypocritically one thing to one man and another to another. It is a matter in the modern phrase, of being able to get alongside anyone. The man who can never see anything but his own point of view and who never makes any attempt to understand the mind and heart of others, will never make a pastor or an evangelist or even a friend.

Boswell somewhere speaks of "the art of accommodating oneself to others." That was an art which Dr. Johnson possessed in a supreme degree, for, not only was he a great talker, but he was also a great listener with a supreme ability to get alongside any man. A friend said of him that he had the art of "leading people to talk on their favourite subjects, and on what they knew best." Once a country clergyman complained to Mrs. Thrale's mother of the dullness of his people. "They talk of runts" (young cows), he said bitterly. "Sir," said the old lady, "Mr. Johnson would have learned to talk of runts." To the countryman he would have become a countryman. Robert Lynd points out how Johnson would discuss the digestive apparatus of a dog with a country parson; how he talked dancing with a dancing master; how he talked on farm management, thatching, the process of malting, the manufacture of gunpowder, the art of tanning. He talks of Johnson's "readiness to throw himself into the interests of other people. He was a man who would have enjoyed discussing the manufacture of spectacles with a spectacle-maker, law with a lawyer, pigs with a pig-breeder, diseases with a doctor, or ships with a ship-builder. He knew that in conversation it is only more blessed to give than to receive."

We can never attain to any kind of evangelism or friendship without speaking the same language and thinking the same thoughts as the other man. Someone once described teaching, medicine and the ministry as "the three patronizing professions." So long as we patronize people and make no effort to understand them, we can never get anywhere with them. Paul, the master missionary, who won more men for Christ than any other man, saw how essential it was to become all things to all men. One of our greatest necessities is to learn the art of getting alongside people; and the trouble so often is that we do not even try.

A REAL FIGHT

1 *Corinthians* 9: 24–27

Are you not aware that those who run in the stadium all run, but only one receives the prize? So run that you may win the prize. Now every athlete in the games practises complete self-discipline. They therefore do so to win a crown that quickly fades away; we do so to win a crown that never fades. I therefore so run as one who knows his goal; I fight, not like one who shadow-boxes; but I batter my body; I make it my slave; lest after I have preached to others I myself should fail to stand the test.

PAUL takes another line. He insists to those Corinthians who wanted to take the easy way that no man will ever get any- where without the sternest self-discipline. Paul was always fascinated by the picture of the athlete. An athlete must train with intensity if he is to win his contest; and Corinth knew how thrilling contests could be, for at Corinth the Isthmian games, second only to the Olympic games, were held. Further- more, the athlete undergoes this self-discipline and this training to win a crown of laurel leaves that within days will be a withered chaplet. How much more should the Christian discipline himself to win the crown which is eternal life.

In this passage Paul sets out a kind of brief philosophy of life.

(i) Life is a battle. As William James put it, "If this life be not a real fight, in which something is eternally gained for the universe by success, it is not better than a game of private theatricals from which one may withdraw at will. But it *feels* like a fight—as if there were something really wild in the universe which we, with all our idealities and faithfulnesses, are needed to redeem." As Coleridge had it, "So far from the world being a goddess in petticoats, it is rather a devil in a strait waistcoat." A flabby soldier cannot win battles; a slack trainer cannot win races. We must regard ourselves always as men engaged upon a campaign, as men pressing onwards to a goal.

(ii) To win the fight and to be victorious in the race demands discipline. We have to discipline our bodies; it is one of the neglected facts of the spiritual life that very often spiritual depression springs from nothing else than physical unfitness. If a man is going to do his best work in anything he must bring to it a body as fit as he can make it. We have to discipline our minds; it is one of the tragedies of life that men may refuse to think until they become incapable of thinking. We can never solve problems by refusing to see them or by running away from them. We must discipline our souls; we can do so by facing life's sorrows with calm endurance, its temptations with the strength God gives, its disappointments with courage.

(iii) We need to know our goal. A distressing thing is the obvious aimlessness of the lives of so many people; they are drifting anywhere instead of going somewhere. Maarten Maartens has a parable. "There was a man once, a satirist. In the natural course of time his friends slew him, and he died. And the people came and stood round about his corpse. 'He treated the whole round world as his football,' they said indignantly, 'and he kicked it.' The dead man opened one eye. 'But,' he said, *'always towards the goal.'*" Someone once drew a cartoon showing two men on Mars looking down at the people in this world scurrying here, there and everywhere. One said to the other, "What are they doing?" The other replied, "They are going." "But," said the first, "where are they going?" "Oh," said the other, "they are not going anywhere; they are just going." And to go just anywhere is the certain way to arrive nowhere.

(iv) We need to know the worth of our goal. The great appeal of Jesus was rarely based on penalty and punishment. It was based on the declaration, "Look what you are missing if you do not take my way." The goal is *life*, and surely it is worth anything to win that.

(v) We cannot save others unless we master ourselves. Freud once said, "Psycho-analysis is learnt first of all on oneself, through the study of one's own personality." The Greeks declared that the first rule of life is, "Man know thyself." Certainly we cannot serve others until we have mastered ourselves; we cannot teach what we do not know; we cannot bring others to Christ until we ourselves have found him.

THE PERIL OF OVER-CONFIDENCE

1 *Corinthians* 10: 1–13

> Brothers, I do not want you to forget that all our fathers were under the cloud, and all of them passed through the midst of the sea, and all of them were baptized into Moses in the cloud and in the sea; and all ate the same food which the Spirit of God gave to them; and all drank the same drink which came to them by the action of the Spirit; for they drank of the rock which accompanied them through the action of the Spirit, and that rock was Christ. All the same, with the majority of them God was not well pleased; for they were left dead, strewn in the desert. These things have become examples to us, so that we should not be men who long for evil and forbidden things as they longed after them. Nor must you become idolaters as some of them did, as it stands written, "The people sat down to eat and drink and rose up to enjoy their sport." Nor must we practise fornication, as certain of them practised fornication, with the consequence that twenty-three thousand of them died in one day. Nor must we try the patience of the Lord beyond the limit, as some of them tried it, and in consequence were destroyed by serpents. Nor must you grumble, as certain of them grumbled, and were destroyed by the destroyer. It was to show what can happen that these things happened to them. They were written to warn us upon whom the ends of the ages have come. So then let him who thinks that he stands secure take care lest he fall. No test has come upon you other than that which comes on every man. You can rely on God, for he will not allow you to be tested beyond what you are able to bear, but he will send with the trial an escape route as well, so that you may be able to bear it.

IN this chapter Paul is still dealing with the question of eating meat which has been offered to idols. At the back of this passage lies the over-confidence of some of the Corinthian Christians. Their point of view was, "We have been baptized and are therefore one with Christ; we have partaken of the sacrament and so of the body and the blood of Christ; we are in him and he is in us; therefore we are quite safe; we can eat meat offered to idols and take no harm." So Paul warns of the danger of over-confidence.

When Oliver Cromwell was planning the education of his son Richard, he said, "I would have him learn a little history." And it is to history that Paul goes to show what can happen to people who have been blessed with the greatest privileges. He goes back to the days when the children of Israel were wayfarers in the desert. In those days the most wonderful things happened to them. They had the cloud which showed them the way and protected them in the hour of danger. (*Exodus* 13: 21; 14: 19). They were brought through the midst of the Red Sea (*Exodus* 14: 19–31). Both these experiences had given them a perfect union with Moses the greatest of leaders and law-givers, until it could be said that they were baptized into him as the Christian is baptized into Christ. They had eaten of the manna in the wilderness (*Exodus* 16: 11–15). In verse 5 Paul speaks of them drinking of the rock which followed them. This is taken not from the Old Testament itself but from Rabbinic tradition. *Numbers* 20: 1–11 tells how God enabled Moses to draw water from the rock for the thirsty people; the Rabbinic tradition was that that rock thereafter followed the people and always gave them water to drink. That was a legend which all the Jews knew.

All these privileges the children of Israel possessed, and yet in spite of them they failed most signally. When the people were too terrified to go forward into the Promised Land and all the scouts except Joshua and Caleb brought back a pessimistic report, God's judgment was that that whole generation would die in the desert. (*Numbers* 14: 30–32). When Moses was on Mount Sinai receiving the law, the people seduced Aaron into making a golden calf and worshipping it. (*Exodus* 32: 6). They were guilty of fornication, even in the desert, with the Midianites and the Moabites and thousands perished in the judgment of God. (*Numbers* 25: 1–9). (It is to be noted in passing that *Numbers* 25: 9 says twenty-four thousand perished; Paul says twenty-three thousand. The explanation is simply that Paul is quoting from memory. He rarely quotes scripture with verbatim accuracy; no one did in those days. There was no such thing as a concordance to help find a passage easily; scripture was not written in books, which had not yet been invented, but on unwieldy rolls.) They were wasted with serpents because they grumbled on the way (*Numbers* 21: 4–6). When Korah, Dathan and Abiram led a grumbling revolt, judgment fell on many and they died. (*Numbers* 16).

The history of Israel shows that people who enjoyed the greatest privileges of God were far from being safe from temptation; special privilege, Paul reminds the Corinthians, is no guarantee whatever of security.

We must note the temptations and the failures which Paul singles out.

(i) There is the temptation to idolatry. We do not now worship idols so blatantly; but if a man's god be that to which he gives all his time and thought and energy, men still worship the works of their own hands more than they worship God.

(ii) There is the temptation to fornication. So long as a man is a man there come to him temptations from his lower self. Only a passionate love of purity can save him from impurity.

(iii) There is the temptation to try God too far. Consciously or unconsciously many a man trades on the mercy of God. At the back of his mind there is the idea, "It will be all right; God will forgive." It is at his peril that he forgets that there is a holiness as well as a love of God.

(iv) There is the temptation to grumble. There are still many who greet life with a whine and not with a cheer.

So Paul insists on the need of vigilance. "Let him who thinks he stands secure take care lest he fall." Again and again a fortress has been stormed because its defenders thought that it was impregnable. In *Revelation* 3: 3 the risen Christ warns the Church of Sardis to be on the watch. The Acropolis of Sardis was built on a jutting spur of rock that was held to be impregnable. When Cyrus was besieging it, he offered a special reward to any who could find a way in. A certain soldier, Hyeroeades by name, was watching one day and saw a soldier in the Sardian garrison drop his helmet accidentally over the battlements. He saw him climb down after it and marked his path. That night he led a band up the cliffs by that very path and when they reached the top they found it quite unguarded; so they entered in and captured the citadel, which had been counted too safe. Life is a chancy business; we must be ever on the watch.

Paul concludes this section by saying three things about temptation.

(i) He is quite sure that temptation will come. That is part of life. But the Greek word which we translate temptation means far more a *test*. It is something designed, not to make us fall, but to test us, so that we emerge from it stronger than ever.

(ii) Any temptation that comes to us is not unique. Others have endured it and others have come through it. A friend tells how he was once driving Lightfoot, the great Bishop of Durham, in a horse carriage along a very narrow mountain road in Norway. It got so narrow that there were only inches between the wheels of the carriage and the cliffs on one side and the precipice on the other. He suggested in the end that Lightfoot would be safer to get out and walk. Lightfoot surveyed the situation and said, "Other carriages must have taken this road. Drive on." In the Greek Anthology there is an epigram which gives the epitaph of a shipwrecked sailor, supposedly from his own lips. "A shipwrecked mariner on this coast bids you set sail," he says. His bark may have been lost but many more have weathered the storm. When we are going through it, we are going through what others have, in the grace of God, endured and conquered.

(iii) With the temptation there is always a way of escape. The word is vivid (*ekbasis*). It means *a way out of a defile, a mountain pass*. The idea is of an army apparently surrounded and then suddenly seeing an escape route to safety. No man need fall to any temptation, for with the temptation there is the way out, and the way out is not the way of surrender nor of retreat, but the way of conquest in the power of the grace of God.

THE SACRAMENTAL OBLIGATION

1 *Corinthians* 10: 14–22

So then, my beloved ones, avoid everything that has to do with idols. I speak as I would to sensible men; pass your own judgment on what I am saying. Is not this blessed cup on which we ask the blessing, a very sharing in the blood of Jesus Christ? Is not the bread which we break a very sharing in the body of Christ? Just as the broken bread is one, so we, though we are many, are one body. For we all share in the one bread. Look at the nation of Israel in the racial sense. Do not those who eat of the sacrifices become sharers with the altar in them? What then am I saying? Am I saying that a thing which has been offered to idols is actually a real sacrifice? Am I saying that an idol is actually something? I do not say that, but I do say that what pagans sacrifice they sacrifice to demons and not to God; and I do not want you to share things with the demons. You cannot drink the cup of the Lord and the cup of demons. Or are we too to provoke the jealousy of the Lord? Surely you do not think that you are stronger than he is?

BEHIND this passage there are three ideas; two of them are peculiar to the age in which Paul lived; one is forever true and valid.

(i) As we have seen, when sacrifice was offered, part of the meat was given back to the worshipper to hold a feast. At such a feast it was always held that the god himself was a guest. More, it was often held that, after the meat had been sacrificed, the god himself was in it and that at the banquet he entered into the very bodies and spirits of those who ate. Just as an unbreakable bond was forged between two men if they ate each other's bread and salt, so a sacrificial meal formed a real communion between the god and his worshipper. The person who sacrificed was in a real sense a sharer with the altar; he had a mystic communion with the god.

(ii) At this time the whole world believed in demons. These demons might be good or bad, but more often they were bad. They were spirits who were intermediate between the gods

and men. For the Greek every spring, every grove, every
mountain, every tree, every stream, every pool, every rock,
every place had its demon. "There were gods in every fountain
and every mountain summit; gods breathing in the wind and
flashing in the lightning; gods in the ray of the sun and the
star; gods heaving in the earthquake and the storm." The
world was packed with demons. For the Jew there were the
shedim. These were evil spirits who haunted empty houses,
who lurked "in the crumbs on the floor, in the oil in the
vessels, in the water which we would drink, in the diseases
which attack us, in the air, in the room, by day and by night."

Paul believed in these demons; he called them "principalities
and powers." His point of view was this—an idol was nothing
and stood for nothing; but the whole business of idol
worship was the work of the demons; through it they
seduced men from God. When they were worshipping idols,
men thought they were worshipping gods; in fact they were
being deluded by these malignant demons. Idol worship
brought a man into contact, not with God, but with demons;
and anything to do with it had the demonic taint on it. Meat
offered to idols was nothing, but the fact remained it had
served the purposes of demons and was therefore a polluted
thing.

(iii) Out of this ancient set of beliefs comes one permanent
principle—a man who has sat at the table of Jesus Christ
cannot go on to sit at the table which is the instrument of
demons. If a man has handled the body and blood of
Christ there are things he cannot touch.

One of the great statues of Christ is that by Thorwaldsen;
after he had carved it, he was offered a commission to
carve a statue of Venus for the Louvre. His answer, was "The
hand that carved the form of Christ can never carve the form
of a heathen goddess."

When Prince Charlie was fleeing for his life he found
refuge with the eight men of Glenmoriston. They were outlaws
and criminals every one; there was a price of £30,000 on
Charlie's head; they had not a shilling among them; but for

weeks they hid him and kept him safe and not a man
betrayed him. The years passed on until the rebellion was but
an old, unhappy memory. One of the eight men, Hugh
Chisholm by name, found his way to Edinburgh. People were
interested now in his story of the prince and they talked to him.
He was poor and sometimes they would give him money. But
always Hugh Chisholm would shake hands with his left hand.
He said that when Prince Charlie left the eight men he shook
hands with them; and Hugh had sworn that he would never
again give to any man the hand he had given to his prince.

It was true in Corinth and it is true today, that the man
who has handled the sacred things of Christ cannot soil his
hands with mean and unworthy things.

THE LIMITS OF CHRISTIAN FREEDOM

1 *Corinthians* 10: 23—11: 1

All things are allowed to me, but all things are not good for me.
All things are allowed, but all things do not build up. Let no one
think only of his own good, but let him think of the good of
the other man too. Eat everything that is sold in the market place,
and don't ask fussy questions for conscience sake; for the earth and
its fulness belong to god. If one of the pagans invites you to a meal,
and you are willing to go, eat anything that is put before you, and
don't ask questions for conscience sake. But if anyone says to you,
"This is meat that was part of a sacrifice," don't eat it, for the
sake of him who told you and for conscience sake. I don't mean
your own conscience, but the conscience of the other man, for why
has my liberty to be subject to the judgment of any man's
conscience? If I partake of something after I have given thanks for
it, how can I unjustly be criticized for eating that for which I gave
thanks? So then, whether you eat or whether you drink or
whatever you do, do all things to God's glory. Live in such a way
that you will cause neither Jew nor Greek nor church member to
stumble, just as I in all things try to win the approval of all men, for
I am not in this job for what I can get out of it, but for what benefits I
can bring to the many, that they may be saved. So then show yourselves to be imitators of me, as I am of Christ.

PAUL brings to an end this long discussion of the question of meat offered to idols with some very practical advice.

(i) His advice is that a Christian can buy anything that is sold in the shops and ask no questions. It was true that the meat sold in the shops might well have formed part of a sacrifice or have been slaughtered in the name of some god lest the demons enter into it; but it is possible to be too fussy and to create difficulties where none need exist. After all, in the last analysis, all things are God's.

(ii) If the Christian accepts an invitation to dinner in the house of a pagan, let him eat what is put before him and ask no questions. But, if he is deliberately informed that the meat is part of a sacrifice, he must not eat it. The assumption is that he is told by one of these brothers who cannot rid his conscience of the feeling that to eat such meat is wrong. Rather than bring worry to such a man the Christian must not eat.

(iii) So once again out of an old and remote situation emerges a great truth. Many a thing that a man may do with perfect safety as far as he himself is concerned, he must not do if it is going to be a stumbling-block to someone else. There is nothing more real than Christian freedom; but Christian freedom must be used to help others and not to shock or hurt them. A man has a duty to himself but a still greater duty to others.

We must note to where that duty extends.

(i) Paul insisted that a Corinthian Christian must be a good example to the *Jews*. Even to his enemies a man must be an example of the fine things.

(ii) The Corinthian Christian had a duty to the *Greeks*; that is to say he had to show a good example to those who were quite indifferent to Christianity. It is in fact by that example that many are won. There was a minister who went far out of his way to help a man who had nothing to do with the Church and rescued him from a difficult situation. That man began to come to Church and in the end made an astonishing request. He asked to be made an elder that he might spend his life showing his gratitude for what Christ through his servant had done for him.

(iii) The Corinthian Christian had a duty to his *fellow Church member*. It is the plain fact of life that somebody takes the cue for his conduct from everyone of us. We may not know it; but a younger or a weaker brother is often looking to us for a lead. It is our duty to give that lead which will strengthen the weak and confirm the waverer and save the tempted from sin.

We can do all things to the glory of God only when we remember the duty we must discharge to our fellow men; and we will do that only when we remember that our Christian freedom is given to us not for our own sake but for the sake of others.

Chapters 11 to 14 are amongst the most difficult in the whole epistle for a modern person in the western world to understand; but they are also among the most interesting, for they deal with the problems which had arisen in the Corinthian Church in connection with public worship. In them we see the infant Church struggling with the problem of offering a fitting and a seemly worship to God. It will make the section easier to follow if we set out at the beginning the various parts of which it is composed.

(i) 11: 2—11: 16 deals with the problem of whether or not women should worship with their heads uncovered.

(ii) 11: 17—11: 23 deals with problems which have arisen in connection with the *Agape* or Love Feast, the weekly common meal which the Christian congregation held.

(iii) 11: 24—11: 34 deals with the correct observance of the Sacrament of the Lord's Supper.

(iv) 12 discusses the problem of welding into one harmonious whole those who possess all kinds of different gifts. It is here that we have the great picture of the Church as the Body of Christ, and of each member as a limb in that body.

(v) 13 is the great hymn of love which shows men the more excellent way.

(vi) 14: 1—14: 23 deals with the problem of speaking with tongues.

(vii) 14: 24—14: 33 insists on the necessity of orderliness in public worship and seeks to bring under necessary discipline the overflowing enthusiasm of a newly born Church.

(viii) 14: 24—14: 36 discusses the place of women in the public worship of God in the Church of Corinth.

THE NECESSARY MODESTY

1 *Corinthians* 11: 2–16

> I praise you because you remember me in all things and because you hold fast to the traditions as I handed them down to you. But I want you to know that Christ is the head of every man, and that the man is the head of the woman, and that God is the head of Christ. Every man who prays or preaches with his head *covered* shames his head. Every woman who prays or preaches with her head *uncovered* shames her head, for she is in exactly the same case as a woman whose head has been shaved; for, if a woman does not cover her head, let her have her hair cut also. If it is shameful for a woman to have her hair cut or to be shaved, let her have her head covered. A man ought not to cover his head because he is the image and the glory of God; but woman is the glory of man; for the man did not come from the woman but the woman from the man; for the man was not created for the sake of the woman but woman for the sake of man. For this reason a woman ought to retain upon her head the sign that she is under someone else's authority, for the sake of the angels. All the same it is true that, in the Lord, woman is nothing without man nor man without woman; for just as woman came from man, so man is born through woman, and all things are from God. Use your own judgment on this. Is it fitting for a woman to pray to God uncovered? Does not the very nature of things teach us that it is a dishonour to a man if he lets his hair grow long? But if a woman lets her hair grow long it is her glory, because her hair was given to her for a covering. All the same, if anyone wishes to go on arguing for the sake of arguing, it is sufficient to say that we have no such custom, nor have the Churches of God.

THIS is one of these passages which have a purely local and temporary significance; they look at first sight as if they had only an antiquarian interest because they deal with a situation which has long since ceased to have any relevance for us; and yet such passages have a very great interest because they shed a flood of light on the domestic affairs and problems of the early Church; and, for him who has eyes to see, they have a very great importance, because Paul solves the problems by principles which are eternal.

The problem was whether or not in the Christian Church a woman had the right to take part in the service unveiled. Paul's answer was bluntly this—the veil is always a sign of subjection, worn by an inferior in the presence of a superior; now woman is inferior to man, in the sense that man is head of the household; therefore it is wrong for a man to appear at public worship veiled and equally wrong for a woman to appear unveiled. It is very improbable that in the twentieth century we are likely to accept this view of the inferiority and subordination of women. But we must read this chapter in the light not of the twentieth century but of the first, and as we read it we must remember three things.

(i) We must remember the place of the veil in the East. To this day eastern women wear the *yashmak* which is a long veil leaving the forehead and the eyes uncovered but reaching down almost to the feet. In Paul's time the eastern veil was even more concealing. It came right over the head with only an opening for the eyes and reached right down to the feet. A respectable eastern woman would never have dreamed of appearing without it. Writing in Hastings' *Dictionary of the Bible,* T. W. Davies says, "No·respectable woman in an eastern village or city goes out without it, and, if she does, she is in danger of being misjudged. Indeed English and American missionaries in Egypt told the present writer that their own wives and daughters when going about find it often best to wear the veil."

The veil was two things. (*a*) It was a sign of inferiority. (*b*) But it was also a great protection. Verse 10 is very difficult to translate. We have translated it: "For this reason a woman ought to retain upon her head the sign that she is under someone else's authority," but the Greek literally means that a woman ought to retain "her authority upon her head." Sir William Ramsay explains it this way—"In Oriental lands the veil is the power and honour and dignity of the woman. With the veil on her head she can go anywhere in security and profound respect. She is not seen; it is a mark of thoroughly bad manners to observe a veiled woman in the street. She is alone. The rest of the people around are non-existent to her, as she is to them. She is supreme in the crowd. . . . But without the veil the woman is a thing of nought, whom anyone may insult. . . . A woman's authority and dignity vanish along with the all-covering veil that she discards."

In the East, then, the veil is all-important. It does not only mark the inferior status of a woman; it is the inviolable protection of her modesty and chastity.

(ii) We must remember the status of women in Jewish eyes. Under Jewish law woman was vastly inferior to man. She had been created out of Adam's rib (*Genesis* 2: 22, 23) and she had been created to be the helpmeet of man (*Genesis* 2: 18). There was a Rabbinic piece of fanciful exegesis which said, "God did not form woman out of the head lest she should become proud; nor out of the eye lest she should lust; nor out of the ear lest she should be curious; nor out of the mouth lest she should be talkative; nor out of the heart lest she should be jealous; nor out of the hand lest she should be covetous; nor out of the foot lest she should be a wandering busybody; but out of a rib which was always covered; therefore modesty should be her primary quality."

It is the unfortunate truth that in Jewish law a woman was a thing and was part of the property of her husband over which he had complete rights of disposal. It was true that in the synagogue, for instance, women had no share whatever in the worship but were segregated completely from the men in a shut-off gallery or other part of the building.

In Jewish law and custom it was unthinkable that women should claim any kind of equality with men.

In verse 10 there is the curious phrase that women should be veiled "for the sake of the angels." It is not certain what this means, but probably it goes back to the strange old story in *Genesis* 6: 1 and 2 which tells how the angels fell a prey to the charms of mortal women and so sinned; it may well be that the idea is that the unveiled woman is a temptation even to the angels, for an old Rabbinic tradition said that it was the beauty of women's long hair which tempted the angels.

(iii) It must always be remembered that this situation arose in *Corinth*, probably the most licentious city in the world. Paul's point of view was that in such a situation it was far better to err on the side of being too modest and too strict rather than to do anything which might either give the heathen a chance to criticize the Christians as being too lax or be a cause of temptation to the Christians themselves.

It would be quite wrong to make this passage of universal application; it was intensely relevant to the Church of Corinth but it has nothing to do with whether or not women should wear hats in church at the present day. But for all its local significance it has three great permanent truths in it.

(i) It is always better to err on the side of being too strict than on the side of being too lax. It is far better to abandon rights which may be a stumbling-block to some than to insist on them. It is the fashion to decry convention; but a man should always think twice before he defies it and shocks others. True, he must never be the slave of convention, but conventions do not usually come into being for nothing.

(ii) Even after he has stressed the subordination of women, Paul goes on to stress even more directly the essential partnership of man and woman. Neither can live without the other. If there be subordination, it is in order that the partnership may be more fruitful and more lovely for both.

(iii) Paul finishes the passage with a rebuke to the man who argues for the sake of argument. Whatever the differences that may arise between men, there is no place in the Church for the deliberately contentious man or woman. There is a time to stand on principle; but there is never a time to be contentiously argumentative. There is no reason why people should not differ and yet remain at peace.

THE WRONG KIND OF FEAST

1 *Corinthians* 11: 17–22

> When I give you this instruction, I am not praising you, because when you meet together it is actually doing you more harm than good. Firstly, I hear that when you meet together in assembly, there are divisions among you; and to some extent I believe it. There are bound to be differences of opinion among you, so that it may become clear which of you are of tried and sterling quality. So then when you assemble together in the same place it is certainly not the *Lord's* meal that you eat; for each of you, when you eat, is in a hurry to get his own meal first, and the result is that some go hungry and some drink until they are drunk. Have you not your own houses for eating and drinking? Have you no reverence for the assembly of God? Are you going to shame those who are poor? What am I to say to you? Am I to commend you in this? I certainly do not.

THE ancient world was in many ways much more social than ours is. It was the regular custom for groups of people to meet together for meals. There was, in particular, a certain kind of feast called an *eranos* to which each participant brought his own share of the food, and in which all the contributions were pooled to make a common meal. The early Church had such a custom, a feast called the *Agape* or Love Feast. To it all the Christians came, bringing what they could, the resources were pooled and they sat down to a common meal. It was a lovely custom; and it is to our loss that the custom has vanished. It was a way of producing and nourishing real Christian fellowship.

But in the Church at Corinth things had gone sadly wrong with the Love Feast. In the Church there were rich and poor; there were those who could bring plenty, and there were slaves who could bring hardly anything at all. In fact for many a poor slave the Love Feast must have been the only decent meal in the whole week. But in Corinth the art of sharing had got lost. The rich did not share their food but ate it in little exclusive groups by themselves, hurrying through it in case they had to share, while the poor had next to nothing. The result was that the meal at which the social differences between members of the Church should have been obliterated only succeeded in aggravating these same differences. Unhesitatingly and unsparingly Paul rebukes this.

(i) It may well be that the different groups were composed of those who held different opinions. A great scholar has said, "To have religious zeal, without becoming a religious partisan, is a great proof of true devotion." When we think differently from a man, we may in time come to understand him and even to sympathize with him, if we remain in fellowship with him and talk things over with him; but, if we shut ourselves off from him and form our own little group while he remains in his, there is never any hope of mutual understanding.

> He drew a circle that shut me out—
> Rebel, heretic, thing to flout—
> But love and I had the wit to win—
> We drew a circle that took him in.

(ii) The early Church was the one place in all the ancient world where the barriers were down. That world was very rigidly divided; there were the free men and the slaves; there were the Greeks and the barbarians—the people who did not speak Greek; there were the Jews and the Gentiles; there were the Roman citizens and the lesser breeds without the law; there were the cultured and the ignorant. The Church was the one place where all men could and did come together. A great Church historian has written about these early Christian congregations, "Within their own limits they had solved almost by the way the social problem which baffled Rome and baffles Europe still. They had lifted woman to her rightful place, restored the dignity of labour, abolished beggary, and drawn the sting of slavery. The secret of the revolution is that the selfishness of race and class was forgotten in the Supper of the Lord, and a new basis for society found in love of the visible image of God in men for whom Christ died."

A church where social and class distinctions exist is no true church at all. A real church is a body of men and women united to each other because all are united to Christ. Even the word used to describe the sacrament is suggestive. We call it the Lord's *Supper;* but *supper* is to some extent misleading. Usually to us it is not the main meal of the day. But the Greek word is *deipnon.* For the Greek the breakfast was a meal where all that was eaten was a little bread dipped in wine; the midday meal was eaten anywhere, even on the street or in a city square; the *deipnon* was the main meal of the day, where people sat down with no sense of hurry and not only satisfied their hunger but lingered long together. The very word shows that the Christian meal ought to be a meal where people linger long in each other's company.

(iii) A church is no true church if the art of sharing is forgotten. When people wish to keep things to themselves and to their own circle they are not even beginning to be Christian. The true Christian cannot bear to have too much while others have too little; he finds his greatest privilege not in jealously guarding his privileges but in giving them away.

THE LORD'S SUPPER

1 Corinthians 11: 23–34

For I received of the Lord that which I also handed on to you, that the Lord Jesus, on the night on which he was being delivered up, took bread, and, after he had given thanks, he broke it and said, "This is my body which is for you; this do that you may

remember me." In the same way, after the meal, he took the cup
and said, "This cup is the new covenant and it cost my blood. Do
this, as often as you drink it, so that you will remember me." For
as often as you eat this bread and drink this cup you do proclaim
the death of the Lord until he will come. Therefore whoever eats
this bread and drinks this cup of the Lord in an unfitting way is
guilty of a sin against the body and blood of the Lord. But let a
man examine himself, and so let him eat of that bread and drink
of that cup. For he who eats and drinks as some of you do, eats
and drinks judgment to himself, because he does not discern what
the body means. It is because of this that many among you are ill
and weak and some have died. But if we truly discerned what we
are like we would not be liable to judgment. But in this very
judgment of the Lord we are being disciplined that we may not be
finally condemned along with the world. So then, my brothers,
when you come together wait for each other. If anyone is hungry
let him eat at home, so that you may not meet together in such
a way as to render yourselves liable to judgment. As for the other
matters, I will put them in order when I shall have come.

No passage in the whole New Testament is of greater interest
than this. For one thing, it gives us our warrant for the
most sacred act of worship in the Church, the Sacrament of
the Lord's Supper; and, for another since the letter to the
Corinthians is earlier than the earliest of the gospels, this is
actually the first recorded account we possess of any word of
Jesus.

The Sacrament can never mean the same for every person;
but we do not need fully to understand it to benefit from it.
As someone has said, "We do not need to understand the
chemistry of bread in order to digest it and to be nourished
by it." For all that we do well to try at least to understand
something of what Jesus meant when he spoke of the bread
and the wine as he did.

"This is my body," he said of the bread. One simple fact
precludes us from taking this with a crude literalism. When
Jesus spoke, he was still in the body; and there was nothing
clearer than that his body and the bread were at that moment
quite different things. Nor did he simply mean, "This stands

for my body." In a sense that is true. The broken bread of the Sacrament does stand for the body of Christ; but it does more. To him who takes it into his hands and upon his lips with faith and love, it is a means not only of memory but of living contact with Jesus Christ. To an unbeliever it would be nothing; to a lover of Christ it is the way to his presence.

"This cup," said Jesus, in the usual version, "is the new covenant in my blood." We have translated it slightly differently, "This cup is the new covenant and it cost my blood." The Greek preposition *en* most commonly means *in;* but it can, and regularly does, mean *at the cost or price of,* especially when it translates the Hebrew preposition *be.* Now a covenant is a relationship entered into between two people. There was an old covenant between God and man and that old relationship was based on *law.* In it God chose and approached the people of Israel and became in a special sense their God; but there was a condition, that, if this relationship was going to last, they must keep his law. (cp. *Exodus* 24: 1–8). With Jesus a new relationship is opened to man, dependent not on law but on love, dependent not on man's ability to keep the law—for no man can do that—but on the free grace of God's love offered to men.

Under the old covenant a man could do nothing other than fear God for he was ever in default since he could never perfectly keep the law; under the new covenant he comes to God as a child to a father. However you look at things, *it cost the life of Jesus to make this new relationship possible.* "The blood is the life," says the law (*Deuteronomy* 12: 23); it cost Jesus's life, his blood, as the Jew would put it. And so the scarlet wine of the sacrament stands for the very life-blood of Christ without which the new covenant, the new relationship of man to God, could never have been possible.

This passage goes on to talk about eating and drinking this bread and wine unworthily. The unworthiness consisted in the fact that the man who did so did "not discern the Lord's body." That phrase can equally well mean two things; and each is so real and so important that it is quite likely that both are intended.

(i) It may mean that the man who eats and drinks unworthily does not realize what the sacred symbols mean. It may mean that he eats and drinks with no reverence and no sense of the love that these symbols stand for or the obligation that is laid upon him.

(ii) It may also mean this. The phrase *the body of Christ* again and again stands for the Church; it does so, as we shall see, in chapter 12. Paul has just been rebuking those who with their divisions and their class distinctions divide the Church; so this may mean that he eats and drinks unworthily who has never realized that the whole Church is the body of Christ but is at variance with his brother. Every man in whose heart there is hatred, bitterness, contempt against his brother man, as he comes to the Table of our Lord, eats and drinks unworthily. So then to eat and drink unworthily is to do so with no sense of the greatness of the thing we do, and to do so while we are at variance with the brother for whom also Christ died.

Paul goes on to say that the misfortunes which have fallen upon the Church at Corinth may be due to nothing else than the fact that they come to this sacrament while they are divided among themselves; but these misfortunes are sent not to destroy them but to discipline them and to bring them back to the right way.

We must be clear about one thing. The phrase which forbids a man to eat and drink unworthily does not shut out the man who is a sinner and knows it. An old highland minister seeing an old woman hesitate to receive the cup, stretched it out to her, saying, "Take it, woman; it's for sinners; it's for you." If the Table of Christ were only for perfect people none might ever approach it. The way is never closed to the penitent sinner. To the man who loves God and his fellow men the way is ever open, and his sins, though they be as scarlet, shall be white as snow.

THE CONFESSION OF THE SPIRIT

1 *Corinthians* 12: 1–3

> Brothers, I do not want you to be ignorant about manifestations
> of the Spirit. You know that when you were heathens you were
> led away to dumb idols, just as any impulse moved you. I want
> you therefore to know that no one, speaking through the Spirit of
> God, can say, "Accursed be Jesus," and no one can say, "Jesus is
> Lord," unless through the Holy Spirit.

IN the Church of Corinth the most amazing things were
happening through the action of the Holy Spirit, but in an
age of ecstasy and of enthusiasm there can be hysterical
excitement and self-delusion as well as the real thing, and in
this and the next two chapters Paul deals with true manifestations of the Spirit.

This is a very interesting passage because it gives us two
phrases which were battle cries.

(i) There is the phrase *Accursed be Jesus*. There could be
four ways in which this terrible phrase might arise.

(*a*) It would be used by the Jews. The synagogue prayers
included regularly a cursing of all apostates; and Jesus would
come under that. Further, as Paul knew so well (*Galatians*
3: 13), the Jewish law laid it down, "Cursed be everyone
who hangs on a tree." And Jesus had been crucified. It
would be no uncommon thing to hear the Jews pronouncing
their anathemas on this heretic and criminal whom the
Christians worshipped.

(*b*) It is by no means unlikely that the Jews would make
proselytes attracted by Christianity either pronounce this curse
or suffer excommunication from all Jewish worship. When
Paul was telling Agrippa about his persecuting days, he said,
"I often punished them in every synagogue and *I forced them
to blaspheme.*" (*Acts* 26: 11). It must often have been a
condition of remaining within the synagogue that a man
should pronounce a curse on Jesus Christ.

(*c*) Whatever was true when Paul was writing, it is certainly
true that later on, in the sore days of persecution, Christians

were compelled either to curse Christ or to die. In the time of Trajan, it was the test of Pliny, governor of Bithynia, to demand that a person accused of being a Christian should curse Christ. When Polycarp, Bishop of Smyrna, was arrested, the demand of the proconsul Statius Quadratus was, "Say, 'Away with the atheists,' swear by the godhead of Caesar, and blaspheme Christ." And it was the great answer of the aged bishop, "Eighty and six years have I served Christ, and he has never done me wrong. How can I blaspheme my King who saved me?" There certainly came a time when a man was confronted with the choice of cursing Christ or facing death.

(*d*) There was the possibility that, even in the Church, someone in a semi-mad frenzy might cry out, "Accursed be Jesus." In that hysterical atmosphere anything might happen and be claimed to be the work of the Spirit. Paul lays it down that no man can say a word against Christ and attribute it to the influence of the Spirit.

(ii) Beside this there is the Christian battle cry, *Jesus is Lord*. In so far as the early Church had a creed at all, that simple phrase was it. (cp. *Philippians* 2: 11). The word for Lord was *kurios* and it was a tremendous word. It was the official title of the Roman Emperor. The demand of the persecutors always was, "Say, 'Caesar is Lord (*kurios*).'" It was the word by which the sacred name Jehovah was rendered in the Greek translation of the Old Testament scriptures. When a man could say, "Jesus is Lord," it meant that he gave to Jesus the supreme loyalty of his life and the supreme worship of his heart.

It is to be noted that Paul believed that a man could say, "Jesus is Lord," only when the Spirit enabled him to say it. The Lordship of Jesus was not so much something which he discovered for himself as something which God, in his grace, revealed to him.

GOD'S DIFFERING GIFTS

1 *Corinthians* 12: 4–11

> There are distinctions between different kinds of special gifts, but there is one and the same Spirit. There are distinctions between different kinds of service, but there is one and the same Lord. There are distinctions between different kinds of effects, but it is one and the same God who causes them all in every man. To each man there is given his own manifestation of the Spirit, and always towards some beneficial end. To one man there is given through the Spirit the word of wisdom; to another, the word of knowledge, by the same Spirit; to still another, faith, by the same Spirit; to another, the special gifts of healing through one and the same Spirit; to another, the ability to produce wonderful deeds of power; to another, prophecy; to another, the ability to distinguish between different kinds of spirits; to another, different kinds of tongues; to another, the power to interpret tongues. One and the same Spirit produces all these effects, sharing them out individually to each man, as the Spirit wishes.

PAUL'S idea in this section is to stress the essential unity of the Church. The Church is the Body of Christ and the characteristic of a healthy body is that every part in it performs its own function for the good of the whole; but unity does not mean uniformity, and therefore within the Church there are differing gifts and differing functions. But every one of them is a gift of the same Spirit and designed, not for the glory of the individual member of the Church, but for the good of the whole.

Paul begins by saying that all special gifts (*charismata*) come from God and it is his belief that they must, therefore, be used in God's service. The fault of the Church, in modern times at least, is that it has interpreted the idea of special gifts far too narrowly. It has too often acted on the apparent assumption that the special gifts which it can use consist of things like speaking, praying, teaching, writing—the more or less intellectual gifts. It would be well if the Church would realize that the gifts of the man who can work with his hands,

are just as special gifts from God. The mason, the carpenter,
the electrician, the painter, the engineer, the plumber all have
their special gifts, which are from God and can be used for
him.

It is of the greatest interest to examine the list of special
gifts which Paul gives, because from it we learn much about
the character and work of the early Church.

He begins with two things which sound very like each
other—*the word of wisdom* and *the word of knowledge*. The
Greek word we have translated *wisdom* is *sophia*. It is defined
by Clement of Alexandria as "the knowledge of things human
and divine and of their causes." Aristotle described it as
"striving after the best ends and using the best means." This
is the highest kind of wisdom; it comes not so much from
thought as from communion with God. It is the wisdom which
knows God. *Knowledge*—the Greek word is *gnosis*—is a much
more practical thing. It is the knowledge which knows what
to do in any given situation. It is the practical application to
human life and affairs of *sophia*. The two things are necessary—
the *wisdom* which knows by communion with God the deep
things of God, and the *knowledge* which, in the daily life of
the world and the Church, can put that wisdom into practice.

Next on the list comes *faith*. Paul means more than what we
might call ordinary faith. It is the faith which really produces
results. It is not just the intellectual conviction that a thing is
true; it is the passionate belief in a thing which makes a man
spend all that he is and has on it. It is the faith which
steels the will and nerves the sinew of a man into action.

> O God, when the heart is warmest,
> And the head is clearest,
> Give me to act;
> To turn the purposes Thou formest
> Into fact!

It is the faith which turns the vision into deeds.

Next Paul speaks of *special gifts of healings*. The early
Church lived in a world where healing miracles were a

common-place. If a Jew was ill he was much more likely to go to the Rabbi than to the doctor; and he would most likely be healed. Aesculapius was the Greek God of healing. People went to his temples, usually spending whole nights there, to be healed, and often they were. To this day we find among the ruins of these temples votive tablets and inscriptions commemorating healings; and no one goes to the trouble and expense of erecting an inscription for nothing. In the Temple at Epidaurus there is an inscription which tells how a certain Alketas, "although blind saw the dream vision. The god seemed to come to him and to open his eyes with his fingers, and he first saw the trees that were in the temple. At day-break he went away cured." In the temple at Rome there is an inscription, "To Valerius Aper, a blind soldier, the god gave an oracle to come and take blood of a white cock with honey and to mix them into a salve and anoint his eyes for three days, and he received his sight and came and gave thanks publicly to the god." It was an age of cures.

There is not the slightest doubt that gifts of healing did exist in the early Church; Paul would never have cited them unless they were real. In the letter of James (5: 14) there is an instruction that if a man is ill he must come to the elders and they will anoint him with oil. It is the simple historical fact that until the ninth century the Sacrament of Unction was for healing; and only then did it become the Sacrament of Extreme Unction, and a preparation for death. The Church never altogether lost this gift of healing; and in recent times it has been somewhat rediscovered. Montaigne, one of the wisest writers who ever wrote, said about a boy's education, "I would have his limbs trained no less than his brains. It is not a mind we are educating nor a body; it is a man. And we must not split him in two." For too long the Church split man into a soul and a body, and accepted responsibility for his soul but not for his body. It is good that in our time we have once again learned to treat man as a whole.

Next Paul lists *wonderful deeds of power*. Almost certainly he refers to *exorcisms*. In those days many illnesses, often all illnesses, and especially mental illnesses, were attributed to the work of demons; and it was one of the functions of the Church to exorcise these demons. Whether or not they were in fact real, the person so possessed was convinced that they were, and the Church could and did help him. Exorcism is still very much a reality in the mission field; and at all times it is the function of the Church to minister to a mind diseased and disturbed.

Paul goes on to mention *prophecy*. It would give a better idea of the meaning of this word if we translated it *preaching*. We have too much associated *prophecy* with the foretelling of what was to happen. But at all times *prophecy* has been far more *forthtelling* than *foretelling*. The prophet is a man who lives so close to God that he knows his mind and heart and will, and so can make them known to men. Because of that his function is twofold. (*a*) He brings rebuke and warning, telling men that their way of action is not in accordance with the will of God. (*b*) He brings advice and guidance, seeking to direct men into the ways God wishes them to go.

Paul then mentions *the ability to distinguish between different kinds of spirits*. In a society where the atmosphere was tense and where all kinds of manifestations were normal, it was necessary to distinguish between what was real and what was merely hysterical, between what came from God and what came from the devil. To this day, when a thing is outside our ordinary orbit, it is supremely difficult to tell whether it is from God or not. The one principle to observe is that we must always try to understand before we condemn.

Lastly Paul lists *the gift of tongues* and *the ability to interpret them*. This matter of *tongues* was causing a great deal of perplexity in the Church at Corinth. What happened was this—at a church service someone would fall into an ecstasy and pour out a torrent of unintelligible sounds in no known language. This was a highly-coveted gift because it was supposed to be due to the direct influence of the Spirit of God. To the congregation it was of course completely meaningless. Sometimes the person so moved could interpret his own outpourings, but usually it required someone else who had the gift of interpretation. Paul never questioned the reality of the gift of tongues, but he was well aware that it had its dangers, for ecstasy and a kind of self-hypnotism are very difficult to distinguish.

The picture we get is of a Church vividly alive. Things happened; in fact astonishing things happened. Life was heightened and intensified. There was nothing dull and ordinary about the early Church. Paul knew that all this vivid, powerful activity was the work of the Spirit who gave to each man his gift to use for all.

THE BODY OF CHRIST

1 *Corinthians* 12: 12–31

Just as the body is one, although it has many members, and just as all the members of the body, though they are many, are one body, so also is Christ. For by the one Spirit we have all been baptized in such a way as to become one body, whether we be Jews or Greeks, whether we be slaves or free men; and we have all been watered by the one Spirit. For the body does not consist of one member but of many. If the foot were to say, "Because I am not the hand I am not of the body," it is not because of that not part of the body. And if the ear were to say, "Because I am not the eye, I am not part of the body," it is not because of that not part of the body. If the whole body were an eye, where would the sense of hearing be? If the whole body consisted only of the sense of hearing, where would the sense of smell be? But, as it is, God has arranged the members, each individual one of them, as he willed. If everything were one member where would the body be? But, as it is, there are many members but one body. The eye cannot say to the hand, "I do not need you." Or again, the head cannot say to the feet, "I do not need you." Rather indeed those parts of the body which seem to be weaker are all the more essential; and to those parts of the body which seem to be rather without honour we apportion a very special honour; and the uncomely parts of the body have a special comeliness, while the comely parts need no special consideration. God has so compounded the body, giving a special honour to that part of it which seemed to lack all honour, so that there should be no division in the body, but that the members should all have the same care for each other. So, if one member suffers, all the members suffer with it; and if one member is glorified all the members share its joy. You are the body of Christ and each of you is a member of it. So God appointed in the Church some, in the first place, as apostles; in the second place, prophets; in the third place, teachers; then the power to work wonders; then special gifts of healings; the ability to help; the ability to administer; different kinds of tongues. Surely all are not apostles? Surely all are not prophets? Surely all are not teachers? Surely all have not the power to do wonderful things? Surely all do not possess the gifts of healings? Surely all do not speak with tongues? Surely all cannot interpret? Long for the yet greater gifts. I show you a still more excellent way.

HERE is one of the most famous pictures of the unity of the Church ever written. Men have always been fascinated by the way in which the different parts of the body co-operate. Long ago Plato had drawn a famous picture in which he had said that the head was the citadel; the neck, the isthmus between the head and the body; the heart, the fountain of the body; the pores, the lanes of the body; the veins, the canals of the body. So Paul drew his picture of the Church as a body. A body consists of many parts but there is in it an essential unity. Plato had pointed out that we do not say, "My finger has a pain," we say, "I have a pain." There is an *I*, a personality, which gives unity to the many and varying parts of the body. What the *I* is to the body, Christ is to the Church. It is in him that all the diverse parts find their unity.

Paul goes on to look at this in another way. "You," he says, "are the body of Christ." There is a tremendous thought here. Christ is no longer in this world in the body; therefore if he wants a task done within the world he has to find a man to do it. If he wants a child taught, he has to find a teacher to teach him; if he wants a sick person cured, he has to find a physician or surgeon to do his work; if he wants his story told, he has to find a man to tell it. Literally, we

A5

have to be the body of Christ, hands to do his work, feet to run upon his errands, a voice to speak for him.

> "He has no hands but our hands
>   To do his work today;
> He has no feet but our feet
>   To lead men in his way;
> He has no voice but our voice
>   To tell men how he died;
> He has no help but our help
>   To lead them to his side."

Here is the supreme glory of the Christian man—he is part of the body of Christ upon earth.

So Paul draws a picture of the unity which should exist inside the Church if it is to fulfil its proper function. A body is healthy and efficient only when each part is functioning perfectly. The parts of the body are not jealous of each other and do not covet each other's functions. From Paul's picture we see certain things which ought to exist in the Church, the body of Christ.

(i) We ought to realize that *we need each other*. There can be no such thing as isolation in the Church. Far too often people in the Church become so engrossed in the bit of the work that they are doing and so convinced of its supreme importance that they neglect or even criticize others who have chosen to do other work. If the Church is to be a healthy body, we need the work that everyone can do.

(ii) We ought to *respect each other*. In the body there is no question of relative importances. If any limb or any organ ceases to function, the whole body is thrown out of gear. It is so with the Church. "All service ranks the same with God." Whenever we begin to think about our own importance in the Christian Church, the possibility of really Christian work is gone.

(iii) We ought *to sympathize with each other*. If any one part of the body is affected, all the others suffer in sympathy because they cannot help it. The Church is a whole. The person who cannot see beyond his or her own organization, the person who cannot see beyond his or her congregation, worse still, the person who cannot see beyond his or her own family circle, has not even begun to grasp the real unity of the Church.

At the end of the passage Paul speaks of various forms of service in the Church. Some he has already mentioned, but some are new.

(i) At the head of everything he puts the *apostles*. They were beyond question the greatest figures in the Church. Their authority was not confined to one place; they had no settled and localized ministry; their writ ran through the whole Church. Why should that be? The essential qualification of an apostle was that he must have companied with Jesus during his earthly life and been a witness of the Resurrection (*Acts* 1: 22). The apostles were those who had the closest contact with Jesus in the days of his flesh and in the days of his risen power. Jesus never wrote a word on paper; instead he wrote his message upon men, and these men were the apostles. No human ceremony can ever give a man real authority; that must always come from the fact that he has companied with Christ. Once someone said to Alexander Whyte after a service, "Dr. Whyte, you preached today as if you had come straight from the presence." "Perhaps I did," answered Whyte softly. The man who comes from the presence of Christ has apostolic authority no matter what may be his Church denomination.

(ii) We have already spoken about the prophets, but now Paul adds *teachers*. It is impossible to exaggerate their importance. These were the men who had to build up the converts won by the preaching of the evangelists and the apostles. They had to instruct men and women who knew literally nothing about Christianity. Their supreme importance lies in this—the first gospel, Mark's, was not written until about A.D. 60, that is to say, not until about thirty years after the crucifixion of Jesus. We have to think ourselves back to a time when printing did not exist, when books had to be hand-written and were scarce, when a volume the size of the New Testament would cost pounds to buy, when ordinary folk could never hope to possess a book. As a result the story of Jesus had to be handed down in the beginning by word of mouth. That was the teacher's task; and we must remember this—a scholar will learn more from a good teacher than from any book. We have books in plenty nowadays, but it is still true that it is through people that a man really learns of Christ.

(iii) Paul speaks of *helpers*. These were people whose duty it was to succour the poor, the orphan, the widow and the stranger. From the very beginning Christianity was an intensely practical thing. A man may be a poor speaker and have no gift of teaching; but it is open to everyone to help.

(iv) Paul speaks of what the Revised Standard Version calls administrators (*kuberneseis*). The Greek is very interesting; it literally refers to the work of a pilot who steers the ship through the rocks and shoals to harbour. Paul is referring to the people who carry out the administration of the Church. It is a supremely essential work. In the foreground the preacher and the teacher hold the limelight; but they could never do their work at all unless in the background there were those who shouldered the routine day to day administration. There are parts of the body which are never seen but whose function is more important than any other; there are those who serve the Church in ways that win no publicity, but without whose service the Church could not go on.

But in the end Paul is going to go on to speak of a greater gift than all the others. The danger always is that those who have different gifts will be at variance with each other, and so the effective working of the body will be hindered. Love is the only thing which can bind the Church into a perfect unity; and Paul goes on to sing his hymn to love.

THE HYMN OF LOVE

1 *Corinthians* 13

I may speak with the tongues of men and of angels, but if I have not love, I am become no better than echoing brass or a clanging cymbal. I may have the gift of prophecy, I may understand all sacred secrets and all knowledge, I may have faith enough to remove mountains, but if I have not love I am nothing. I may dole out all that I have, I may surrender my body that I may be burned, but if I have not love it is no good to me.

Love is patient; love is kind; love knows no envy; love is no braggart; it is not inflated with its own importance; it does not behave gracelessly; it does not insist on its rights; it never flies into a temper; it does not store up the memory of any wrong it has received; it finds no pleasure in evil-doing; it rejoices with the truth; it can endure anything; it is completely trusting; it never ceases to hope; it bears everything with triumphant fortitude.

Love never fails. Whatever prophecies there are, they will vanish away. Whatever tongues there are, they will cease. Whatever knowledge we have, it will pass away. It is only part of the truth that we know now and only part of the truth that we can forthtell to others. But when that which is complete shall come, that which is incomplete will vanish away. When I was a child I used to speak like a child; I used to think like a child; I used to reason like a child. When I became a man I put an end to childish things. Now we see only reflections in a mirror which leave us with nothing but riddles to solve, but then we shall see face to face. Now I know in part; but then I will know even as I am known. Now faith, hope, love remain—these three; but the greatest of these is love.

FOR many this is the most wonderful chapter in the whole New Testament and we will do well to take more than one day to study words whose full meaning not a lifetime itself would be sufficient to unveil.

Paul begins by declaring that a man may possess any spiritual gift, but if it is unaccompanied by love it is useless.

(i) He may have the gift of *tongues*. A characteristic of heathen worship, especially the worship of Dionysus and Cybele, was the clanging of cymbals and the braying of trumpets. Even the coveted gift of tongues was no better than the uproar of heathen worship if love was absent.

(ii) He may have the gift of *prophecy*. We have already seen that prophecy corresponds most closely to preaching. There are two kinds of preachers. There is the preacher whose one aim is to save the souls of his people and who woos them with the accents of love. Of no one was that more true than of Paul himself. Myers, in his poem *St. Paul,* draws the picture of him looking at the Christless world,

> "Then with a thrill the intolerable craving
>   Shivers throughout me like a trumpet call—
> O to save these—to perish for their saving—
>   Die for their lives, be offered for them all."

On the other hand there is the preacher who dangles his hearers over the flames of hell and gives the impression that he would rejoice in their damnation as much as in their salvation. It is told that Sir George Adam Smith once asked a member of the Greek Church, which has suffered much at the hands of Islam, why God had created so many Mohammedans, and received the answer, "To fill up hell." The preaching which is all threat and no love may terrify but it will not save.

(iii) He may have the gift of *intellectual knowledge.* The permanent danger of intellectual eminence is intellectual snobbery. The man who is learned runs the grave danger of developing the spirit of contempt. Only a knowledge whose cold detachment has been kindled by the fire of love can really save men.

(iv) He may have a passionate *faith.* There are times when faith can be cruel. There was a man who visited his doctor and was informed that his heart was tired and he must rest. He telephoned his employer, a notable Christian figure, with the news, only to receive the answer, "I have an inward strength which enables me to carry on." These were the words of faith but a faith which knew no love and was therefore a hurting thing.

(v) He may practise what men call *charity;* he may dole out his goods to the poor. There is nothing more humiliating than this so-called charity without love. To give as a grim duty, to give with a certain contempt, to stand on one's own little eminence and throw scraps of charity as to a dog, to give and to accompany the giving with a smug moral lecture or a crushing rebuke, is not charity at all—it is pride, and pride is always cruel for it knows no love.

(vi) He may give his body to be burned. Possibly Paul's thoughts are going back to Shadrach, Meshach and Abed-nego and the burning fiery furnace (*Daniel* 3). Perhaps more likely, he is thinking of a famous monument in Athens called "The Indian's Tomb." There an Indian had burned himself in public on a funeral pyre and had caused to be engraved on the monument the boastful inscription: "Zarmano-chegas, an Indian from Bargosa, according to the traditional customs of the Indians, made himself immortal and lies here." Just possibly, he may have been thinking of the kind of Christian who actually courted persecution. If the motive which makes a man give his life for Christ is pride and self-display, then even martyrdom becomes valueless. It is not cynical to remember that many a deed which looks sacrificial has been the product of pride and not of devotion.

Hardly any passage in scripture demands such self-examination from the good man as this.

THE NATURE OF CHRISTIAN LOVE

1 Corinthians 13: 4–7

IN verses 4–7 Paul lists fifteen characteristics of Christian love.

Love is patient. The Greek word (*makrothumein*) used in the New Testament always describes patience with *people* and not patience with circumstances. Chrysostom said that it is the word used of the man who is wronged and who has it easily in his power to avenge himself and who yet will not do it. It describes the man who is slow to anger and it is used of God himself in his relationship with men. In our dealings with men, however refractory and however unkind and hurting they are, we must exercise the same patience as God exercises with us. Such patience is not the sign of weakness but the sign of strength; it is not defeatism but rather the only way to victory. Fosdick points out that no one treated Lincoln with more contempt than did Stanton. He called him "a low cunning clown", he nicknamed him "the original gorilla" and said that Du Chaillu was a fool to wander about Africa trying to capture a gorilla when he could have found one so easily at Springfield, Illinois. Lincoln said nothing. He made Stanton his war minister because he was the best man for the job and he treated him with every courtesy. The years wore on. The night came when the assassin's bullet murdered Lincoln in the theatre. In the little room to which the President's body was taken stood that same Stanton, and, looking down on Lincoln's silent face, he said through his tears, "There lies the greatest ruler of men the world has ever seen." The patience of love had conquered in the end.

Love is kind. Origen had it that this means that love is "sweet to all." Jerome spoke of what he called "the benignity" of love. So much Christianity is good but unkind. There was no more religious a man than Philip the Second of Spain, and yet he founded the Spanish Inquisition and thought he was serving God by massacring those who thought differently from him. The famous Cardinal Pole declared that murder and adultery could not compare in heinousness with heresy. Apart altogether from that persecuting spirit, there is in so many good people an attitude of criticism. So many good Church people would have sided with the rulers and not with Jesus if they had had to deal with the woman taken in adultery.

Love knows no envy. It has been said that there are really only two classes of people in this world—"those who are millionaires and those who would like to be." There are two kinds of envy. The one covets the possessions of other people; and such envy is very difficult to avoid because it is a very human thing. The other is worse—it grudges the very fact that others should have what it has not; it does not so much want things for itself as wish that others had not got them. Meanness of soul can sink no further than that.

Love is no braggart. There is a self-effacing quality in love. True love will always be far more impressed with its own unworthiness than its own merit. In Barrie's story Sentimental Tommy used to come home to his mother after some success at school and say, "Mother, am I no' a wonder?" Some people confer their love with the idea that they are conferring a favour. But the real lover cannot ever get over the wonder that he is loved. Love is kept humble by the consciousness that it can never offer its loved one a gift which is good enough.

Love is not inflated with its own importance. Napoleon always advocated the sanctity of the home and the obligation of public worship—for others. Of himself he said, "I am not a man like other men. The laws of morality do not apply to me." The really great man never thinks of his own importance. Carey, who began life as a cobbler, was one of the greatest missionaries and certainly one of the greatest linguists the world has ever seen. He translated at least parts of the Bible into no fewer than thirty-four Indian languages. When he came to India, he was regarded with dislike and contempt. At a dinner party a snob, with the idea of humiliating him, said in a tone that everyone could hear, "I suppose, Mr. Carey, you once worked as a shoe-maker." "No, your lordship," answered Carey, "not a shoe-maker, only a cobbler." He did not even claim to make shoes—only to mend them. No one likes the "important" person. Man "dressed in a little brief authority" can be a sorry sight.

Love does not behave gracelessly. It is a significant fact that in Greek the words for *grace* and for *charm* are the same. There is a kind of Christianity which takes a delight in being blunt and almost brutal. There is strength in it but there is no winsomeness. Lightfoot of Durham said of Arthur F. Sim, one of his students, "Let him go where he will, his face will be a sermon in itself." There is a graciousness in Christian love which never forgets that courtesy and tact and politeness are lovely things.

Love does not insist upon its rights. In the last analysis, there are in this world only two kinds of people—those who always insist upon their privileges and those who always remember their responsibilities; those who are always thinking of what life owes them and those who never forget what they owe to life. It would be the key to almost all the problems which surround us today if men would think less of their rights and more of their duties. Whenever we start thinking about "our place", we are drifting away from Christian love.

Love never flies into a temper. The real meaning of this is that Christian love never becomes exasperated with people. Exasperation is always a sign of defeat. When we lose our tempers, we lose everything. Kipling said that it was the test of a man if he could keep his head when everyone else was losing his and blaming it on him, and if when he was hated he did not give way to hating. The man who is master of his temper can be master of anything.

Love does not store up the memory of any wrong it has received. The word translated *store up* (*logizeshthai*) is an accountant's word. It is the word used for entering up an item in a ledger so that it will not be forgotten. That is precisely what so many people do. One of the great arts in life is to learn what to forget. A writer tells how "in Polynesia, where the natives spend much of their time in fighting and feasting, it is customary for each man to keep some reminders of his hatred. Articles are suspended from the roofs of their huts to keep alive the memory of their wrongs—real or imaginary." In the same way many people nurse their wrath to keep it warm; they brood over their wrongs until it is impossible to forget them. Christian love has learned the great lesson of forgetting.

Love finds no pleasure in evil-doing. It might be better to translate this that love finds no pleasure in anything that is wrong. It is not so much delight in doing the wrong thing that is meant, as the malicious pleasure which comes to most of us when we hear something derogatory about someone else. It is one of the queer traits of human nature that very often we prefer to hear of the misfortune of others rather

than of their good fortune. It is much easier to weep with
them that weep than to rejoice with those who rejoice.
Christian love has none of that human malice which finds
pleasure in ill reports.

Love rejoices with the truth. That is not so easy as it sounds.
There are times when we definitely do not want the truth to
prevail; and still more times when it is the last thing we
wish to hear. Christian love has no wish to veil the truth; it
has nothing to conceal and so is glad when the truth prevails.

Love can endure anything. It is just possible that this may
mean "love can cover anything," in the sense that it will never
drag into the light of day the faults and mistakes of others.
It would far rather set about quietly mending things than
publicly displaying and rebuking them. More likely it means
that love can bear any insult, any injury, any disappointment.
It describes the kind of love that was in the heart of Jesus
himself,

> "Thy foes might hate, despise, revile,
> Thy friends unfaithful prove;
> Unwearied in forgiveness still,
> Thy heart could only love."

Love is completely trusting. This characteristic has a twofold
aspect. (i) *In relation to God* it means that love takes God at
his word, and can take every promise which begins "Whoso-
ever" and say, "That means me." (ii) *In relation to our fellow
men* it means that love always believes the best about other
people. It is often true that we make people what we believe
them to be. If we show that we do not trust people, we may
make them untrustworthy. If we show people that we trust
them absolutely, we may make them trustworthy. When
Arnold became headmaster of Rugby he instituted a completely new way of doing things. Before him, school had
been a terror and a tyranny. Arnold called the boys together
and told them that there was going to be much more liberty
and much less flogging. "You are free," he said, "but you are
responsible—you are gentlemen. I intend to leave you much

to yourselves, and put you upon your honour, because I believe that if you are guarded and watched and spied upon, you will grow up knowing only the fruits of servile fear; and when your liberty is finally given you, as it must be some day, you will not know how to use it." The boys found it difficult to believe. When they were brought before him they continued to make the old excuses and to tell the old lies. "Boys," he said, "if you say so, it must be true—I believe your word." The result was that there came a time in Rugby when boys said, "It is a shame to tell Arnold a lie—he always believes you." He believed in them and he made them what he believed them to be. Love can ennoble even the ignoble by believing the best.

Love never ceases to hope. Jesus believed that no man is hopeless. Adam Clark was one of the great theologians but at school he was very slow to learn. One day a distinguished visitor paid a visit to the school, and the teacher singled out Adam Clark and said, "That is the stupidest boy in the school." Before he left the school, the visitor came to the boy and said kindly, "Never mind, my boy, you may be a great scholar some day. Don't be discouraged but try hard, and keep on trying." The teacher was hopeless, the visitor was hopeful, and—who knows?—it may well have been that word of hope which made Adam Clark what he one day became.

Love bears everything with triumphant fortitude. The verb used here (*hupomenein*) is one of the great Greek words. It is generally translated *to bear* or *to endure;* but what it really describes is not the spirit which can passively bear things, but the spirit which, in bearing them, can conquer and transmute them. It has been defined as "a masculine constancy under trial." George Matheson, who lost his sight and who was disappointed in love, wrote in one of his prayers that he might accept God's will, "Not with dumb resignation but with holy joy; not only with the absence of murmur but with a song of praise." Love can bear things, not merely with passive resignation, but with triumphant fortitude, because it knows that "a father's hand will never cause his child a needless tear."

One thing remains to be said—when we think of the qualities of this love as Paul portrays them we can see them realized in the life of Jesus himself.

THE SUPREMACY OF LOVE

1 *Corinthians* 13: 8–13

IN verses 8–13 Paul has three final things to say of this Christian love.

(i) He stresses its *absolute permanency*. When all the things in which men glory have passed away love will still stand. In one of the most wonderfully lyrical verses of scripture *The Song of Solomon* (8: 7) sings, "Many waters cannot quench love, neither can floods drown it." The one unconquerable thing is love. That is one of the great reasons for believing in immortality. When love is entered into, there comes into life a relationship against which the assaults of time are helpless and which transcends death.

(ii) He stresses its *absolute completeness*. As things are, what we see are reflections in a mirror. That would be even more suggestive to the Corinthians than it is to us. Corinth was famous for its manufacture of mirrors. But the modern mirror as we know it, with its perfect reflection, did not emerge until the thirteenth century. The Corinthian mirror was made of highly polished metal and, even at its best, gave but an imperfect reflection. It has been suggested that what this phrase means is that we see as through a window made with horn. In those days windows were so made and all that could be seen through them was a dim and shadowy outline. In fact the Rabbis had a saying that it was through such a window that Moses saw God.

In this life Paul feels we see only the reflections of God and are left with much that is mystery and riddle. We see that reflection in God's world, for the work of anyone's hands tells us something about the workman, we see it in the Gospel and we see it in Jesus Christ. Even if in Christ we have the perfect revelation, our seeking minds can grasp it only in part, for the finite can never grasp the infinite. Our knowledge is still like the knowledge of a child. But the way of love will lead us in the end to a day when the veil is drawn aside and we see face to face and know even as we are known. We cannot ever reach that day without love, because God is love and only he who loves can see him.

(iii) He stresses its *absolute supremacy*. Great as faith and hope are, love is still greater. Faith without love is cold, and hope without love is grim. Love is the fire which kindles faith and it is the light which turns hope into certainty.

THE FALSE AND THE TRUE WORSHIP

1 *Corinthians* 14: 1–19

> Pursue this love. Covet the spiritual things, especially the gift of forthtelling the truth to others. For he who speaks in a tongue does not speak to men but to God, for no one can understand. By the Spirit he speaks things which only the initiated can understand. But he who forthtells the truth to men speaks something which builds them up and encourages them and comforts them. He who speaks in a tongue builds up his own spiritual life, but he who forthtells the truth builds up the spiritual life of the Church. I wish that you could all speak with tongues, but I wish still more that you could all forthtell the truth. He who forthtells the truth is greater than he who speaks with tongues, unless the tongues are interpreted so that the Church may receive spiritual upbuilding. Now, brothers, if I come to you speaking with tongues what good would I do you? I cannot do you any good unless I speak to you through some special message given to me direct by God, or with some special knowledge, or with the forthtelling of the truth, or with teaching. There are instruments which, though they are lifeless, have a voice—for example, the flute and the harp—but if they do not observe the correct intervals between the notes, how can the tune that is being played on the flute or the harp be recognized? If the trumpet gives a meaningless sound who will prepare for the battle? So, too, if you produce in a tongue speech the meaning of which cannot be grasped, how can what is being said be

understood? You might as well be talking to the air. There are so many voices—whatever the number of them may be—in the world and nothing is without a voice. So then if I do not understand what the voice is trying to say, I will be a foreigner to him who speaks and he who speaks will be a foreigner as far as I am concerned. So, when you are eager for spiritual gifts, be eager to excel in gifts which are useful for the upbuilding of the Church. Therefore let him who speaks in a tongue pray to be able to interpret what he says, for, if I pray in a tongue, my spirit prays, but my mind gets no benefit at all. What then emerges from all this? I will pray with the spirit, but I will pray with my mind too. I will sing with the spirit, but I will sing with my mind too. For if you are blessing God in the spirit, how can the man who occupies the position of a simple layman say the customary Amen to your thanksgiving, since he does not understand what you are saying? It is a fine thing that you give thanks, but the other man receives no spiritual upbuilding. I thank God that I can speak with tongues more than any of you. But in any Christian gathering I would rather speak five words with my intelligence, so that I may teach others as well, rather than ten thousand words in a tongue.

THIS chapter is very difficult to understand because it deals with a phenomenon which, for most of us, is outside our experience. Throughout Paul sets two spiritual gifts in comparison with each other.

First there is *speaking with tongues*. This phenomenon was very common in the early Church. A man became worked up to an ecstasy and in that state poured out a quite uncontrollable torrent of sounds in no known language. Unless these sounds were interpreted, no one had any idea what they meant. Strange as it may seem to many of us, in the early Church this was a highly coveted gift. It was dangerous. For one thing, it was abnormal and was greatly admired and therefore the person who possessed it was very liable to develop a certain spiritual pride; and for another thing, the very desire to possess it produced, at least in some, a kind of self-hypnotism and deliberately induced hysteria which issued in a completely false and synthetic speaking with tongue.

Over against this speaking with tongues, Paul sets the gift of *prophecy*. In the translation we have not used the word *prophecy*, for that would have further complicated an already complicated situation. In this case, and in fact usually, it has nothing to do with foretelling the future but everything to do with forthtelling the will and the message of God. We have already said that *preaching* very nearly gives the meaning, but in this case we have kept the literal meaning and have translated it *forthtelling*.

In this whole section Paul deals with the dangers of the gift of speaking with tongues, and the superiority of the gift of forthtelling the truth in such a way that all can understand it.

We can best follow Paul's line of thought by analysing the section.

He begins by declaring that tongues are addressed to God and not to men, for men cannot understand them. If a man exercises this gift of tongues he may be enriching his own spiritual experience, but he is certainly not enriching the souls of the congregation because to them it is unintelligible; on the other hand, the gift of forthtelling the truth produces something which everyone can understand and which profits every man's soul.

Paul goes on to use certain illustrations and analogies. He is going to come to them; but if he came speaking with tongues what use would that be? They would have no idea what he was talking about. Take the case of a musical instrument. If it obeys the normal laws of harmony, it can produce a melody; but, if it does not, it produces simply a chaos of sound. Take the case of a trumpet. If it plays the correct call, it can summon men to advance, to retreat, to sleep, to wake. But if it produces simply a medley of meaningless sound, no man can know what to do. There are in this world many kinds of speech; but if two men meet each other who do not understand each other's language, the speech of each sounds like gibberish to the other and makes no sense.

Paul does not deny that the gift of tongues exists. Nor can anyone say that with him it is a case of sour grapes, for he possesses the gift more than anyone else does; but he insists that any gift to be of value must benefit the whole congregation, and therefore, if the gift of tongues is used, it is useless unless it is interpreted. Whether a man is speaking or praying or singing, he must do it not only with his spirit, but with his *mind*. He must know what is going on and others must be able to understand it. And so Paul reaches the blunt conclusion that in a Christian congregation it is better to speak a few intelligible sentences than to pour out a flood of unintelligible sounds.

Out of this difficult section emerge certain valuable truths.

Verse 3 succinctly lays down the aim of all preaching. It is threefold. (i) It must aim *to build up;* to increase a man's knowledge of Christian truth and his ability to live the Christian life. (ii) It must aim *to encourage.* In every group of people there are those who are depressed and discouraged. Dreams will not come true; effort seems to have achieved so little; self-examination serves to show nothing but failures and inadequacies. Within the Christian fellowship, a man should find something to cheer his heart and nerve his arm. It was said of a certain preacher that he preached the gospel as if he were announcing a deep depression off Iceland. A service may begin by humbling a man through showing him his sin, but it is a failure unless it ends by pointing him to the grace of God that can enable him to conquer it. (iii) It must aim *to comfort.* "Never morning wore to evening but some heart did break." There are what Virgil called, "the tears of things." In any company of people there will always be some whom life has hurt; and within the Christian fellowship they must be able to find beauty for their ashes, the oil of joy for mourning and the garment of praise for the spirit of their heaviness.

Verse 5 gives us the things which for Paul were the background and the substance of all preaching. (i) It comes from *a direct revelation from God.* No man can speak to others unless God has first spoken to him. It was said of a great preacher that ever and again he paused as if listening for a voice. We never give to men or to scholars truth which we have produced, or even discovered; we transmit truth which has been given to us. (ii) It may bring *some special knowledge.* No man can possibly be an expert in everything, but every man has special knowledge of something. It has been said that any man can write an interesting book if he will simply set down completely honestly all that has happened to him. The experiences of life give something special to each one of us, and the most effective preaching is simply witness to what we have found to be true. (iii) It consists of *forthtelling the truth.* In the early Church the first preaching given to any fellowship was a simple proclamation of the facts of the Christian story. Certain things are beyond argument. "Tell me of your certainties," said Goethe, "I have doubts enough of my own." However we may finish, it is well to begin with the facts of Christ. (iv) It goes on to *teaching.* There comes a time when a man has to ask, "What is the meaning of these facts?" Simply because we are thinking creatures, religion implies theology. And it may well be that the faith of many people collapses and the loyalty of many people grows cold because they have not thought things out and thought them through.

From the whole passage two broad principles regarding Christian worship emerge.

(i) *Worship must never be selfish.* All that is done in it must be done for the sake of all. No man in worship, whether he leads it or shares in it, has any right to direct it according to his own personal preferences. He must seek the good of the whole worshipping fellowship. The great test of any part of worship is, "Will this help *everyone?*" It is not, "Will this display my special gifts?" It is, "Will this bring all here nearer to each other and nearer to God?"

(ii) *Worship must be intelligible.* The great things are essentially the simple things; the noblest language is essentially the simplest language. In the end only what satisfies my mind can comfort my heart, and only what my mind can grasp can bring strength to my life.

THE EFFECTS OF FALSE AND TRUE WORSHIP

1 *Corinthians* 14: 20–25

> Brothers, don't be childish in your judgment. True, you must be innocent babes as far as evil goes, but in your judgments you must be mature men. In the law it stands written, "With people of a foreign tongue and with the lips of aliens I will speak to this people, and not even so will they listen to me, says the Lord." So you see tongues are meant for a sign not to believers but to unbelievers.
>
> Suppose, then, the whole Christian congregation meets together, and suppose all speak with tongues, and suppose some simple folk or some pagans come in, will they not say that you are raving mad? But suppose all forthtell the truth, and then suppose some pagan or some simple person comes in, his sin will be brought home to him by all, he will be brought to judgment by all, the hidden things of his heart will be brought to light, and so, falling upon his face, he will worship God, and will tell all men that God is really among you.

PAUL is still dealing with this question of speaking with tongues. He begins with an appeal to the Corinthians not to be childish. This passion for and over-evaluation of speaking with tongues is really a kind of childish ostentation.

Paul then finds an argument in the Old Testament. We have seen over and over again how Rabbinic exegesis—and Paul was a trained Rabbi—can find in the Old Testament hidden meanings which were certainly not originally there. He goes back to *Isaiah* 28: 9–12. God, through his prophet, is threatening the people. Isaiah has preached to them in their own Hebrew language and they have not listened. Because of their disobedience, the Assyrians will come and conquer them and occupy their cities and then they will have to listen to language which they cannot understand. They will have to listen to the foreign tongues of their conquerors speaking unintelligible things; and not even that terrible experience will make an unbelieving people turn to God. So Paul uses the argument that tongues were meant for a hard-hearted and unbelieving people and were, in the end, ineffective to them.

Then he uses a very practical argument. If any stranger, or any simple person, came into a Christian assembly where everyone was pouring out a flood of unintelligible sounds, he would think that the place was a madhouse. But if the truth of God was being soberly and intelligibly proclaimed, the result would be very different. He would be brought face to face with himself and with God.

Verses 24 and 25 give us a vivid summary of what happens when the truth of God is intelligibly proclaimed.

(i) *It convicts a man of his sin.* He sees what he is and is appalled. Alcibiades, the spoilt darling of Athens, was the friend of Socrates, and sometimes he used to say to him, "Socrates, I hate you, for every time I meet you you make me see what I am." "Come," said the woman of Samaria in shamed amazement, " see a man who told me all that I ever did." (*John* 4: 29). The first thing the message of God does is to make a man realize that he is a sinner.

(ii) *It brings a man under judgment.* He sees that he must answer for what he has done. So far he may have lived life with no thought of its end. He may have followed the impulses of the day and seized its pleasures. But now he sees that the day has an ending, and there stands God.

(iii) *It shows a man the secrets of his own heart.* The last thing we face is our own hearts. As the proverb has it, "There are none so blind as those who will not see." The Christian message compels a man to that searing, humiliating honesty which will face himself.

(iv) *It brings a man to his knees before God.* All Christianity begins with a man on his knees in God's presence. The gateway to that presence is so low that we can enter it only upon our knees. When a man has faced God and faced himself, all that is left for him to do is to kneel and to pray, "God be merciful to me a sinner."

The test of any act of worship is, "Does it make us feel the presence of God?" Joseph Twitchell tells how he went to visit Horace Bushnell when Bushnell was an old man. At night Bushnell took him out for a walk on the hillside. As they walked in the dark, suddenly Bushnell said, "Let us kneel and pray," and they did. Twitchell, telling of it afterwards, said, "I was afraid to stretch out my hand in the darkness in case I should touch God." When we feel as near to God as that, we have really and truly shared in an act of worship.

PRACTICAL ADVICE

1 *Corinthians* 14: 26–33

> What then emerges from all this, brothers? Whenever you meet together, let each have his psalm, let each have his teaching, let each have his message direct from God, let each have his tongue, let each have his interpretation. Let all things be done for the spiritual upbuilding of the congregation. If anyone speaks with a tongue, let it be two, or at the most three, and let them do it by turns, and let one interpret. If there is no interpreter present, let him who has the gift of tongues keep silent in the congregation, and let him speak to God when he is by himself. Let two or three forthtellers of the truth speak, and let the others exercise the gift of discernment. If someone who is seated is conscious that he has been given a special message, let the first be silent, for you can all forthtell the truth one by one so that all may learn and may be encouraged—and the spirits of those who forthtell the truth are under control of those who do forthtell the truth, for God is not the God of disorder but the God of peace, as we see that he is in all the congregation of his dedicated people.

PAUL comes near to the end of this section with some very practical advice. He is determined that anyone who possesses a gift should receive every chance to exercise it; but he is equally determined that the services of the Church should not become a kind of competitive disorder. Only two or three are to exercise the gift of tongues, and then only if there is someone there to interpret. All have the gift of forthtelling the truth, but again only two or three are to exercise it; and if someone in the congregation has the conviction that he has received a special message, the man who is speaking must give way to him and give him the opportunity to express it. The

man who is speaking can perfectly well do so, and need not
say that he is carried away by inspiration and cannot stop,
because the preacher is able to control his own spirit. There
must be liberty but there must be no disorder. The God of
peace must be worshipped in peace.

There is no more interesting section in the whole letter than
this, for it sheds a flood of light on what an early church
service was like. There was obviously great freedom and an
informality about it. From this passage two great questions
emerge.

(i) Clearly the early Church had no professional ministry.
True, the apostles stood out with special authority; but at this
stage there was no professional local ministry. It was open to
anyone who had a gift to use it. Has the Church been right
or wrong in instituting a professional ministry? Clearly it is
essential that, in our busy age when men are so preoccupied
with material things, one should be set apart to live close to
God and to bring to his fellows the truth and the guidance
and the comfort which God gives to him. But there is the
obvious danger that when a man becomes a professional
preacher he may sometimes be in the position of having to
say something when he has really nothing to say. However
that may be, it must remain true that if a man has a message
to give his fellow men no ecclesiastical rules and regulations
should be able to stop him giving it. It is a mistake to think
that only the professional ministry can ever bring God's truth
to men.

(ii) There was obviously a flexibility about the order of
service in the early Church. Everything was informal enough
to allow any man who felt that he had a message to give to
give it. It may well be that we set far too much store on
dignity and order nowadays, and have become the slaves of
orders of service. The really notable thing about an early
Church service must have been that almost everyone came
feeling that he had both the privilege and the obligation of
contributing something to it. A man did not come with the
sole intention of being a passive listener; he came not only to

receive but to give. Obviously this had its dangers, for it is clear that in Corinth there were those who were too fond of the sound of their own voices; but nonetheless the Church must have been in those days much more the real possession of the ordinary Christian. It may well be that the Church lost something when she delegated so much to the professional ministry and left so little to the ordinary Church member; and it may well be that the blame lies not with the ministry for annexing those rights but with the laity for abandoning them, certainly it is all too true that many Church members think far more of what the Church can do for them than of what they can do for the Church, and are very ready to criticize what is done but very unready to take any share in doing the Church's work themselves.

FORBIDDEN INNOVATIONS

1 *Corinthians* 14: 34–40

Let women keep silent in the congregation, for it is not permitted to them to speak, but let them be in subjection even as the law says. If they wish to learn about anything, let them question their husbands at home. It is a shameful thing for a woman to speak in the congregation. Was it from you that God's word went out? Or, was it to you alone that it came?

If anyone thinks that he is a forthteller of the truth, or that he has a special spiritual gift, let him understand what I write to you because it is the Lord's command. If anyone does not understand it, let him remain in his ignorance.

So then, my brothers, be eager to have the gift of forthtelling the truth and do not forbid speaking with tongues. Let everything be done with propriety and with order.

THERE were innovations threatening in the Church at Corinth which Paul did not like. In effect, he asks what right they had to make them. Were they the originators of the Christian Church? Had they a monopoly of the gospel truth? They had received a tradition and to it they must be obedient.

No man ever rose completely above the background of the age in which he lived and the society in which he grew up; and Paul, in his conception of the place of women within the Church, was unable to rise above the ideas which he had known all his life.

We have already said that in the ancient world the place of women was low. In the Greek world Sophocles had said, "Silence confers grace upon a woman." Women, unless they were very poor or very loose in their morals, led a very secluded life in Greece. The Jews had an even lower idea of women. Amongst the Rabbinic sayings there are many which belittle their place. "As to teaching the law to a woman one might as well teach her impiety." To teach the law to a woman was "to cast pearls before swine." The Talmud lists among the plagues of the world "the talkative and the inquisitive widow and the virgin who wastes her time in prayers." It was even forbidden to speak to a woman on the street. "One must not ask a service from a woman, or salute her."

It was in a society like that that Paul wrote this passage. In all likelihood what was uppermost in his mind was the lax moral state of Corinth and the feeling that absolutely nothing, must be done which would bring upon the infant Church the faintest suspicion of immodesty. It would certainly be very wrong to take these words out of their context and make them a universal rule for the Church.

Paul goes on to speak with a certain sternness. He is quite certain that, even if a man has spiritual gifts, that gives him no right to be a rebel against authority. He is conscious that the advice he has given and the rules he has laid down have come to him from Jesus Christ and his Spirit, and if a man refuses to understand them he must be left in his wilful ignorance.

So Paul draws to an end. He makes it clear that he has no wish to quench anyone's gift; the one thing he strives for is the good order of the Church. The great rule which he in effect lays down is that a man has received from God whatever gift he may possess, not for his own sake, but for the sake of the Church. When a man can say, "To God be the glory," then and only then will he use his gifts aright within the Church and outside it.

JESUS'S RESURRECTION AND OURS

1 CORINTHIANS 15 is both one of the greatest and one of the most difficult chapters in the New Testament. Not only is it in itself difficult, but it has also given to the creed a phrase which many people have grave difficulty in affirming, for it is from this chapter that we mainly derive the idea of *the resurrection of the body*. The chapter will be far less difficult if we study it against its background, and even that troublesome phrase will become quite clear and acceptable when we realize what Paul really meant by it. So then, before we study the chapter, there are certain things we would do well to have in mind.

(i) It is of great importance to remember that the Corinthians were denying not the Resurrection of Jesus Christ but the resurrection of the body; and what Paul was insistent upon was that if a man denied the resurrection of the body he thereby denied the Resurrection of Jesus Christ and therefore emptied the Christian message of its truth and the Christian life of its reality.

(ii) In any early Christian church there must have been two backgrounds, for in all churches there were Jews and Greeks.

First, there was the Jewish background. To the end of the day the Sadducees denied that there was any life after death at all. There was therefore one line of Jewish thought which completely denied both the immortality of the soul and the resurrection of the body (*Acts* 23: 8). In the Old Testament there is very little hope of anything that can be called life after death. According to the general Old Testament belief all men, without distinction, went to Sheol after death. Sheol, often wrongly translated Hell, was a gray land beneath the world, where the dead lived a shadowy existence, without strength, without light, cut off alike from men and from God. The

Old Testament is full of this bleak, grim pessimism regarding what is to happen after death.

> For in death there is no remembrance of thee: in Sheol who can give thee praise? (*Psalm* 6: 5).

> What profit is there in my death if I go down to the pit? Will the dust praise thee? Will it tell of thy faithfulness? (*Psalm* 30: 9).

> Dost thou work wonders for the dead? Do the shades rise up to praise thee? Is thy steadfast love declared in the grave? Or thy faithfulness in Abaddon? Are thy wonders known in the darkness, or thy saving help in the land of forgetfulness? (*Psalm* 88: 10–12).

> The dead do not praise the Lord, nor do any that go down into silence. (*Psalm* 115: 17).

> For Sheol cannot thank thee, death cannot praise thee; those who go down to the pit cannot hope for thy faithfulness. (*Isaiah* 38: 18).

> Look away from me, that I may know gladness, before I depart and be no more. (*Psalm* 39: 13).

> But he who is joined with all the living has hope; for a living dog is better than a dead lion. For the living know that they will die; but the dead know nothing. . . . Whatever your hand finds to do do it with your might; for there is no work, or thought, or knowledge, or wisdom, in Sheol to which you are going. (*Ecclesiastes* 9: 4, 5, 10).

> Who shall give praise to the Most High in the grave? (*Ecclesiasticus* 17: 27).

> The dead that are in the grave, whose breath is taken from their bodies, will give unto the Lord neither glory nor righteousness. (*Baruch* 2: 17).

J. E. McFadyen, a great Old Testament scholar, says that this lack of a belief in immortality in the Old Testament is due "to the power with which those men apprehended God in this world." He goes on to say, "There are few more wonderful things than this in the long story of religion, that for centuries men lived the noblest lives, doing their duties and bearing their sorrows, without hope of future reward; and they did this because in all their going out and coming in they were very sure of God."

It is true that in the Old Testament there are some few, some very few, glimpses of a real life to come. There were times when a man felt that, if God be God at all, there must be something which would reverse the incomprehensible verdicts of this world. So Job cries out,

> Still, I know One to champion me at last,
> to stand up for me upon earth.
> This body may break up, but even then
> my life shall have a sight of God.
>
> (*Job* 19: 25–27. Moffatt).

The real feeling of the saint was that even in this life a man might enter into a relationship with God so close and so precious that not even death could break it.

> My body also dwells secure. For thou dost not give me up to Sheol, or let thy godly one see the Pit. Thou dost show me the path of life; in thy presence there is fulness of joy; in thy right hand there are pleasures for evermore. (*Psalm* 16: 9–11).

> Thou dost hold my right hand. Thou dost guide me with thy counsel, and afterward thou wilt receive me to glory. (*Psalm* 73: 24).

It is also true that in Israel the immortal hope developed. Two things helped that development. (*a*) Israel was the chosen people, and yet her history was one continued tale of disaster. Men began to feel that it required another world to redress the balance. (*b*) For many centuries it is true to say that the individual hardly existed. God was the God of the nation and the individual was an unimportant unit. But as the centuries went on religion became more and more personal. God became not the God of the nation but the friend of every individual; and so men began dimly and instinctively to feel that once a man knows God and is known by him, a relationship has been created which not even death can break.

(iii) When we turn to the Greek world, we must firmly grasp one thing, which is at the back of the whole chapter. The Greeks had an instinctive fear of death. Euripides wrote, "Yet mortals, burdened with countless ills, still love life. They long for each coming day, glad to bear the thing they know, rather than face death the unknown." (Fragment 813). But on the whole the Greeks, and that part of the world influenced by Greek thought, did believe in the immortality of the soul. But for them the immortality of the soul involved the complete dissolution of the body.

They had a proverb, "The body is a tomb." "I am a poor soul," said one of them, "shackled to a corpse." "It pleased me," said Seneca, "to enquire into the eternity of the soul—nay! to believe in it. I surrendered myself to that great hope." But he also says, "When the day shall come which shall part this mixture of divine and human, here, where I found it, I will leave my body, myself I will give back to the gods." Epictetus writes, "When God does not supply what is necessary, he is sounding the signal for retreat—he has opened the door and says to you 'Come!' But whither? To nothing terrible, but to whence you came, to the things which are dear and kin to you, to the elements. What in you was fire shall go to fire, earth to earth, water to water." Seneca talks about things at death "being resolved into their ancient elements." For Plato "the body is the antithesis of the soul, as the source of all weaknesses as opposed to what alone is capable of independence and goodness." We can see this best in the Stoic belief. To the Stoic God was fiery spirit, purer than anything on earth. What gave men life was that a spark of this divine fire came and dwelt in a man's body. When a man died, his body simply dissolved into the elements of which it was made, but the divine spark returned to God and was absorbed in the divinity of which it was a part.

For the Greek immortality lay precisely in getting rid of the body. For him the resurrection of the body was unthinkable. Personal immortality did not really exist because that which gave men life was absorbed again in God the source of all life.

(iv) Paul's view was quite different. If we begin with one immense fact, the rest will become clear. The Christian belief is that after death individuality will survive, that you will still be you and I will still be I. Beside that we have to set another immense fact. To the Greek the body could not be consecrated. It was matter, the source of all evil, the prison-house of the soul. But to the Christian the body is not evil. Jesus, the Son of God, has taken this human body upon him and therefore it is not contemptible because it has been inhabited by God. To the Christian, therefore the life to come involves the total man, body and soul.

Now it is easy to misinterpret and to caricature the doctrine of the resurrection of the body. Celsus, who lived about A.D. 220, a bitter opponent of Christianity, did this very thing long ago. How can those who have died rise with their identical bodies? he demands. "Really it is the hope of worms! For what soul of a man would any longer wish for a body that had rotted?" It is easy to cite the case of a person smashed up in an accident or dying of cancer.

But Paul never said that we would rise with the body with which we died. He insisted that we would have a spiritual body. What he really meant was that a man's *personality* would survive. It is almost impossible to conceive of personality without a body, because it is through the body that the personality expresses itself. What Paul is contending for is that after death the individual remains. He did not inherit the Greek contempt of the body but believed in the resurrection of the whole man. He will still be himself; he will survive as a person. That is what Paul means by the resurrection of the body. Everything of the body and of the soul that is necessary to make a man a person will survive, but, at the same time, all things will be new, and body and spirit will alike be very different from earthly things, for they will alike be divine.

THE RISEN LORD

1 *Corinthians* 15: 1–11

Brothers, I want to make clear to you the nature of the good news that I preached to you, that gospel which you also received, and in which you stand, and through which you are saved. I want to make clear to you what account I gave you of the good news, an account which can save you if you hold fast to it, unless your belief is a random and haphazard thing. In the very forefront of it I handed on to you what I myself received, that Christ died for our sins according to the scriptures, and that he was laid in the tomb, and that he was raised up on the third day according to the scriptures, and that he was seen by Cephas and then by The Twelve, and that then he was seen by more than five hundred brothers all at the one time, of whom the majority are still alive, although some have fallen asleep. After that he was seen by James, and then by all the apostles, and last of all, as if by the abortion of the apostolic family, he was seen by me too. For I am the least of the apostles; in fact I am not fit to be called an apostle because I persecuted the Church of God. It is by the grace of God that I am what I am, and his grace to me has not proved ineffective, but I have toiled more exceedingly than all of them; but it was not I who achieved anything but God's grace working with me. So then, whether I be the preacher or they, this is what we preach and this is what we have believed.

PAUL is recapitulating the good news which he first brought to the Corinthians. It was not news which he had invented but news which had first been delivered to him, and it was news of a Risen Lord.

In verses 1 and 2 Paul says an extremely interesting series of things about the good news.

(i) It was something which the Corinthians had *received*. No man ever invented the gospel for himself; in a sense no man ever discovers it for himself. It is something which he receives. Therein indeed is the very function of the Church. The Church is the repository and the transmitter of the good news. As one of the old fathers had it, "No man can have God for his Father, unless he has the Church for his mother." The good news is something that is received within a fellowship.

(ii) It was something in which the Corinthians *stood*. The very first function of the good news was to give a man stability.

In a slippery world it kept him on his feet. In a tempting world it gave him resistance power. In a hurting world it enabled him to endure a broken heart or an agonized body and not to give in. Moffatt finely translates *Job* 4: 4, "Your words have kept men on their feet." That is precisely what the gospel does.

(iii) It was something in which they were *being saved*. It is interesting to note that in the Greek this is a present tense, and not past. It would be strictly correct to translate it not, "in which you have been saved," but, "in which you are being saved." Salvation goes from glory to glory. It is not something which is ever completed in this world. There are many things in this life which we can exhaust, but the meaning of salvation is something which a man can never exhaust.

(iv) It was something to which a man had *to hold tenaciously*. Life makes many an attempt to take away our faith. Things happen to us and to others which baffle our understanding; life has its problems to which there seems no solution and its questions to which there seems no answer; life has its dark places where there seems to be nothing to do but hold on. Faith is always a *victory*, the victory of the soul which tenaciously maintains its clutch on God.

(v) It was something which *must not be held haphazardly and at random*. The faith which collapses is the faith which has not thought things out and thought them through. For so many of us faith is a superficial thing. We tend to accept things because we are told them and to possess them merely at secondhand. If we undergo the agony of thought there may be much that we must discard, but what is left is really ours in such a way that nothing can ever take it from us.

In Paul's list of appearances of the Risen Lord two are specially interesting.

(i) There is the appearance to *Peter*. In the earliest account of the Resurrection story, the word of the messenger in the empty tomb is, "Go, tell his disciples *and Peter*." (*Mark* 16: 7). In *Luke* 24: 34 the disciples say, "The Lord has risen indeed and has appeared to *Simon*." It is an amazing thing that one of the first appearances of the Risen Lord was to the disciple who had denied him. There is all the wonder of the love and grace of Jesus Christ here. Others might have hated Peter forever, but the one desire of Jesus was to set this erratic disciple of his upon his feet. Peter had wronged Jesus and then had wept his heart out; and the one desire of this amazing Jesus was to comfort him in the pain of his disloyalty. Love can go no further than to think more of the heartbreak of the man who wronged it than of the hurt that it itself has received.

(ii) There is the appearance to *James*. Without doubt this James is the brother of our Lord. It is quite clear from the gospel narrative that Jesus's own family did not understand him and were even actively hostile to him. *Mark* 3: 21 tells us that they actually sought to restrain him because they believed him to be mad. *John* 7: 5 tells us that his brothers did not believe in him. One of the earliest of those gospels which did not succeed in getting into the New Testament is the Gospel according to the Hebrews. Only fragments of it remain. One fragment, preserved by Jerome, reads, "Now the Lord, when he had given the linen cloth unto the servant of the priest, went unto James and appeared unto him (for James had sworn that he would not eat bread from that hour wherein he had drunk the Lord's cup until he should see him risen again from among them that sleep)." So, the story runs, "Jesus went to James and said, 'Bring ye a table and bread.' And he took bread and blessed it and broke it and gave it unto James the Just and said unto him, 'My brother, eat thy bread, for the Son of Man is risen from among them that sleep.' " We can only conjecture what lies behind this. It may well be that the last days turned James's contempt into wondering admiration so that when the end came, he was so torn with remorse for the way in which he had treated his brother that he swore that he would starve unless he came back to forgive him. Here once again we have the amazing grace and love of Christ. He came to bring peace to the troubled soul of the man who had called him mad and who had been his opponent.

It is one of the most heart-moving things in all the story of Jesus that two of his first appearances, after he rose from the tomb, were to men who had hurt him and were sorry for it. Jesus meets the penitent heart far more than halfway.

Finally, in this passage we have a vivid light thrown on the character of Paul himself. To him it was the most precious thing in the world that Jesus had appeared also to him. That was at one and the same time the turning point and the dynamic moment of his life. But verses 9–11 tell us much about him.

(i) They tell us of his utter *humility*. He is the least of the apostles; he has been glorified with an office for which he is not worthy. Paul would never have claimed to be a self-made man. It was by the grace of God that he was what he was. He is perhaps even accepting a taunt made against him. It would seem that he was a little and an unhandsome man (2 *Corinthians* 10: 10). It may be that the Jewish Christians who wished to impose the law upon Christian converts and who hated his doctrine of free grace, declared that, so far from being born again, Paul was an abortion. He, for his part, was so conscious of his own unworthiness that he felt no one could say anything too bad about him. Charles Gore once said, "On a general review of life we can seldom feel that we are suffering unmerited wrong." Paul felt like that. His was not the pride which resented the criticisms and the taunts of men, but the humility which felt that it deserved them.

(ii) They tell us at the same time of *the consciousness of his own worth*. He was well aware that he had laboured beyond them all. His was not a false modesty. But even at that, he spoke always, not of what he had done, but of what God had enabled him to do.

(iii) They tell of *his sense of fellowship*. He did not regard himself as an isolated phenomenon with a message that was unique. He and the other apostles preached the same gospel. His was the greatness which bound him closer

A6

to the Christian fellowship; there is always something lacking in the greatness which divides a man from his fellows.

IF CHRIST BE NOT RAISED

1 *Corinthians* 15: 12–19

> If it is continually proclaimed that Christ has been raised from the dead, how can some among you say that the resurrection of the dead does not exist? If the resurrection from among the dead does not exist, then not even Christ has been raised. And if Christ has not been raised, then the proclamation of the faith is emptied of its meaning, and your faith has been emptied of its meaning too. If that is so we are shown to have borne false witness about God, because we witnessed about God, that he raised Christ, whom he did not raise, if indeed the dead are not raised up. If the dead are not raised, not even Christ has been raised; and if Christ has not been raised your faith is worthless, you are still in your sins; and, if that is so, those who died trusting in Christ have perished. If it is only in this life that we have hope in Christ, then we are more to be pitied than all men.

PAUL attacks the central position of his opponents at Corinth. They said flatly, "Dead men do not rise again." Paul's answer is, "If you take up that position it means that Jesus Christ has not risen again; and if that be so, the whole Christian faith is wrecked."

Why did Paul regard a belief in the Resurrection of Jesus as so essential? What great values and great truths does it conserve? It proves four great facts, which can make all the difference to a man's view of life here and hereafter.

(i) The Resurrection proves that *truth is stronger than falsehood*. According to the Fourth Gospel, Jesus said to his enemies, "Now you seek to kill me, a man who has told you the truth." (*John* 8: 40). Jesus came with the true idea of God and of goodness; his enemies procured his death because they did not want their own false view destroyed. If they had succeeded in finally obliterating him, falsehood would have been stronger than truth. On one occasion the Earl of Morton, regent of Scotland, sent for Andrew Melville, the great Reformation leader. "Ther will never be quyetnes in this countrey," said Morton, "till halff a dissone of you be hangit or banished the countrey." "Tushe! sir," said Melville, "threaten your courtiers in that fashion. It is the same to me whether I rot in the air or in the ground. . . . Yet God be glorified, it will nocht ly in your power to hang nor exyll his treuthe!" The Resurrection is the final guarantee of the indestructibility of the truth.

(ii) The Resurrection proves *that good is stronger than evil.* Again to quote the Fourth Gospel, Jesus is represented as saying to his enemies, "You are of your father, the devil." (*John* 8: 44). The forces of evil crucified Jesus and if there had been no Resurrection these forces would have been triumphant. J. A. Froude, the great historian, wrote, "One lesson, and only one, history may be said to repeat with distinctness, that the world is built somehow on moral foundations, that in the long run it is well with the good, and in the long run it is ill with the wicked." But if the Resurrection had not taken place, that very principle would have been imperilled, and we could never again be certain that goodness is stronger than evil.

(iii) The Resurrection proves that *love is stronger than hatred.* Jesus was the love of God incarnate.

> "Love came down at Christmas,
> Love all lovely, Love Divine."

On the other hand, the attitude of those who procured his crucifixion was an almost virulent hatred, so bitter that in the end it was capable of ascribing the loveliness and graciousness of his life to the power of the devil. If there had been no Resurrection, it would have meant that the hatred of man in the end conquered the love of God. The Resurrection is the triumph of love over all that hatred could do. This very beautiful poem sums up the whole matter.

"I heard two soldiers talking
As they came down the hill,
The sombre hill of Calvary,
Bleak and black and still.
And one said, 'The night is late,
These thieves take long to die.'
And one said, 'I am sore afraid,
And yet I know not why.'

I heard two women weeping
As down the hill they came,
And one was like a broken rose,
And one was like a flame.
One said, 'Men shall rue
This deed their hands have done.'
And one said only through her tears,
'My son! my son! my son!'

I heard two angels singing
Ere yet the dawn was bright,
And they were clad in shining robes,
Robes and crowns of light.
And one sang, 'Death is vanquished,'
And one in golden voice
Sang, 'Love hath conquered, conquered all,
O heaven and earth rejoice! ' "

The Resurrection is the final proof that love is stronger than hate.

(iv) The Resurrection proves that *life is stronger than death.* If Jesus had died never to rise again, it would have proved that death could take the loveliest and best life that ever lived and finally break it. During the second world war a certain city church in London was all set out for harvest thanksgiving. In the centre of the gifts was a sheaf of corn. The service was never held, for, on the Saturday night, a savage air raid laid the church in ruins. The months passed and the spring came, and someone noticed that, on the bomb site where the church had stood, there were shoots of green. The summer came and the shoots flourished and in the autumn there was a flourishing patch of corn growing amidst the rubble. Not even the bombs and the destruction could kill the life of the corn and its seeds. The Resurrection is the final proof that life is stronger than death.

Paul insisted that if the Resurrection of Jesus was not a fact the whole Christian message was based on a lie, that many thousands had died trusting in a delusion, that without it the greatest values in life have no guarantee. "Take away the Resurrection," he said, "and you destroy both the foundation and the fabric of the Christian faith."

THE FIRST-FRUITS OF THOSE THAT SLEEP

1 *Corinthians* 15: 20–28

> Now then Christ has been raised from among the dead, the first-fruits of those who sleep. For, since it was through one man that death came, it was also through one man that the resurrection of the dead came. For just as in Adam all die, so also in Christ all will be made alive. Each comes in his own rank. Christ is the first-fruits, and then those who belong to Christ will be raised when he comes. After that comes the final end, when he will hand over the Kingdom to God, his father, when he has reduced to helplessness every other rule, and every other authority and power. For he must reign until he puts all his enemies under his feet. Death will be the last enemy to be reduced to helplessness. For God has subjected all things to him. (When we say that all things have been subjected to him, that of course does not include him who subjected them to him). But when all things have been subjected to him, then the Son himself will be subjected to him who subjected all things to him, so that God may be all in all.

THIS again is a very difficult passage because it deals with ideas which are strange to us.

It speaks of Christ as "the first-fruits of them that sleep." Paul is thinking in terms of a picture which every Jew would recognize. The Feast of the Passover had more than one significance. It commemorated the deliverance of the children of Israel from Egypt. But it was also a great harvest festival. It fell just at the time when the barley harvest was due to be ingathered. The law laid it down, "You shall bring the sheaf of the first-fruits of your harvest to the priest; and he shall wave the sheaf before the Lord, that you may find acceptance; on the morrow after the Sabbath the priest shall wave it." (*Leviticus* 23: 10, 11). Some sheaves of barley must be reaped from a common field. They must not be taken from a garden or an orchard or from specially prepared soil. They must come from a typical field. When the barley was cut, it was brought to the Temple. There it was threshed with soft canes so as not to bruise it. It was then parched over the fire in a perforated pan so that every grain was touched by the fire. It was then exposed to the wind so that the chaff was blown away. It was then ground in a barley mill and its flour was offered to God. That was the first-fruits.

It is significant to note that not until after that was done could the new barley be bought and sold in the shops and bread be made from the new flour. The first-fruits were a sign of the harvest to come; and the Resurrection of Jesus was a sign of the resurrection of all believers which was to come. Just as the new barley could not be used until the first-fruits had been duly offered, so the new harvest of life could not come until Jesus had been raised from the dead.

Paul goes on to use another Jewish idea. According to the old story in *Genesis* 3: 1–19 it was through Adam's sin that death came into the world as its direct consequence and penalty. The Jews believed that all men literally sinned in Adam; we see that his sin might transmit to his descendants *the tendency* to sin. As Aeschylus said, "The impious deed leaves after it a larger progeny, all in the likeness of the parent stock." As George Eliot wrote, "Our deeds are like children that are born to us, they live and act apart from our will; nay, children may be strangled, but deeds never. They have an indestructible life both in and out of our consciousness."

Nobody would be likely to deny that a child can inherit a tendency to sin and that the father's sins are literally visited upon the children. No one would deny that a child can inherit the consequences of a father's sin, for we know all too well how physical conditions which are the consequence of an immoral life can be transmitted to the child. But the Jew meant more than that. He had a tremendous sense of solidarity. He was sure that no man could ever do anything that could affect only himself. And he held that all men sinned in Adam. The whole world of men was, as it were, in him; and when he sinned all sinned.

That may seem a strange idea to us and unfair. But that was the Jewish belief. All had sinned in Adam, therefore all were under the penalty of death. With the coming of Christ that chain was broken. Christ was sinless and conquered death. Just as all men sinned in Adam, so all men escape from sin in Christ; and just as all men died in Adam, so all men conquered death in Christ. Our unity with Christ is just as real as our unity with Adam and this destroys the evil effect of the old.

So we get two contrasting sets of facts. First, there is Adam—sin—death. Second, there is Christ—goodness—life. And just as we were all involved in the sin of him who was first created, we are all involved in the victory of him who re-created mankind. However we may estimate that way of thinking today, it was convincing to those who heard it for the first time; and, whatever else is doubtful, it remains true that with Jesus Christ a new power came into the world to liberate men from sin and death.

Verses 24–28 read very strangely to us. We are used to thinking of the Father and the Son on terms of equality. But here Paul clearly and deliberately subordinates the Son to the Father. What he is thinking of is this. We can use only human terms and analogies. God gave to Jesus a task to do, to defeat sin and death and to liberate man. The day will come when that task will be fully and finally accomplished, and then, to put it in pictorial terms, the Son will return to the Father like a victor coming home and the triumph of God will be complete. It is not a case of the Son being subject to the Father as a slave or even a servant is to a master. It is a case of one who, having accomplished the work that was given him to do, returns with the glory of complete obedience as his crown. As God sent forth his Son to redeem the world, so in the end he will receive back a world redeemed; and then there will be nothing in heaven or in earth outside his love and power.

IF THERE IS NO RESURRECTION

1 *Corinthians* 15: 29–34

> If there is no resurrection, what will those who are baptized for the dead do? If the dead are not raised at all, why do people get themselves baptized for them? Every day I take my life in my hands, I swear it by the pride which I have in you in Christ Jesus our Lord. What good is it to me—looking at it from the human point of view—if at Ephesus I had to fight with beasts in the arena? If the dead are not raised, let us eat and drink for tomorrow we die. Don't deceive yourselves—evil friendships destroy good characters. Turn to sober living, as it is only right that you should, and don't go on sinning. Some of you boast about your knowledge, but you have not a vestige of knowledge about God. It is to shame you that I speak.

ONCE again this passage begins with a very difficult section. People have always been puzzled about what *being baptized for the dead* means, and even yet the problem is not definitely settled. The preposition *for* in the phrase for the dead is the Greek *huper*. In general this word can have two main meanings. When used of place, it can mean *above* or *over*. Far more commonly it is used of persons or things and means *instead of* or *on behalf of*. Remembering these two meanings, let us look at some of the ways this phrase has been understood.

(i) Beginning from the meaning of *over* or *above,* some scholars have suggested that it refers to those *who get themselves baptized over the graves of the martyrs*. The idea is that there would be something specially moving in being baptized on sacred ground with the thought of the unseen cloud of witnesses all around. It is an attractive and rather lovely idea, but at the time Paul was writing to the Corinthians persecution had not yet broken out in anything like a big way. Christians might suffer ostracism and social persecution, but the time of the martyrs had not yet come.

(ii) It is in any event much more natural to take *huper* in the sense of *instead of* or *on behalf of*. If we take it that way there are three possibilities. It is suggested that the phrase refers to those *who get themselves baptized in order to fill up the vacant places in the Church which the dead have left*. The idea is that the new believer, the young Christian, comes into the Church like a new recruit to take the place of the veterans who have served their campaign and earned their release. There is a great thought there. The Church ever needs its replacements and the new member is like the volunteer who fills up the depleted ranks.

(iii) It is suggested that the phrase means *those who get themselves baptized out of respect for and affection for the dead*. Again there is a precious truth here. Many of us came into the Church because we knew and remembered that some loved one had died praying and hoping for us. Many have in the end given their lives to Christ because of the unseen influence of one who has passed over to the other side.

(iv) All these are lovely thoughts, but in the end we think that this phrase can refer to only one custom, which has quite correctly passed out of Church practice altogether. In the early Church there was vicarious baptism. If a person died who had intended to become a member of the Church and was actually under instruction, sometimes someone else underwent baptism for him. The custom sprang from a superstitious view of baptism, that, without it, a person was necessarily excluded from the bliss of heaven. It was to safeguard against this exclusion that sometimes people volunteered to be baptized literally on behalf of those who had died. Here Paul neither approves nor disapproves that practice. He merely asks if there can be any point in it if there is no resurrection and the dead never rise again.

From that he passes on to one of the great motives of the Christian life. In effect he asks, "Why should a Christian accept the perils of the Christian life if it is all to go for nothing?" He quotes his own experience. Every day he is in jeopardy of his life. Something terrible of which the New Testament has no record happened to Paul at Ephesus. He refers to it again in 2 *Corinthians* 1: 8–10: he says that in Asia, that is in Ephesus, he was in such dire peril that he despaired of life and had the sentence of death passed upon him. To this day in Ephesus there is a building known as Paul's prison. Here he calls his peril *fighting with beasts*. The word he uses is that used of a gladiator in the arena. The later legends tell us that he actually did so fight and that he was wondrously preserved because the beasts would not attack him. But Paul was a Roman citizen and no Roman citizen could be compelled to fight in the arena. Much more likely he used the phrase as a vivid picture of being threatened by men who were as savage for his life as a wild beast might have been. In any event he demands, "To what end is all the peril and the suffering if there is no life beyond?"

The man who thinks that this life is all, and that there is nothing to follow it, may well say, "Eat, drink and be merry for tomorrow we die." The Bible itself quotes those who speak like that. "Come," they say, "let us get wine, let us fill ourselves with strong drink; and tomorrow will be like this day, great beyond measure." (*Isaiah* 56: 12). The preacher, who held that death was extinction, wrote, "There is nothing better for a man than that he should eat and drink, and find enjoyment from his toil." (*Ecclesiastes* 2: 24, cp. 3: 12; 5: 18; 8: 15; 9: 7). Jesus himself told about the rich fool who forgot eternity and took as his motto, "Eat, drink and be merry." (*Luke* 12: 19).

Classical literature is full of this spirit. Herodotus, the Greek historian, tells of a custom of the Egyptians. "In social meetings among the rich, when the banquet is ended, a servant carries round to the several guests a coffin, in which there is a wooden image of a corpse, carved and painted to resemble nature as nearly as possible, about a cubit or two cubits in length. As he shows it to each guest in turn, the servant says, 'Gaze here, and drink and be merry, for when you die, such will you be.'" Euripides writes in the *Alcestis* (781–789, A. S. Way's translation):

> "From all mankind the debt of death is due,
> For of all mortals is there one that knows
> If through the coming morrow he shall live?
> For trackless is the way of fortune's feet,
> Not to be taught nor won by art of man.
> This hearing then, and learning it of me,
> Make merry, drink; the life from day to day
> Account thine own, all else in fortune's power."

Thucydides (2: 53) tells how, when the mortal plague came to Athens, people committed every shameful crime and eagerly snatched at every lustful pleasure because they believed that life was short and they would never have to pay the penalty. Horace (Odes 2: 13; 13) gives as his philosophy, "Tell them to bring wines and perfumes and the too-short-lived blossoms of the lovely rose while circumstances and age and the black threads of the three sisters (the Fates) still allow us to do so." In one of the most famous poems in the world the Latin poet Catullus wrote, "Let us live, my Lesbia, and let us love, and let us value the tales of austere old men at a single halfpenny. Suns can set and then return again, but for us, when once our brief light sets, there is but one perpetual night through which we must sleep."

Take away the thought of a life to come and this life loses its values. Take away the idea that this life is a preparation for a greater life to follow and the bonds of honour and morality are loosened. It is useless to argue that this should not be so and that men should not be good and honourable simply for the sake of some reward. The fact remains that the man who believes that this is the only world tends to live as if the things of this world are all that matter.

So Paul insists that the Corinthians must not associate with those who say that there is no resurrection; for this would

be to risk an infection which can pollute life. To say that
there is no resurrection is not a sign of superior knowledge;
it is a sign of utter ignorance of God. Paul is unleashing the
lash that very shame may bring these wanderers back into
the right way.

THE PHYSICAL AND THE SPIRITUAL

1 *Corinthians* 15: 35–49

But perhaps someone says, "In what form are the dead raised?
With what kind of body do they come?" That is a foolish
question. When you sow a seed, it cannot be made alive, unless it
first dies. It is not the body which is going to come into existence
that is sown, but a seed which is not clothed in a body at all, it
may be of corn, or of some other of the crops. But God gives it
a body as he wills, and to each of the seeds he gives its own
body. All flesh is not the same flesh. But there is one kind of
flesh of men, and another of beasts, and another of birds, and
another of fishes. There are heavenly bodies and there are earthly
bodies. The splendour of the heavenly bodies is one thing, and the
splendour of the earthly bodies is another. The sun has one
splendour and the moon another splendour and the stars another
splendour. I say stars, not star, for star differs from star in
splendour. There is the same difference between this body and the
body we shall have in the resurrection of the dead. Our body is
like the seed. It is sown in corruption; it is raised in incorruption:
it is sown in dishonour; it is raised in glory: it is sown in
weakness; it is raised in power: it is sown a physical body; it is
raised a spiritual body. For if a physical body exists, so does a
spiritual one. For it stands written, "The first man, Adam, became
a living soul. The last Adam became a life-giving spirit." It is not
the spiritual that comes first, but the physical, and after that the
spiritual. The first man is of the earth and was made of earth;
the second man is from heaven. Such as are made of earth are
like earth; such as are heavenly, are like the heavenly one; and,
as we have borne the image of that which is of earth, so we
shall also bear the image of him who is of heaven.

BEFORE we begin to try to interpret this section we would do well to remember one thing—all through it Paul is talking about things that no one really knows anything about. He is talking not about verifiable matters of fact, but about matters of faith. Trying to express the inexpressible and to describe the indescribable, he is doing the best he can with the human ideas and human words that are all that he has to work with. If we remember that, it will save us from a crudely literalistic interpretation and make us fasten our thoughts on the underlying principles in Paul's mind. In this section he is dealing with people who say, "Granted that there is a resurrection of the body, with what kind of body do people rise again?" His answer has three basic principles in it.

(i) He takes the analogy of a seed. The seed is put in the ground and dies, but in due time it rises again; and does so with a very different kind of body from that with which it was sown. Paul is showing that, at one and the same time, there can be dissolution, difference and yet continuity. The seed is dissolved; when it rises again, there is a vast difference in its body; and yet, in spite of the dissolution and the difference, it is the same seed. So our earthly bodies will dissolve; they will rise again in very different form; but it is the same person who rises. Dissolved by death, changed by resurrection, it is still we who exist.

(ii) In the world, even as we know it, there is not one kind of body; each separate part of creation has its own. God gives to each created thing a body suitable for its part in creation. If that be so, it is only reasonable to expect that he will give us a body fitted for the resurrection life.

(iii) In life there is a development. Adam, the first man, was made from the dust of the earth (*Genesis* 2: 7). But Jesus is far more than a man made from the dust of the earth. He is the incarnation of the very Spirit of God. Now, under the old way of life, we were one with Adam, sharing his sin, inheriting his death and having his body; but, under the new way of life, we are one with Christ and we shall therefore share his life and his being. It is true that we have a physical body to begin with, but it is also true that one day we shall have a spiritual body.

All through this section Paul has maintained a reverent and wise reticence as to what that body will be like; it will be spiritual, it will be such as God knows that we need and we will be like Christ. But in verses 42–44 he draws four contrasts which shed light on our future state.

(i) The present body is corruptible; the future body will be incorruptible. In this world everything is subject to change and decay. "Youth's beauty fades, and manhood's glory fades," as Sophocles had it. But in the life to come there will be a permanence in which beauty will never lose its sheen.

(ii) The present body is in dishonour; the future body will be in glory. It may be that Paul means that in this life it is through our bodily feelings and passions that dishonour can so easily come; but in the life to come our bodies will no longer be the servants of passion and of impulse but the instruments of the pure service of God, than which there can be no greater honour.

(iii) The present body is in weakness; the future body will be in power. It is nowadays fashionable to talk of man's power, but the really remarkable thing is his weakness. A draught of air or a drop of water can kill him. We are limited in this life so often simply because of the necessary limitations of the body. Time and time again our physical constitution says to our visions and our plans, "Thus far and no farther." We are so often frustrated because we are what we are. But in the life to come the limitations will be gone. Here we are compassed about with weakness; there we will be clad with power.

> "All we have hoped or willed or dreamed of good
>   shall exist;
> The high that proved too high, the heroic for earth
>   too hard."

On earth we have the "broken arcs"; in the life to come "the perfect round."

(iv) The present body is a natural body; the future body will be a spiritual body. By that, it may be, Paul meant that here we are but imperfect vessels and imperfect instruments for the Spirit; but in the life to come we will be such that the Spirit can truly fill us, as can never happen here, and the Spirit can truly use us, as is never possible now. Then we will be able to render the perfect worship, the perfect service, the perfect love that now can only be a vision and a dream.

THE CONQUEST OF DEATH

1 *Corinthians* 15: 50–58

> Brothers, I say this, that flesh and blood cannot inherit the Kingdom of God, nor can corruption inherit incorruption. Look now—I tell you something which only the initiated can understand. We shall not all die, but we shall all be changed, in a moment of time, in the twinkling of an eye, at the last trumpet. For the trumpet shall sound and the dead shall be raised up incorruptible and we shall be changed. For this corruptible must put on incorruption, and this mortal must put on immortality, then the word which stands written will happen, "Death has been swallowed up in victory." O death, where is your victory? O death, where is your sting? The sting of death is sin; and the strength of sin is the law. Thanks be to God who gives us the victory through our Lord Jesus Christ. So then, beloved brothers, show yourselves steady, immovable, always excelling in the work of the Lord, knowing that in the Lord your toil does not go for nothing.

ONCE again we must remember that Paul is dealing with things which defy language and baffle expression. We must read this as we would read great poetry, rather than as we would dissect a scientific treatise. The argument follows a series of steps until it reaches its climax.

(i) Paul insists that, as we are, we are not fit to inherit the Kingdom of God. We may be well enough equipped to get on with the life of this world, but for the life of the world to come we will not do. A man may be able to run enough to catch his morning train and yet need to be very different to be able to run enough for the Olympic games. A man may write well enough to amuse his friends and yet need to be very different to write something which men will not willingly let die. A man may talk well enough in the circle of his club and yet need to be very different to hold his own in a circle of real experts. A man always needs to be changed to enter into a higher grade of life; and Paul insists that before we can enter the Kingdom of God we must be changed.

(ii) Further he insists that this shattering change is going to come in his own lifetime. In this he was in error; but he looked to that change coming when Jesus Christ came again.

(iii) Then Paul goes on triumphantly to declare that no man need fear that change. The fear of death has always haunted men. It haunted Dr. Johnson, one of the greatest and best men who ever lived. Once Boswell said to him that there had been times when he had not feared death. Johnson answered that "he never had a moment in which death was not terrible to him." Once Mrs. Knowles told him that he should not have a horror for that which is the gate of life. Johnson answered, "No rational man can die without uneasy apprehension." He declared that the fear of death was so natural to man that all life was one long effort not to think about it.

Wherein lies the fear of death? Partly it comes from fear of the unknown. But still more it comes from the sense of sin. If a man felt that he could meet God easily then to die would be only, as Peter Pan said, a great adventure. But where does that sense of sin come from? It comes from a sense of being under the law. So long as a man sees in God only the law of righteousness, he must ever be in the position of a criminal before the bar with no hope of acquittal. But this is precisely what Jesus came to abolish. He came to tell us that God is not law, but love, that the centre of God's being is not legalism but grace, that we go out, not to a judge, but to a Father who awaits his children coming home. Because of that Jesus gave us the victory over death, its fear banished in the wonder of God's love.

(iv) Finally, at the end of the chapter, Paul does what he always does. Suddenly the theology becomes a challenge; suddenly the speculations become intensely practical; suddenly the sweep of the mind becomes the demand for action. He ends by saying, "If you have all that glory to look forward to, then keep yourself steadfast in God's faith and service, for if you do, all your effort will not be in vain." The Christian life may be difficult, but the goal is infinitely worth the struggle.

> "A hope so great and so divine,
>   May trials well endure;
> And purge the soul from sense and sin,
>   As Christ himself is pure."

PRACTICAL PLANS

1 *Corinthians* 16: 1–12

With regard to the collection for the people of Christ, do you too follow the instructions which I gave to the Churches of Galatia. Every first day of the week each of you must put by and save up whatever his prosperity demands, so that there may be no need to take collections when I arrive. Whenever I arrive, I will send whoever you approve by letter to take your gifts to Jerusalem. If it is fitting for me to go, too, they will travel with me. I will come to you after I have passed through Macedonia. Possibly I may stay with you, or I may even spend the winter with you so that you may speed me on my way wherever I go. I do not want to see you now in the passing, for I hope to stay some time with you, if the Lord permits it. I will stay in Ephesus until Pentecost, for a great and effective door stands open to me, although my opponents are many.

If Timothy comes, see that he may be able to stay with you without fear. He is doing God's work just as I, too, am doing it, so let no one look down on him. Speed him on his way with the blessing of peace that he may come to me, for I and the brothers are eagerly waiting for him. With regard to Apollos, the brother,

I have strongly urged him to go to you with the brothers, but he was all against coming to you just now, but will come when the time is convenient.

THERE is nothing more typical of Paul than the abrupt change between chapter 15 and chapter 16. Chapter 15 has been walking in the loftiest realms of thought and theology, and discussing the life of the world to come. Chapter 16 deals with the most practical things in the most practical way and is concerned with the everyday life of this world and the administration of the Church. There is no reach of thought too high for Paul to scale and no practical detail of administration too small for him to remember. He was very far from being one of those visionaries, who are at home in the realms of theological speculation and quite lost in practical matters. There might be times when his head was in the clouds but his feet were always planted firmly on the solid earth.

He begins by dealing with the collection for the poor saints at Jerusalem. This was an undertaking very dear to Paul's heart. (cp. *Galatians* 2: 10; *2 Corinthians* chapters 8 and 9; *Romans* 15: 25; *Acts* 24: 17). There was a certain brotherliness in the ancient world. In the Greek world there were associations called *eranoi*. If a person fell on evil days or was in sudden need, his friends would club together to raise an interest-free loan to help him. The synagogue had officials whose duty it was to collect from those who had and to share out to those who had not. Quite frequently Jews who had gone abroad and prospered sent their envoys to Jerusalem with contributions for the Temple and for the poor. Paul did not want the Christian Church to be behind the Jewish and the heathen world in generosity.

But to him this collection for the poor at Jerusalem meant more than that. (i) It was a way of demonstrating the unity of the Church. It was a way of teaching the scattered Christians that they were not members of a congregation only, but members of a Church, each part of which had obligations to the rest. The narrowly congregational outlook was far from the Pauline conception of the Church. (ii) It was a way of putting into effect the practical teaching of Christianity. By arranging this collection Paul was providing his converts with an opportunity of translating into action the teaching of Christ on the virtue of love.

It has been pointed out that, in different letters and speeches, Paul uses no fewer than nine different words to describe this collection.

(i) Here he calls it a *logia;* the word means *an extra collection.* A *logia* was something which was the opposite of a tax which a man had to pay; it was an extra piece of giving. A man never satisfies his Christian duty by discharging the obligations which he can legally be compelled to fulfil. The question of Jesus was, "What more are you doing than others?" (*Matthew* 5: 47).

(ii) Sometimes he calls it a *charis* (1 *Corinthians* 16: 3; 2 *Corinthians* 8: 4). As we have already seen, the characteristic of *charis* is that it describes *a free gift freely given.* The really lovely thing is not something extracted from a man, however large it be, but something given in the overflowing love of a man's heart, however small it be. We must note that Paul does not lay down a flat rate which each Corinthian Christian must give; he tells them that they must give as their prosperity demands. A man's heart must tell him what to give.

(iii) Sometimes he uses the word *koinonia* (2 *Corinthians* 8: 4; 9: 13; *Romans* 15: 6). *Koinonia* means *fellowship,* and the essence of fellowship is *sharing.* Christian fellowship is based on the spirit which cannot hug to itself that which it has, but which regards all its possessions as things to be shared with others. Its dominating question is not, "What can I keep?" but, "What can I give?"

(iv) Sometimes he uses the word *diakonia* (2 *Corinthians* 8: 4; 9: 1, 12, 13). *Diakonia* means practical Christian service. It is from its kindred word *diakonos* that we get our English word *deacon.* It may sometimes happen that the limitations of life prevent us from rendering personal service and it may often happen that our money can go where we cannot go.

(v) Once he uses the word *hadrotes,* whose meaning is

abundance (2 *Corinthians* 8: 20). In that passage Paul speaks of the envoys of the Church who accompany him to guarantee that he does not misuse the *abundance* which is entrusted to him. Paul would never have desired an abundance for himself. He was content with what he could earn with the toil of his hands and the sweat of his brow. But he was glad in heart when he had abundance to give away. It is a grim commentary on human nature that, when a man is dreaming of what he would do if he was a millionaire, he almost always begins by thinking what he would buy for himself, and seldom of what he would give away.

(vi) Sometimes he uses the word *eulogia,* which in this case means *bounty* (2 *Corinthians* 9: 5). There is a kind of giving which is not a bounty. The gift is given as a bleak and unavoidable duty, given with a grudge and with no delight. All true giving is a bounty which we are supremely glad to give.

(vii) Sometimes he uses the word *leitourgia* (2 *Corinthians* 9: 12). In classical Greek this is a word with a noble history. In the great days of Athens there were generous citizens who volunteered out of their own pockets to shoulder the expenses of some enterprise on which the city was engaged. It might be to defray the expenses of training the chorus for some new drama or some team to compete for the honour of the city in the games; it might be to pay for the outfitting and manning of a trireme or man-of-war in time of the city's peril. A *leitourgia* was originally a service of the state voluntarily accepted. Christian giving is something which should be volunteered. It should be accepted as a privilege to help in some way the household of God.

(viii) Once he speaks of this collection as *eleemosune* (*Acts* 24: 17). That is the Greek word for *alms.* So central was alms-giving to the Jewish idea of religion, that the Jew could use the same word for *almsgiving* and *righteousness.*

> "Alms given to a father shall not be blotted out,
> And it shall stand firm as a substitute for sin;
> In the day of trouble it shall be remembered,

Obliterating thine iniquities as the heat the
hoar frost" (*Ecclesiasticus* 14: 15).

The Jew would have said, "How can a man show that he is
a good man except by being generous?"

(ix) Lastly he uses the word *prosphora* (*Acts* 24: 17). The
interesting thing is that *prosphora* is the word for *an offering
and a sacrifice*. In the realest sense that which is given to a
man in need is a sacrifice to God. The best of all sacrifices
to him, after the sacrifice of the penitent heart, is kindness
shown to one of his children in trouble.

At the end of this section Paul commends two of his
helpers. The first is *Timothy*. Timothy had the disadvantage
of being a young man. The situation in Corinth was difficult
enough for the experienced Paul; it would be infinitely worse
for Timothy. Paul's commendation is that they are to respect
Timothy, not for his own sake, but for the sake of the work
that he is doing. It is not the man who glorifies the work but
the work which glorifies the man. There is no dignity like the
dignity of a great task. The second is *Apollos*. Apollos emerges
from this passage as a man of great wisdom. Right at the
beginning of this letter we saw that there was a party in
Corinth who, quite without the sanction of Apollos, had
attached themselves to his name. Apollos knew that, and, no
doubt, he wished to stay away from Corinth, lest that party
try to annex him. He was wise enough to know that, when a
Church is torn with party politics, there is a time when it is
wiser and more far-sighted to stay away.

CLOSING WORDS AND GREETINGS

1 *Corinthians* 16: 13–21

Be on the alert; stand fast in the faith; play the man; be strong.
Let all your affairs be transacted in love.

Brothers I urge you—(you know the family of Stephanas was
the first-fruits of God's harvest in Achaea and that they have laid

themselves out to be of help to Christ's people)—that you too may be obedient to such men and to all who share in the common work of the gospel and who toil for it. I rejoice at the arrival of Stephanas, Fortunatus and Achaicus, because they filled up all the gaps in my news about you. They have refreshed my spirit and yours. Give full acknowledgment to such men.

The Churches of Asia send you their greetings. Aquila and Prisca send you many greetings in the Lord together with the Church that is in their house. All the brothers send their greetings. Greet each other with a holy kiss.

Here is my greeting written in the handwriting of me Paul. If anyone does not love the Lord let him be accursed. The Lord is at hand. The grace of the Lord Jesus Christ be with you. My love be with you all in Christ Jesus. Amen.

THIS is an interesting passage because its very practical nature and its ordinariness shed a vivid light on the day to day life of the early Church.

Paul begins with a series of five imperatives. It may well be that all the first four have a military background and are like a commander's orders to his soldiers. "As a sentinel, be ever on the alert. When under attack, stand fast in the faith and yield not an inch. In time of battle, play a hero's part. Like a well-equipped and well-trained soldier, be strong to fight for your King." Then the metaphor changes. Whatever the Christian soldier be to those persons and things which threaten the Christian faith from the outside, to those within the Church he must be a comrade and a lover. In the Christian life there must be the courage which will never retreat and the love which will never fail.

To Paul in Ephesus there had come Stephanas, Fortunatus and Achaicus, and they had brought him first-hand information which filled in the gaps in his knowledge of what was happening at Corinth. His commendation of Stephanas is very interesting. Stephanas deserved respect because he had put himself at the service of the Church. In the early Church willing and spontaneous service was the beginning of official office. A man became a leader of the Church, not so much by man-made appointment, as by the fact that his life and work marked him out as one whom all men must respect. T. C. Edwards says, "In the Church many *work*, but few *toil*."

Verses 19 and 20 are a series of greetings. Greetings are sent from Aquila and Priscilla. These two people, man and wife, move across the background of Paul's letters and the Book of Acts. They were Jews, and, like Paul, were tent-makers. Originally they had been settled in Rome, but in A.D. 49 or 50 Claudius, the Roman Emperor, had issued a decree banishing all Jews from Rome. Aquila and Priscilla found their way to Corinth, and it was there that Paul first met them (*Acts* 18: 2). From Corinth they found their way to Ephesus, from which now Paul sends their greetings to their old associates in Corinth. From *Romans* 16: 3 we find that they found their way back to Rome and settled there again. One of the interesting things about Aquila and Priscilla is that they show us how easy and natural travel was even at that time. They followed their trade from Palestine to Rome, from Rome to Corinth, from Corinth to Ephesus, and from Ephesus back to Rome.

There is one great thing about these two. In those early days there were no church buildings. It is, in fact, not until the third century that we hear about a church building at all. The little congregations met in private houses. If a house had a room big enough, it was there that the Christian fellowship met. Now wherever Aquila and Priscilla went, their home became a church. When they are in Rome, Paul sends greetings to them and to the church that is their house (*Romans* 16: 3–5). When he writes from Ephesus, he sends greetings from them and from the church that is in their house. Aquila and Priscilla were two of these wonderful people who make their homes centres of Christian light and love, who welcome many guests because Christ is always their unseen guest, who make their houses havens of rest and peace and friendship for the lonely and the tempted and the sad and the depressed. A great compliment Homer paid one of his characters was to say of him, "He dwelt in a house by the side of the road and he was the friend of wayfaring men." The Christian wayfarer ever found an inn of peace where Aquila and Priscilla lived. God grant to us to make our homes like that!

"Greet each other," writes Paul, "with a holy kiss." The kiss of peace was a lovely custom of the early Church. It may have been a Jewish custom which the early Church took over. It was apparently given at the end of the prayers and just before the congregation partook of the sacrament. It was the sign and symbol that they sat at the table of love joined together in perfect love. Cyril of Jerusalem writes of it, "Do not think that this kiss is like the kiss given to each other by mutual friends in the market place." It was not given promiscuously. Certainly in later times it was not given between men and women, but between man and man, and woman and woman. Sometimes it was given not on the lips but on the hand. It came to be called simply "The Peace." Surely never did a church need to be recalled to that lovely custom more than this Church at Corinth, so torn with strife and dissension.

Why did that lovely custom pass from the Church's life? First, it faded because, lovely though it was, it was obviously liable to abuse, and, still more, it was liable to misinterpretation by heathen slanders. Second, it faded because the Church became less and less of a fellowship. In the little house churches, where friend met with friend and all were closely bound together, it was the most natural thing in the world; but, when the house fellowship became a vast congregation and the little room became a great church, the intimacy went lost and the kiss of peace went lost with it. It may well be that with our vast congregations we have lost something, for the bigger and more scattered a congregation is the more difficult it is for it to be a fellowship, where people really know and really love each other. And yet a church which is a collection of strangers, or, at the best, of acquaintances, is not a true church in the deepest sense.

And so to the end. Paul sends his own autograph greeting on the last page of the letter which some secretary had taken down for him. He warns them against anyone who does not love Christ. And then he writes in Aramaic the phrase, "Maran atha," which most probably means, "The Lord is at hand." It is strange to meet with an Aramaic phrase in a Greek letter to a Greek church. The explanation is that that phrase had become a watchword and a password. It summed up the vital hope of the early Church, and Christians identified each other by it, in a language which the heathen could not understand.

Two last things Paul sends to the folk at Corinth—the grace of Christ and his own love. He might have had occasion to warn, to rebuke, to speak with righteous anger, but the last word is love.

2 CORINTHIANS

COMFORTED TO COMFORT

2 Corinthians 1: 1-7

Paul, an apostle of Christ Jesus through God's will, and Timothy, the brother you all know, send this letter to the Church of God which is at Corinth, together with all God's dedicated people who are in the whole of Achaea. Grace be to you and peace from God our Father, and from the Lord Jesus Christ.

Blessed be the God and Father of our Lord Jesus Christ, the Father who is ever compassionate and the God who sends all comfort, he who comforts us in all our affliction, so that we are able to comfort those who are in any kind of affliction, through that comfort with which we ourselves are comforted by God. For, even as the things which Christ had to suffer have overflowed to us, so the comfort which we can bring you also overflowed through Christ. If we are undergoing affliction it is that we may be the better able to comfort you and bring you salvation. If we are comforted, it is that we may be the better able to bring to you that comfort whose effectiveness is demonstrated by your ability triumphantly to endure the hard experiences which we also are going through. So our hope concerning you is well-grounded, for we know that just as you share the sufferings which we undergo, you also share the source of comfort we possess.

BEHIND this passage there is a kind of summary of the Christian life.

(i) Paul writes as a man who knows trouble to those who are in trouble. The word that he uses for affliction is *thlipsis*. In ordinary Greek this word always describes actual physical pressure on a man. R. C. Trench writes, "When, according to the ancient law of England, those who wilfully refused to plead had heavy weights placed on their breasts, and were so pressed and crushed to death, this was literally *thlipsis*."

Sometimes there falls upon a man's spirit the burden and the mystery of this unintelligible world. In the early years of Christianity the man who chose to become a Christian chose to face trouble. There might well come to him abandonment by his own family, hostility from his heathen neighbours, and persecution from the official powers. Samuel Rutherford wrote to one of his friends, "God has called you to Christ's side, and the wind is now in Christ's face in this land: and seeing ye are with him ye cannot expect the lee-side or the sunny side of the brae." It is always a costly thing to be a real Christian, for there can be no Christianity without its cross.

(ii) The answer to this suffering lies in endurance. The Greek word for this endurance is *hupomone*. The keynote of *hupomone* is not grim, bleak acceptance of trouble but triumph. It describes the spirit which can not only accept suffering but triumph over it. Someone once said to a sufferer, "Suffering colours life, doesn't it?" The sufferer replied, "Yes, but I propose to choose the colour." As the silver comes purer from the fire, so the Christian can emerge finer and stronger from hard days. The Christian is the athlete of God whose spiritual muscles become stronger from the discipline of difficulties.

(iii) But we are not left to face this trial and to provide this endurance alone. There comes to us the comfort of God. Between verses 3 and 7 the noun *comfort* or the verb *to comfort* occurs no fewer than nine times. *Comfort* in the New Testament always means far more than soothing sympathy.

Always it is true to its root meaning, for its root is the Latin *fortis* and *fortis* means *brave*. Christian comfort is the comfort which brings courage and enables a man to cope with all that life can do to him. Paul was quite sure that God never sends a man a vision without the power to work it out and never sends him a task without the strength to do it.

Even apart from that, there is always a certain inspiration in any suffering which a man's Christianity may incur, for such suffering, as Paul puts it, is the overflow of Christ's suffering reaching to us. It is a sharing in the suffering of Christ. In the old days of chivalry, the knights used to come demanding some specially difficult task, in order that they might show their devotion to the lady whom they loved. To suffer for Christ is a privilege. When the hard thing comes, the Christian can say, as Polycarp, the aged Bishop of Smyrna, said when they bound him to the stake, "I thank thee that thou hast judged me worthy of this hour."

(iv) The supreme result of all this is that we gain the power to comfort others who are going through it. Paul claims that the things which have happened to him and the comfort which he has received have made him able to be a source of comfort to others. Barrie tells how his mother lost her dearest son, and then he says, "That is where my mother got her soft eyes and why other mothers ran to her when they had lost a child." It was said of Jesus, "Because he himself has gone through it, he is able to help others who are going through it." (*Hebrews* 2: 18). It is worth while experiencing suffering and sorrow if that experience will enable us to help others struggling with life's billows.

DRIVEN BACK ON GOD

2 Corinthians 1: 8–11

> I want you to know, brothers, about the terrible experience which happened to us in Asia, an experience in which we were excessively

weighted down till it was beyond bearing, so that we despaired even of life. The only verdict we could give on our condition was the verdict of death; but this happened in order that we should not trust in ourselves but in the God who raises the dead. It was he who rescued us from so terrible a death, and who will rescue us. We hope in him that he will continue to rescue us, while you lend the help of your prayers for us, so that thanks on our behalf will be given from many faces and through many people for the gift of God's grace which came to us.

THE most extraordinary thing about this passage is that we have no information at all about this terrible experience which Paul went through at Ephesus. Something happened to him which was almost beyond bearing. He was in such danger that he believed that sentence of death had been passed on him and that there was no escape, and yet, beyond this passing reference and some others like it in these letters, we have no account of what happened.

There is a very human tendency to make the most of anything that we have to go through. Often a person who has undergone a quite simple operation will make it a subject of conversation for a long time to come. H. L. Gee tells of two men who met to transact some business in days of war. The one was full of how the train in which he had travelled had been attacked from the air. He would not stop talking about the excitement, the danger, the narrow escape. The other in the end said quietly, "Well, let's get on with our business now. I'd like to get away fairly early because my house was demolished by a bomb last night."

People who have really suffered usually do not talk about it very much. King George the Fifth had as one of his rules of life, "If I have to suffer let me be like a well-bred animal and go and suffer in silence and alone." Paul made no parade of his sufferings, and we who have so much less to suffer should follow his example.

But Paul saw that the terrifying experience he had gone through had had one tremendous use—*it had driven him back to God* and demonstrated to him his utter dependence on him.

The Arabs have a proverb, "All sunshine makes a desert." The danger of prosperity is that it encourages a false independence; it makes us think that we are well able to handle life alone. For every one prayer that rises to God in days of prosperity, ten thousand rise in days of adversity. As Lincoln had it, "I have often been driven to my knees in prayer because I had nowhere else to go." It is often in misfortune that a man finds out who are his true friends, and it often needs some time of adversity to show us how much we need God.

The outcome was that Paul had an unshakable confidence in God. He knew now beyond all argument what he could do for him. If God could bring him through that, he could bring him through anything. The joyful cry of the Psalmist is, "Thou hast delivered my soul from death, my eyes from tears, my feet from stumbling." (*Psalm* 116: 8.) What really converted John Bunyan was when he heard some old women sitting in the sun "talking about what God had done for their souls." The confidence of the Christian in God is not a thing of theory and speculation; it is a thing of fact and experience. He knows what God has done for him and therefore he is not afraid.

Finally, Paul asks for the prayers of the Corinthians. As we have noted before, the greatest of the saints is not ashamed to ask for the prayers of the least of the brethren. We may have very little to give our friends; but, however little of this world's goods we possess, we may give them the priceless treasure of our prayers.

OUR ONLY BOAST

2 Corinthians 1: 12–14

> The only boast we make is this—and it is backed by the witness of our conscience—that in the world we have behaved ourselves with the holiness and the purity of God, not with a wisdom dominated by human motives, but with the grace of God, and especially so

towards you. We have written no other things to you than those which you read and understand, and I hope that you will go on to understand even their deepest meanings and significances, just as you have already understood them at least in part, because we are your boast, as you are ours, in the day of Christ.

HERE we begin to catch the undertones of the accusations that the Corinthians were levelling against Paul and of the slanders with which they were trying to besmirch him.

(i) They must have been saying that there was more in Paul's conduct than met the eye. His answer is that he has lived with the holiness and the purity of God. *There were no hidden actions in Paul's life*. We might well add a new beatitude to the list, "Blessed is the man who has nothing to hide." It is an old jest to tell of how a man went from door to door saying, "Flee! All is discovered!" and how the most unlikely people fled. It is said that once an architect offered to build a Greek philosopher a house so constructed that it would be impossible to see into it. "I will give you double your fee," said the philosopher, "if you will build me a house into every room of which everyone can see." The word Paul uses for *purity* (*eilikrineia*) is most interesting. It may describe something which can bear the test of being held up to the light of the sun and looked at with the sun shining through it. Happy is the man whose every action will bear the light of day and who, like Paul, can claim that there are no hidden actions in his life.

(ii) There were those who were attributing hidden motives to Paul. His answer is that his whole conduct is dominated, not by calculating shrewdness, but by the grace of God. *There were no hidden motives in Paul's life*. Burns in another connection points out the difficulty of discovering "the moving why they did it." If we are honest, we will have to admit that we seldom do anything with absolutely unmixed motives. Even when we do something fine, there may be entangled with it motives of prudence, of prestige, of self-display, of fear, of calculation. Men may never see these motives, but, as Thomas Aquinas said, "Man regardeth the deed but God seeth the intention." Purity of action may be difficult, but purity of motive is still more difficult. Such purity can come to us only when we too can say that our old self has died and Christ lives in us.

(iii) There were those who said that Paul in his letters did not quite mean what he said. His answer was that *there were no hidden meanings in his words*. Words are odd things. A man may use them to reveal his thoughts or equally to conceal them. Few of us can honestly say that we mean to the full every word we say. We may say a thing because it is the right thing to say; we may say it for the sake of being agreeable; we may say it for the sake of avoiding trouble. James, who saw the dangers of the tongue more clearly than any man, said, "If any one makes no mistakes in what he says he is a perfect man." (*James* 3: 2.)

In Paul's life there were no hidden actions, no hidden motives and no hidden meanings. That is indeed something to aim at.

GOD'S YES IN JESUS CHRIST

2 Corinthians 1: 15–22

> It was with this confidence that I previously planned to visit you, that I might bring you pleasure for the second time, and so go on to Macedonia by way of you, and be sped by you on my way to Judaea. So then, when I made this plan, surely you cannot think that I did so with a fickle intention? Or can you really think that when I make plans I make them as a worldly man might make them, so that I say yes and no at one and the same time? You can rely on God. You can be quite sure that the message we brought to you does not vacillate between yes and no. For God's Son, Jesus Christ, he who was proclaimed among you through myself and Silvanus and Timothy, was not one who vacillated between yes and no. It was always yes with him. He is the yes to all the promises of God. That is why we can say, "Amen," through him when we speak it to the glory of God. But it is God who

guarantees you with us for Christ, the God who has anointed us
and sealed us, and who has given us the Holy Spirit in our hearts
as the first instalment and pledge of the life that shall be.

AT first sight this is a difficult passage. Behind it lies another
accusation and slander against Paul. Paul had said that he
would visit the Corinthians, but the situation had become so
bitter that he postponed his visit so as not to give them pain
(verse 23). His enemies had promptly accused him of being the
kind of man who made frivolous promises with a fickle
intention and could not be pinned down to a definite yes or no.
That was bad enough, but they went on to argue, "If we
cannot trust Paul's everyday promises, how can we trust the
things he told us about God?" Paul's answer is that we can
rely on God and that there is no vacillation in Jesus between
yes and no.

Then he puts the matter in a vivid phrase—"Jesus is the yes
to every promise of God." He means this—had Jesus never
come we might have doubted the tremendous promises of
God, might have argued that they were too good to be true.
But a God who loves us so much that he gave us his Son is
quite certain to fulfil every promise that he ever made.
He is the personal guarantee of God that the greatest and
the least of his promises are all true.

Although the Corinthians were slandering Paul, there
remains this salutary truth—the trustworthiness of the
messenger affects the trustworthiness of the message. Preaching is always "truth through personality." And if a man
cannot trust the preacher, he is not likely to trust the preacher's
message. Amongst the Jewish regulations regarding the
conduct and character of a teacher, it is laid down that he
must never promise anything to a class which he cannot or will
not do. This would be to accustom the class to falsehood.
Here is a warning that promises should never be lightly given,
for they may well be as lightly broken. Before a man gives
a promise, he should count the cost of keeping it and make
sure that he is able and willing to pay it.

Paul goes on to say two great things.

(i) It is through Jesus that we say "Amen" to the promises of God. We finish our prayers by saying, "through Jesus Christ our Lord. Amen." When we have read scripture we frequently conclude it by saying, "Amen." *Amen* means *So let it be*, and the great truth is that it is not just a formality and a bit of ritual; it is the word that expresses our confidence that we can offer our prayers with every confidence to God and can appropriate with confidence all his great promises, because Jesus is the guarantee that our prayers will be heard and that all the great promises are true.

(ii) Finally, Paul speaks about what the Authorised Version calls the *earnest* of the Spirit. The Greek word is *arrabon*. And an *arrabon* was the first instalment of a payment, paid as a guarantee that the rest was sure to follow. It is a common word in Greek legal documents. A woman selling a cow receives 1,000 drachmae as *arrabon* that the rest of the purchase price will be paid. Some dancing girls being engaged for a village festival receive so much as *arrabon,* which will be included in the final payment, but which is a present guarantee that the contract will be honoured and the full money paid. A certain man writes to his master that he has paid Lampon, the mouse-catcher, an *arrabon* of 8 drachmae so that he will start work and catch the mice while they are still with young. It was the first instalment and the guarantee that the rest would be paid. Everyone knew this word. It is the same idea as is in the Scots word *arles* which was a token payment made when a man was employed or a house bought, and a guarantee that the full contract would be honoured. When Paul speaks of the Holy Spirit as an *arrabon* given us by God, he means that the kind of life we live by the help of the Holy Spirit is the first instalment of the life of heaven and the guarantee that the fullness of that life will some day open upon us. The gift of the Holy Spirit is God's token and pledge of still greater things to come.

WHEN A SAINT REBUKES

2 Corinthians 1 : 23—2 : 4

> I call God to witness against my soul that it was because I
> wished to spare you that I did not come again to Corinth. I am
> not saying this because we have any desire to domineer over your
> faith, but because we desire to labour with you to produce joy.
> As far as faith is concerned, you stand firm. But for my own
> peace of mind I came to this decision—not to come to you again
> in grief. For, if I grieve you, who then is there to make me
> glad, except him who is grieved by what I have done? I write
> this very letter so that when I do come I may not incur grief at the
> hands of those from whom I ought to have joy, for I have never
> lost my confidence in every one of you, and I am still sure that
> my joy and the joy of all of you are one and the same thing. So
> I wrote you a letter out of much affliction and anguish of heart,
> it was through my tears I wrote it, not that I wanted you to be
> grieved, but that I wanted you to know the love I bear
> especially to you.

HERE is the echo of unhappy things. As we have seen in the
introduction, the sequence of events must have been this. The
situation in Corinth had gone from bad to worse. The Church
was torn with party divisions and there were those who
denied the authority of Paul. Seeking to mend matters, Paul
had paid a flying visit to Corinth. So far from mending
things, that visit had exacerbated them and had nearly broken
his heart. In consequence he had written a very severe
letter of rebuke, written with a sore heart and through tears.
It was just for that very reason that he had not fulfilled his
promise to visit them again, for, as things were, the visit could
only have hurt him and them.

Behind this passage lies the whole heart of Paul when he
had to deal in severity with those he loved.

(i) He used severity and rebuke very unwillingly. He used
them only when he was driven to use them and there was
nothing else left to do. There are some people whose eyes are
always focussed to find fault, whose tongues are always tuned

to criticize, in whose voice there is always a rasp and an edge. Paul was not like that. In this he was wise. If we are constantly critical and fault-finding, if we are habitually angry and harsh, if we rebuke far more than we praise, the plain fact is that even our severity loses its effect. It is discounted because it is so constant. The more seldom a man rebukes, the more effective it is when he does. In any event, the eyes of a truly Christian man seek ever for things to praise and not for things to condemn.

(ii) When Paul did rebuke, he did it in love. He never spoke merely to hurt. There can be sadistic pleasure in seeing someone wince at a sharp and cruel word. But Paul was not like that. He never rebuked to cause pain; he always rebuked to restore joy. When John Knox was on his deathbed he said, "God knows that my mind was always void of hatred to the persons of those against whom I thundered my severest judgments." It is possible to hate the sin but love the sinner. The effective rebuke is that given with the arm of love round the other person. The rebuke of blazing anger may hurt and even terrify; but the rebuke of hurt and sorrowing love alone can break the heart.

(iii) When Paul rebuked, the last thing he wanted was to domineer. In a modern novel, a father says to his son, "I'll beat the fear of the loving God into you." The great danger which the preacher and the teacher ever incur is of coming to think that our duty is to compel others to think exactly as we do and to insist that if they do not see things as we see them, they must be wrong. The duty of the teacher is not to impose beliefs on other people, but to enable and to encourage them to think out their own beliefs. The aim is not to produce a pale copy of oneself, but to create an independent human being. One who was taught by that great teacher, A. B. Bruce, said, "He cut the cables and gave us a glimpse of the blue waters." Paul knew that as a teacher he must never domineer, although he must discipline and guide.

(iv) Finally, for all his reluctance to rebuke, for all his desire to see the best in others, for all the love that was in his heart, Paul nonetheless does rebuke when rebuke becomes necessary. When John Knox rebuked Queen Mary for her proposed marriage to Don Carlos, at first she tried anger and outraged majesty and then she tried "tears in abundance." Knox's answer was, "I never delighted in the weeping of any of God's creatures. I can scarcely well abide the tears of my own boys, whom my own hand correcteth, much less can I rejoice in Your Majesty's weeping. But I must sustain, albeit unwillingly, Your Majesty's tears rather than I dare hurt my conscience, or betray my commonwealth through my silence." Not seldom we refrain from rebuke because of mistaken kindness, or because of the desire to avoid trouble. But there is a time when to avoid trouble is to store up trouble and when to seek for a lazy or cowardly peace is to court a still greater danger. If we are guided by love and by consideration, not for our own pride but for the ultimate good of others, we will know the time to speak and the time to be silent.

PLEADING FOR A SINNER'S PARDON

2 Corinthians 2: 5–11

> If anyone has caused grief, it is not I whom he has grieved, but to some extent—not to overstress the situation—all of you. To such a man the punishment that has been imposed by the majority is sufficient, so that, so far from inflicting severer punishment, you must forgive him and comfort him, lest such a one be engulfed by excess of grief. So then, I urge you, let your decision in regard to him be a decision of love. For when I wrote to you my purpose was to test you, to see if you are obedient in all things. Whatever you have forgiven anyone, I too forgive. For what I have forgiven, if I had anything to forgive, I forgave for your sakes, in the presence of Christ, so that we might not be over-reached by Satan, for we well know his intentions.

AGAIN we have a passage which is an echo of trouble and of unhappiness. When Paul had visited Corinth there had been a ring-leader to the opposition. This man had clearly personally insulted Paul who had insisted that discipline must be exercised upon him. The majority of the Corinthians had come to see that his conduct had not only hurt Paul, but had injured the good name of the whole Corinthian Church. Discipline had been exercised, but there were some who felt that it had not been sufficiently severe and who desired to impose a still greater punishment.

It is now that the supreme greatness of Paul emerges. His plea is that enough has been done; the man is now penitent and to exercise still further discipline would do far more harm than good. It might simply drive the man to despair, and to do that is not to serve Christ and the Church, but to offer an opportunity to Satan to lay hold upon the man. Had Paul been actuated by merely human motives he would have gloated over the hard fate of his former enemy. Nowhere does the majesty of his character better emerge than on this occasion, when, in the graciousness of his heart, he pleads for mercy on the man who had hurt him so much. Here is a supreme example of Christian conduct in face of injury and insult.

(i) Paul did not take the matter personally at all. It was not the injury done to his personal feelings which was important. What he was anxious about was the good discipline and the peace of the Church. There are some people who take everything personally. Criticism, even when it is kindly meant and kindly given, they take as a personal insult. Such people do more than any other kind of people to disturb the peace of a fellowship. It would be well to remember that criticism and advice are usually offered, not to hurt us, but to help us.

(ii) Paul's motive in the exercise of discipline was not vengeance but correction; he did not aim to knock a man down, but to help him to get up. His aim was to judge a man, not by the standards of abstract justice, but of Christian love. The fact is that quite often sins are good qualities gone wrong. The man who can plan a successful burglary has initiative and organizing power; pride is a kind of intensification of the independent spirit; meanness is thrift run to seed. Paul's aim in discipline was, not to eradicate such qualities as a man might have, but rather to harness them to higher purposes. The Christian duty is not to render the sinner harmless by battering him into submission, but to inspire him to goodness.

(iii) Paul's insistence was that punishment must never drive to despair and must never take the heart out of a man. The wrong kind of treatment often gives a man the last push into the arms of Satan. Over-severity may well drive him from the Church and its fellowship, while sympathetic amendment might well bring him in. Mary Lamb, who had terrible periods of insanity, was harshly treated by her mother. She used to sigh, "Why is it that I never seem able to do anything to please my mother?" Luther could scarcely bear to pray the Lord's Prayer because his own father had been so stern that the word father painted a picture of grim terror to him. He used to say, "Spare the rod and spoil the child—yes; but, beside the rod keep an apple, to give the child when he has done well." Punishment should encourage and not discourage. In the last analysis, this can happen only when we make it clear that, even when we are punishing a person, we still believe in him.

IN THE TRIUMPH OF CHRIST

2 Corinthians 2: 12–17

When we had come to Troas to tell the good news of Christ, even when a door of opportunity stood open to us in the Lord, I had no rest for my spirit, because I did not find Titus, my brother, there. But thanks be to God who at all times leads us in the train of his triumph in Christ, and who, through us, displays the perfume of the knowledge of him in every place; for we are the sweet scent of Christ in God to those who are destined for salvation and to those who are destined for destruction. To the one we are a perfume from death, to the other a perfume from life to life. And who is adequate for these tasks? We do not, as so many do, make a traffic of the

word of God but, as from utter purity of motives, as from God,
in the very presence of God in Christ we speak.

PAUL begins by telling how his anxiety to know what was
happening in Corinth made him so restless that he could not
wait in Troas, although a fruitful field was there, and sent
him off to meet Titus who had not yet arrived. Then
comes his shout of triumph to God who brought all things to
a happy ending.

Verses 14 to 16 are difficult to understand by themselves,
but when set against the background which was in Paul's
thoughts they become a vivid picture. Paul speaks of being led
in the train of the triumph of Christ; and then he goes on to
speak of being the sweet scent of Christ to men, to some
the perfume of death and to others the perfume of life.

In his mind is the picture of a Roman *Triumph* and of
Christ as a universal conqueror. The highest honour which
could be given to a victorious Roman general was a Triumph.
To attain it he must satisfy certain conditions. He must have
been the actual commander-in-chief in the field. The campaign
must have been completely finished, the region pacified and the
victorious troops brought home. Five thousand of the enemy
at least must have fallen in one engagement. A positive
extension of territory must have been gained, and not merely
a disaster retrieved or an attack repelled. And the victory must
have been won over a foreign foe and not in a civil war.

In a Triumph the procession of the victorious general
marched through the streets of Rome to the Capitol in the
following order. First came the state officials and the senate.
Then came the trumpeters. Then were carried the spoils taken
from the conquered land. For instance, when Titus conquered
Jerusalem, the seven-branched candlestick, the golden table
of the shew-bread and the golden trumpets were carried
through the streets of Rome. Then came pictures of the
conquered land and models of conquered citadels and ships.
There followed the white bull for the sacrifice which would
be made. Then there walked the captive princes, leaders and
generals in chains, shortly to be flung into prison and in all

probability almost immediately to be executed. Then came the lictors bearing their rods, followed by the musicians with their lyres; then the priests swinging their censers with the sweet-smelling incense burning in them. After that came the general himself. He stood in a chariot drawn by four horses. He was clad in a purple tunic embroidered with golden palm leaves, and over it a purple toga marked out with golden stars. In his hand he held an ivory sceptre with the Roman eagle at its top, and over his head a slave held the crown of Jupiter. After him rode his family; and finally came the army wearing all their decorations and shouting *Io triumphe!* their cry of triumph. As the procession moved through the streets, all decorated and garlanded, amid the cheering crowds, it made a tremendous day which might happen only once in a lifetime.

That is the picture that is in Paul's mind. He sees Christ marching in triumph throughout the world, and himself in that conquering train. It is a triumph which, Paul is certain, nothing can stop.

We have seen how in that procession there were the priests swinging the incence-filled censers. To the victors the perfume from the censers would be the perfume of joy and triumph and life; but to the wretched captives who walked so short a distance ahead it was the perfume of death, standing for the past defeat and their coming execution. So Paul thinks of himself and his fellow apostles preaching the gospel of the triumphant Christ. To those who will accept it, it is the perfume of life, as it was to the victors; to those who refuse it, it is the perfume of death, as it was to the vanquished.

Of one thing Paul was certain—not all the world could defeat Christ. He lived not in pessimistic fear, but in the glorious optimism which knew the unconquerable majesty of Christ.

Then once more comes the unhappy echo. There were those who said that he was not fit to preach Christ. There were those who said worse, that he was using the gospel as an excuse to line his own pockets. Again Paul uses the word *eilikrineia* for *purity*. His motives will stand the penetrating rays of the sun; his message is from God, it will stand the very scrutiny of Christ himself. Paul never feared what men might say, because his conscience told him that he had the approval of God and the "Well done!" of Christ.

EACH MAN A LETTER OF CHRIST

2 Corinthians 3: 1–3

> Are we beginning to commend ourselves again? Surely you do not think that we need—as some people need—letters of commendation either to you or from you? You are our letter, written on our hearts, known and read by all men. It is plain to see that you are a letter written by Christ, produced under our ministry, written not with ink, but with the Spirit of the living God, not on tablets of stone, but on tablets which are living, beating, human hearts.

BEHIND this passage lies the thought of a custom which was common in the ancient world, that of sending letters of commendation with a person. If someone was going to a strange community, a friend of his who knew someone in that community would give him a letter of commendation to introduce him and to testify to his character.

Here is such a letter, found among the papyri, written by a certain Aurelius Archelaus, who was a *beneficiarius,* that is a soldier privileged to have special exemption from all menial duties, to his commanding officer, a military tribune called Julius Domitius. It is to introduce and commend a certain Theon. "To Julius Domitius, military tribune of the legion, from Aurelius Archelaus, his *beneficiarius,* greeting. I have already before this recommended to you Theon, my friend, and now also, I ask you, sir, to have him before your eyes as you would myself. For he is a man such as to deserve to be loved by you, for he left his own people, his goods and his business and followed me, and through all things he has kept me safe. I therefore pray you that he may

have the right to come and see you. He can tell you everything about our business . . . I have loved the man . . . I wish
you, sir, great happiness and long life with your family and
good health. Have this letter before your eyes and let it make
you think that I am speaking to you. Farewell."

That was the kind of commendatory letter, or reference, of
which Paul was thinking. There is one such in the New
Testament. *Romans* 16 is a letter of commendation written to
introduce Phoebe, a member of the Church at Cenchrea, to
the Church at Rome.

In the ancient world, as nowadays, sometimes written
testimonials did not mean very much. A man once asked
Diogenes, the Cynic philosopher, for such a letter. Diogenes
answered, "That you are a man he will know at a glance;
but whether you are a good or a bad man he will discover
if he has the skill to distinguish between good and bad, and
if he is without that skill he will not discover the facts even
though I write to him thousands of times." Yet in the
Christian Church such letters were necessary, for even Lucian,
the pagan satirist, noted that any charlatan could make a
fortune out of the simple-minded Christians, because they
were so easily imposed upon.

The previous sentences of Paul's letter seemed to read as
if he was giving himself a testimonial. He declares that he
has no need of such commendation. Then he takes a side-
glance at those who have been causing trouble in Corinth.
"There may be some," he says, "who brought you letters of
commendation or who got them from you." In all probability
these were emissaries of the Jews who had come to undo
Paul's work and who had brought introductory letters from
the Sanhedrin to accredit them. Once Paul had had such
letters himself, when he set out to Damascus to obliterate the
Church. (*Acts* 9: 2). He says that his only testimonial is the
Corinthians themselves. The change in their character and life
is the only commendation that he needs.

He goes on to make a great claim. Every one of them is a
letter of Christ. Long ago Plato had said that the good teacher

does not write his message in ink that will fade; he writes it upon men. That is what Jesus had done. He had written his message on the Corinthians, through his servant, Paul, not with fading ink but with the Spirit, not on tablets of stone as the law was first written, but on the hearts of men.

There is a great truth here, which is at once an inspiration and an awful warning—every man is an open letter for Jesus Christ. Every Christian, whether he likes it or not, is an advertisement for Christianity. The honour of Christ is in the hands of his followers. We judge a shopkeeper by the kind of goods he sells; we judge a craftsman by the kind of articles he produces; we judge a Church by the kind of men it creates; and therefore men judge Christ by his followers. Dick Sheppard, after years of talking in the open air to people who were outside the Church, declared that he had discovered that "the greatest handicap the Church has is the unsatisfactory lives of professing Christians." When we go out into the world, we have the awe-inspiring responsibility of being open letters, advertisements, for Christ and his Church.

THE SURPASSING GLORY

2 *Corinthians* 3: 4-11

We can believe this with such confidence because we believe it through Christ and in the sight of God. It is not that in our own resources we are adequate to reckon up the effect of anything that we have done, as it were personally, but our adequacy comes from God, who has made us adequate to be ministers of the new relationship which has come into existence between him and men. This new relationship does not depend on a written document, but on the Spirit. The written document is a deadly thing; the Spirit is a life-giving power. If the ministry which could only produce death, the ministry which depends on written documents, the ministry which was engraved on stone, came into being with such glory that the children of Israel could not bear to look for any time at the face of Moses, because of the glory which shone upon his face—and it was a glory that was doomed to fade—surely even more will the ministry of the Spirit be clad in glory. For if the

ministry which could not produce anything else but condemnation
was a glory, the ministry which produces the right relationship
between God and man excels still more in glory. For, indeed,
that which was clad with glory no longer enjoys glory because of
this—because of the glory that surpasses it. If that which was
doomed to pass away emerged in glory, much more that which is
destined to remain exists in glory.

THIS passage really falls into two parts. At the beginning of it
Paul is feeling that perhaps his claim that the Corinthians are
a living epistle of Christ, produced under his ministry, may
sound a little like self-praise. So he hastens to insist that
whatever he has done is not his own work but the work of
God. It is God who has made him adequate for the task
which was his. It may be that he is thinking of a fanciful
meaning that the Jews sometimes gave to one of the great
titles of God. God was called *El Shaddai,* which is *The
Almighty,* but sometimes the Jews explained *El Shaddai* to
mean *The Sufficient One.* It is he who is all-sufficient who
has made Paul sufficient for his task.

When Harriet Beecher Stowe produced *Uncle Tom's Cabin,*
300,000 copies were sold in America in one year. It was
translated into a score of languages. Lord Palmerston, who
had not read a novel for thirty years, praised it "not only
for the story, but for the statesmanship." Lord Cockburn, a
Privy Counsellor, declared that it had done more for humanity
than any other book of fiction. Tolstoi ranked it among the
great achievements of the human mind. It certainly did more
than any other single thing to advance the freedom of the
slaves. Harriet Beecher Stowe refused to take any credit for
what she had written. She said, "I, the author of *Uncle Tom's
Cabin?* No, indeed, I could not control the story; it wrote
itself. The Lord wrote it, and I was but the humblest
instrument in his hand. It all came to me in visions, one
after another, and I put them down in words. To him alone
be the praise!"

Her adequacy was of God. It was so with Paul. He never
said, "See what I have done!" He always said, "To God be

the glory!'' He never conceived of himself as adequate for any task; he thought of God as making him adequate. And that is precisely why, conscious as he was of his own weakness, he feared to set his hand to no task. He never had to do it alone; he did it with God.

The second part of the passage deals with the contrast between the old and the new covenant. A covenant means an arrangement made between two people through which they enter into a certain relationship. It is not, in the biblical usage, an ordinary agreement, because the contracting parties enter into an ordinary agreement on equal terms. But in the biblical sense of covenant, it is God who is the prime mover and approaches man to offer him a relationship upon conditions which man could neither initiate nor alter but only accept or reject.

The word Paul uses for *new* when he speaks of the new covenant is the same as Jesus used and it is very significant. In Greek there are two words for new. First, there is *neos,* which means *new in point of time and that alone.* A young person is *neos* because he is a newcomer into the world. Second, there is *kainos,* which means not only new in point of time, but also *new in quality.* If something is *kainos* it has brought a fresh element into the situation. It is the word *kainos* that both Jesus and Paul use of the *new* covenant, and the significance is that the new covenant is not only new in point of time; it is quite different in kind from the old covenant. It produces between man and God a relationship of a totally different kind.

Wherein does this difference lie?

(i) The old covenant was based on a written document. We can see the story of its initiation in *Exodus* 24: 1–8. Moses took the book of the covenant and read it to the people and they agreed to it. On the other hand the new covenant is based on the power of the life-giving Spirit. A written document is always something that is external; whereas the work of the Spirit changes a man's very heart. A man may obey the written code while all the time he wishes to disobey it; but when the Spirit comes into his heart and controls it, not only does he not break the code, he does not even wish to break it, because he is a changed man. A written code can change the law; only the Spirit can change human nature.

(ii) The old covenant was a deadly thing, because it produced a legal relationship between God and man. In effect it said, "If you wish to maintain your relationship with God, you must keep these laws." It thereby set up a situation in which God was essentially judge and man was essentially a criminal, forever in default before the bar of God's judgment.

The old covenant was deadly because it killed certain things. (*a*) It killed *hope*. There was never any hope that any man could keep it, human nature being what it is. It therefore could issue in nothing but frustration. (*b*) It killed *life*. Under it a man could earn nothing but condemnation; and condemnation meant death. (*c*) It killed *strength*. It was perfectly able to tell a man what to do, but it could not help him to do it.

The new covenant was quite different. (*a*) It was a relationship of *love*. It came into being because God so loved the world. (*b*) It was a relationship between *a father and his sons*. Man was no longer the criminal in default, he was the son of God, even if a disobedient son. (*c*) It changed a man's life, not by imposing a new code of laws on him, but *by changing his heart*. (*d*) It therefore not only told a man what to do but gave him the strength to do it. With its commandments *it brought power*.

Paul goes on to contrast the two covenants. The old covenant was born in glory. When Moses came down from the mountain with the Ten Commandments, which are the code of the old covenant, his face shone with such a splendour that no one could look at it (*Exodus* 34: 30). Obviously that was a transient splendour. It did not and it could not last. The new covenant, the new relationship which Jesus Christ makes possible between man and God, has a greater splendour which will never fade because it produces pardon and not condemnation, life and not death.

Here is the warning. The Jews preferred the old covenant, the law; they rejected the new covenant, the new relationship in Christ. Now the old covenant was not a bad thing; but it was only a second-best, a stage upon the way. As a great commentator has put it, "When the sun has risen the lamps cease to be of use." And as has been so truly said, "The second-best is the worst enemy of the best." Men have always tended to cling to the old even when something far better is offered. For long people, on so-called religious grounds, refused to use chloroform. When Wordsworth and the romantic poets emerged, criticism said, "This will never do." When Wagner began to write his music, people would not have it. Churches all over the world cling to the old and refuse the new. Because a thing was always done, it is right, and because a thing was never done, it is wrong. We must be careful not to worship the stages instead of the goal, not to cling to the second-best while the best is waiting, not, as the Jews did, to insist that the old ways are right and refuse the new glories which God is opening to us.

THE VEIL WHICH HIDES THE TRUTH

2 Corinthians 3: 12–18

It is because we possess such a hope that we speak with such freedom. We do not draw a veil over things, as Moses did over his face so that the children of Israel should not gaze at the end of the glory which was doomed to fade away. But their minds were dulled. To this very day the same veil remains, still not drawn aside, when they read the record of the old relationship between God and man, because only in Christ is that veil abolished. Yes, to this day, whenever the books that Moses wrote are read, the veil rests upon their heart. But, whenever a man turns to the Lord, the veil is taken away. The Lord is the Spirit. Where the Spirit of the Lord is, there is liberty. And we all, with no veil upon our faces, see as in a mirror the glory of the Lord, and we go on

changing this image from glory to glory, even as it comes from the
Lord who is the Spirit.

ALL the pictures in this passage emerge directly from the
passage which goes before. Paul begins from the thought that
when Moses came down from the mount the glory upon his
face was so bright that no one could gaze steadily upon it.

(i) He thinks back to *Exodus* 34: 33. The Authorized
Version has it that Moses put a veil upon his face *until* he had
finished speaking; but the correct translation of the Hebrew,
is that Moses, as in the R.S.V., did this *when* he had finished
speaking. Paul takes this to mean that Moses veiled his face
so that the people should not have to see the slow fading of
the glory that once was there. His first thought is that the
glory of the old covenant, the old relationship between God
and men, was essentially a fading one. It was destined to be
overpassed, not as the wrong is overpassed by the right, but
as the incomplete is overpassed by the complete. The revelation
that came by Moses was true and great, but it was only
partial; the revelation that came in Jesus Christ is full and
final. As Augustine so wisely put it long ago, "We do wrong
to the Old Testament if we deny that it comes from the same
just and good God as the New. On the other hand we do
wrong to the New Testament, if we put the Old on a level
with it." The one is a step to glory; the other is the summit
of glory.

(ii) The idea of the veil now takes hold of Paul's mind
and he uses it in different ways. He says that, when the Jews
listen to the reading of the Old Testament, as they do every
Sabbath day in the synagogue, a veil upon their eyes keeps
them from seeing the real meaning of it. It ought to point
them to Jesus Christ, but the veil keeps them from seeing
that. We, too, may fail to see the real meaning of scripture
because our eyes are veiled.

(*a*) They may be veiled by *prejudice*. We, too, often go to
scripture to find support for our own views rather than to
find the truth of God.

(*b*) They may be veiled by *wishful thinking*. Too often we find what we want to find, and neglect what we do not want to see. To take an example, we may delight in all the references to the love and the mercy of God, but pass over all the references to his wrath and judgment.

(*c*) They may be veiled by *fragmentary thinking*. We should always regard the Bible as a whole. It is easy to take individual texts and criticize them. It is easy to prove that parts of the Old Testament are sub-Christian. It is easy to find support for private theories by choosing certain texts and passages and putting others aside. But it is the whole message that we must seek; and that is just another way of saying that we must read all scripture in the light of Jesus Christ.

(iii) Not only is there a veil which keeps the Jews from seeing the real meaning of scripture; there is also a veil which comes between them and God.

(*a*) Sometimes it is the veil of *disobedience*. Very often it is moral and not intellectual blindness which keeps us from seeing God. If we persist in disobeying him we become less and less capable of seeing him. The vision of God is to the pure in heart.

(*b*) Sometimes it is the veil of the *unteachable spirit*. As the Scots saying has it, "There's none so blind as those who winna see." The best teacher on earth cannot teach the man who knows it all already and does not wish to learn. God gave us free will, and, if we insist upon our own way, we cannot learn his.

(iv) Paul goes on to say that we see the glory of the Lord with no veil upon our faces, and because of that we, too, are changed from glory into glory. Possibly what Paul means is that, if we gaze at Christ, we in the end reflect him. His image appears in our lives. It is a law of life that we become like the people we gaze at. People hero-worship someone and begin to reflect his ways. If we contemplate Jesus Christ, in the end we come to reflect him.

Paul sets for many a theological problem when he says, "The Lord is the Spirit." He seems to identify the Risen Lord and the Holy Spirit. We must remember that he was not writing theology; he was setting down experience. And it is the experience of the Christian life that the work of the Spirit and the work of the Risen Lord are one and the same. The strength and guidance we receive come alike from the Spirit and from the Risen Lord.

Where the Spirit is, says Paul, there is liberty. He means that so long as man's obedience to God is conditioned by obedience to a code of laws he is in the position of an unwilling slave. But when it comes from the operation of the Spirit in his heart, the very centre of his being has no other desire than to serve God, for then it is not law but love which binds him. Many things which we would resent doing under compulsion for some stranger are a privilege to do for someone we love. Love clothes the humblest and the most menial tasks with glory. "In God's service we find our perfect freedom."

THE BLINDED EYE

2 Corinthians 4: 1–6

Since therefore this part of God's service has been given to us, even as we have received mercy, we do not lose heart. But we have refused to have anything to do with hidden and shameful methods. We do not act with unscrupulous cleverness. We do not adulterate the word which God gave us to preach. But by making the truth clear, we commend ourselves to the human conscience in all its forms in the sight of God. But if in fact the good news that we preach is veiled to some, it is veiled in the case of those who are doomed to perish. In their case, the god of this world has blinded the minds of those who refuse to believe, in order that upon them there may not dawn the light of the good news which tells of the glory of Christ in whom we can see God. It is not ourselves that we proclaim, but Christ Jesus as Lord, and ourselves your servants for Jesus's sake. This we must do because it is the God who said, "Out of darkness light shall shine," who has shined in our hearts to illumine us with the knowledge of the glory of God in the face of Jesus Christ.

IN this passage Paul has something to say, either directly or by implication, about four different people or sets of people.

(i) Right at the beginning he has something to say about himself. He says that he never loses heart in the great task that has been given to him, and by implication he tells us why. Two things keep him going. (*a*) There is the consciousness of a great task. A man who is conscious of a great task can do amazing things. One of the great works of musical genius is Handel's *Messiah*. It is on record that the whole work was composed and written down in *twenty-two days,* and that during all that time Handel would scarcely consent to eat or to sleep. A great task brings its own strength with it. (*b*) There is the memory of mercy received. It was Paul's aim to spend all his life seeking to do something for the love which had redeemed him.

(ii) Then by implication Paul has something to say about his opponents and his slanderers. Again there is the echo of unhappy things. Behind this we can see that his enemies had levelled three charges against him. They had said that he used underhand methods, that he exercised an unscrupulous cleverness to get his own way, and that he adulterated the message of the gospel. When our motives are misinterpreted, our actions misconstrued and our words twisted out of their real meaning, it is a comfort to remember that this also happened to Paul.

(iii) Paul goes on to speak of those who have refused to accept the gospel. He insists that he has proclaimed the gospel in such a way that any man with any kind of conscience at all is bound to admit its claim and its appeal. Even in spite of that some are deaf to its appeal and blind to its glory. What of them?

Paul says something very difficult about them. He says that the god of this world has blinded their minds so that they cannot believe. All through the Bible the writers are conscious that in this world there is a power of evil. Sometimes that power is called Satan, sometimes the Devil. Three times John makes Jesus speak of *the prince of this world* and of his defeat. (*John* 12: 31, 14: 30, 16: 11). Paul in *Ephesians* 2: 2 speaks of the *prince of the power of the air,* and here he speaks of *the god of this world.* Even in the Lord's Prayer there is a reference to this malign power, for it is most probable that the correct translation of *Matthew* 6: 13 is "Deliver us from *the Evil One.*" At the back of this idea as it emerges in the New Testament there are certain influences.

(*a*) The Persian faith called Zoroastrianism sees the whole universe as a battle-ground between the god of the light and the god of the dark, between Ormuzd and Ahriman. That which settles a man's destiny is the side he chooses in this cosmic conflict. When the Jews were subject to the Persians they came into contact with that idea and it undoubtedly coloured their thinking.

(*b*) Basic to the Jewish faith is the thought of the two ages, the present age and the age to come. By the time of the Christian era, the Jews had come to think of the present age as incurably bad and destined for total destruction when the age to come dawned. It could fitly be said that the present age was under the power of the god of this world and at enmity with the true God.

(*c*) It has to be remembered that this idea of an evil and a hostile power is not so much a theological idea, as a fact of experience. If we regard it in a theological way we are up against serious difficulties. Where did that evil power come from in a universe created by God? What is its ultimate end? But if we regard it as a matter of experience, we all know how real the evil of the world is. Robert Louis Stevenson somewhere says, "You know the Caledonian Railway Station in Edinburgh? One cold, east windy morning I met Satan there."

Everyone knows the kind of experience of which Stevenson speaks. However difficult the idea of a power of evil may be theologically or philosophically, it is one which experience understands only too well. Those who cannot accept the good news of Christ are those who have so given themselves over to the evil of the world that they can no longer hear God's invitation. It is not that God has abandoned them; they by their own conduct have shut themselves off from him.

(iv) Paul has something to say about Jesus. The great thought that he drives home here is that in Jesus Christ we see what God is like. "He who has seen me," said Jesus, "has seen the Father." (*John* 14: 9). When Paul preached he did not say, "Look at me!" He said, "Look at Jesus Christ! and there you will see the glory of God come to earth in a form that a man can understand."

TRIBULATION AND TRIUMPH

2 Corinthians 4: 7–15

> But we have this treasure in earthen vessels, so that the power which surpasses all things may be seen to be of God and not of us. We are sore pressed at every point, but not hemmed in. We are at our wit's end, but never at our hope's end. We are persecuted by men, but never abandoned by God. We are knocked down, but not knocked out. In our bodies we have to run the same risk of death as Jesus Christ did, so that in our body the same life as Jesus lived may be clear for all to see. For all through our lives we are continually handed over to death for Jesus's sake, so that the life also which Jesus gives may be clear for all to see in our mortal flesh. The result is that death operates in us, but life operates in you. Because we have the same spirit of faith as appears in that passage of scripture where it stands written, "I have believed and therefore have I spoken," we, too, believe and therefore speak, for we know that he who raised up the Lord Jesus will raise us up also with Jesus, and will present us with you. Everything that happens to us is for your sake, so that grace may abound more and more, and so swell the thanksgiving which rises from many to the glory of God.

PAUL begins this passage with the thought that it might well be that the privileges which a Christian enjoys might move him to pride. But life is designed to keep a man from pride.

However great his Christian glory he is still a mortal man; still the victim of circumstances; still subject to the chances and the changes of human life; still a mortal body with all that body's weakness and pain. He is like a man with a precious treasure contained in an earthen vessel, which itself is weak and worthless. We talk a great deal about the power of man and about the vast forces which he now controls. But the real characteristic of man is not his power but his weakness. As Pascal said, "A drop of water or a breath of air can kill him."

We have already seen what a proud and glorious thing a triumph was for a Roman general. But there were two things designed to keep the general from pride. First, as he rode in the chariot with the crown held over his head, the populace not only shouted their applause but also, ever and again, they shouted, "Look behind you and remember you will die." Second, at the very end of the procession there came the conquering general's own soldiers, and they did two things as they marched. They sang songs in the general's praise, but they also shouted ribald jests and insults to keep him from too much pride.

Life has surrounded us with infirmity, although Christ has surrounded us with glory, so that we may remember that the infirmity is ours and the glory is God's, and recognize our own utter dependence on him.

Paul goes on to describe this Christian life, in which our infirmity is intermingled with God's glory, in a series of paradoxes.

(i) We are sore pressed at every point but not hemmed in. There are all kinds of pressure on us, but we are never in so tight a corner that there is no way out. It is characteristic of the Christian that, even if his body be confined in some difficult environment or some narrow circumstance, there is always an escape route for his spirit to the spaciousness of God.

Matthew Arnold writes of his meeting with a minister of Christ in the London slums.

> "'Twas August and the fierce sun overhead
> Smote on the squalid slums of Bethnal Green,
> And the pale weaver, through his window seen
> In Spitalfields, look'd thrice dispirited.
>
> I met a preacher there I knew, and said:
> 'Ill and o'erwork'd, how fare you in this scene?'
> 'Bravely,' said he, 'for I of late have been
> Much cheer'd with thoughts of Christ, the living bread'."

His body might be hemmed in in a slum but his soul reached out into the spaciousness of communion with Christ.

(ii) We are persecuted by men but never abandoned by God. One of the most notable things about the martyrs is that it was amidst their sorest times that they had their sweetest times with Christ. As Joan of Arc said when she was abandoned by those who should have stood by her, "It is better to be alone with God. His friendship will not fail me, nor his counsel, nor his love. In his strength, I will dare and dare and dare until I die." As the psalmist wrote, "When my father and my mother forsake me, then the Lord will take me up." (*Psalm* 27: 10). Nothing can alter the loyalty of God.

(iii) We are at our wit's end but never at our hope's end. There are times when the Christian does not know what is to be done, but even then he never doubts that something *can* be done. There are times when he cannot well see where life is going, but he never doubts that it is going somewhere. If he must "stoop into a dark, tremendous sea of cloud", he still knows that he will emerge. There are times when a Christian has to learn the hardest lesson of all, the very lesson which Jesus himself had to learn in Gethsemane—how to accept what he cannot understand and still to say, "God, Thou art love; I build my faith on that."

Francis Thompson wrote of the presence of Christ on the darkest days:

> "But (when so sad thou canst not sadder)
> Cry—and upon thy so sore loss
> Shall shine the traffic of Jacob's ladder
> Pitched betwixt heaven and Charing Cross.

> Yea, in the night, my soul, my daughter,
> Cry—clinging heaven by the hems;
> And lo, Christ walking on the water
> Not of Gennesaret but Thames."

A man may be at his wit's end but he can never be at his hope's end while he has the presence of Christ.

(iv) We are knocked down but not knocked out. The supreme characteristic of the Christian is not that he does not fall, but that every time he falls he rises again. It is not that he is never beaten, but he is never ultimately defeated. He may lose a battle, but he knows that in the end he can never lose the campaign. Browning in his *Epilogue* describes the gallant character:

> "One who never turned his back but marched breast forward,
> Never doubted clouds would break,
> Never dreamed, though right were worsted, wrong would
>   triumph,
> Held we fall to rise, are baffled to fight better,
> Sleep to wake."

After he has stated the great paradoxes of the Christian life Paul goes on to give the secret of his own life, the reasons why he was able to do and to endure as he did.

(i) He was well aware that if a man would share the life of Christ he must share his risks, that if a man wished to live with Christ he must be ready to die with him. Paul knew and accepted the inexorable law of the Christian life—"No Cross, No Crown."

(ii) He faced everything in the memory of the power of God who raised Jesus Christ from the dead. He was able to speak with such courage and such disregard of personal safety because he believed that even if death took him, that God could and would also raise him up. He was certain that he could draw on a power which was sufficient for life and greater than death.

(iii) He bore everything in the conviction that through his sufferings and trials others were being led into the light and love of God. The great Boulder Dam scheme in America brought fertility to vast areas which had once been desert. In the making of it there were inevitably those who lost their lives. When the scheme was completed, a tablet was let into the wall of the dam bearing the names of the workmen who had died, and below stands the inscription: "These died that the desert might rejoice and blossom as the rose." Paul could go through what he did because he knew that it was not for nothing; he knew that it was to bring others to Christ. When a man has the conviction that what is happening to him is happening literally for Christ's sake he can face anything.

THE SECRET OF ENDURANCE

2 Corinthians 4: 16–18

> That is the reason why we do not grow weary. But if indeed our outward frame is wasting away, our inward self is renewed day by day, for the light affliction which at the moment we must endure produces for us in a way that cannot be exaggerated an eternal weight of glory, so long as we do not think of the things which are seen, but of the things which are unseen, for the things which are seen are passing, but the things which are unseen are eternal.

Here Paul sets out the secret of endurance.

(i) All through life it must happen that a man's bodily strength fades away, but all through life it ought to happen that a man's soul keeps growing. The sufferings which leave a man with a weakened body may be the very things which strengthen the sinews of his soul. It was the prayer of the poet, "Let me grow lovely growing old." From the physical point of view life may be a slow but inevitable slipping down the slope that leads to death. But from the spiritual point of view life is a climbing up the hill that leads to the presence of God. No man need fear the years, for they bring him nearer, not to death, but to God.

(ii) Paul was convinced that anything he had to suffer in this world would be as nothing compared with the glory he would enjoy in the next. He was certain that God would never be in any man's debt. Alistair Maclean, minister father of the author of H.M.S. Ulysses and the rest, tells of an old Highland woman who had to leave the clean air and the blue waters and the purple hills and live in the slum of a great city. She still lived close to God, and one day she said, "God will make it up to me, and I will see the flowers again."

In *Christmas Eve* Browning writes of the martyr whose story was set out "on the rude tablet overhead."

> "I was born sickly, poor and mean,
> A slave; no misery could screen
> The holders of the pearl of price
> From Caesar's envy; therefore twice
> I fought with beasts and three times saw
> My children suffer by his law;
> At last my own release was earned;
> I was some time in being burned,
> But at the close a Hand came through
> The fire above my head, and drew
> My soul to Christ, whom now I see.
> Sergius, a brother, writes for me
> This testimony on the wall—
> For me, I have forgot it all."

Earth's suffering was forgotten in the glory of heaven.

It is a notable fact that in all the gospel story Jesus never foretold his death without foretelling his Resurrection. He who suffers for Christ will share his glory. God's own honour is pledged to that.

(iii) For that very reason, a man's eyes must be ever fixed, not on the things that are seen, but on the things that are unseen. The things that are seen, the things of this world, have their day and cease to be; the things that are unseen, the things of heaven, last forever.

There are two ways of looking at life. We can look at it as a slow but inexorable journey away from God. Wordsworth in his *Ode on the Intimations of Immortality* had the idea that when a child came into this world he had some memory of heaven which the years slowly took away from him.

"Trailing clouds of glory do we come,"

but,

"Shades of the prison house begin to close
About the growing boy."

And in the end the man is earthbound and heaven is forgotten. Thomas Hood wrote with wistful pathos:

"I remember, I remember
The fir-trees dark and high.
I used to think their slender spires
Were close against the sky.
It was a childish ignorance
But now 'tis little joy
To know, I'm farther off from heaven
Than when I was a boy."

If we think only of the things that are visible we are bound to see life that way. But there is another way. The writer to the Hebrews said of Moses: "He endured as seeing him who is invisible." (*Hebrews* 11 : 27). Robert Louis Stevenson tells of an old byreman. Someone was sympathizing with him about his daily work amidst the muck of the byre and asking him how he could go on doing it day in and day out, and the old man answered, "He that has something ayont (beyond) need never weary."

JOY AND JUDGMENT TO COME

2 Corinthians 5 : 1–10

For we know that if this earthly house of ours, that tent which is the body is pulled down, we have a building which comes from God, a house not made with hands, eternal and in the heavens. For indeed so long as we are as we are we earnestly long to put on our abode which is from heaven, and if indeed we have put it on we shall not be found naked. For, while we are in this tent of the body, we groan, for life weighs us down, for it is not so much that we desire to be stripped of this house, but rather that we desire to put on our heavenly body over it, so that that which is subject to death may be swallowed up by life. He who has designed us for this very thing is God, who has given us the Spirit as a first instalment of the life to come. So then we are always in good heart, although we know that, while we sojourn here in the body, we are absent from the Lord—for it is by faith we walk and not by sight—but we are in good heart and we are willing rather to depart from the body and to stay with the Lord. So then it is our one ambition, whether we are present with him or absent from him, to be the kind of people in which he can find pleasure. For we must all appear before the judgment seat of Christ, so that each one of us may receive the consequences of the thing we did while we were in the body, consequences which will correspond to what each one of us has done, be it good or bad.

THERE is a very significant progression of thought in this passage, a progression which gives us the very essence of the thought of Paul.

(i) To him it will be a day of joy when he is done with this human body. He regards it as merely a tent, a temporary dwelling place, in which we sojourn till the day comes when it is dissolved and we enter into the real abode of our souls.

We have had occasion before to see how Greek and Roman thinkers despised the body. "The body," they said, "is a tomb." Plotinus could say that he was ashamed that he had a body. Epictetus said of himself, "Thou art a poor soul burdened with a corpse." Seneca wrote, "I am a higher being and born for higher things than to be the slave of my body which I look upon as only a shackle put upon my freedom. . . . In so detestable a habitation dwells the free soul." Even Jewish thought sometimes had this idea. "For the corruptible body presses down upon the soul and the earthly tabernacle weighs down the mind that muses on many things." (*Wisdom* 9: 15).

With Paul there is a difference. He is not looking for a Nirvana with the peace of extinction; he is not looking for absorption in the divine; he is not looking for the freedom of a disembodied spirit; he is waiting for the day when God will give him a new body, a spiritual body, in which he will still be able, even in the heavenly places, to serve and to adore God.

Kipling once wrote a poem in which he thought of all the great things that a man would be able to do in the world to come:

> "When earth's last picture is painted
>   And the tubes are twisted and dried,
> When the oldest colours have faded,
>   And the youngest critic has died,
> We shall rest, and, faith, we shall need it—
>   Lie down for an aeon or two,
> Till the Master of All Good Workmen
>   Shall put us to work anew.
>
> And those that were good shall be happy,
>   They shall sit in a golden chair
> They shall splash at a ten-league canvas
>   With brushes of comets' hair.
> They shall find real saints to draw from,
>   Magdalene, Peter and Paul,
> They shall work for an age at a sitting
>   And never be tired at all.
>
> And only the Master shall praise them,
>   And only the Master shall blame;
> And no one will work for money
>   And no one will work for fame;
> But each for the joy of the working,
>   And each in his separate star,
> Shall draw the thing as he sees it,
>   For the God of things as they are."

That was how Paul felt. He saw eternity not as release into permanent inaction, but as the entry into a body in which service could be complete.

(ii) For all his yearning for the life to come, Paul does not despise this life. He is, he says, in good heart. The reason is that even here and now we possess the Holy Spirit of God, and the Holy Spirit is the *arrabon* (cp. 1: 22), the first instalment of the life to come. It is Paul's conviction that already the Christian can enjoy the foretaste of the life everlasting. It is given to the Christian to be a citizen of two worlds; and the result is, not that he despises this world, but that he finds it clad with a sheen of glory which is the reflection of the greater glory to come.

(iii) Then comes the note of sternness. Even when Paul was thinking of the life to come, he never forgot that we are on the way not only to glory, but also to judgment. "We must all appear before the judgment seat of Christ." The word for judgment seat is *bema*. Paul may be thinking simply of the tribunal of the Roman magistrate before which he himself had stood, or he may be thinking of the Greek way of justice.

All Greek citizens were liable to serve as judges, or, as we would say, as jurymen. When an Athenian sat in judgment on a case he was given two bronze discs. Each had a cylindrical axis. One axis was hollow and that disc stood for condemnation; one was solid and that disc stood for acquittal. On the *bema* there stood two urns. One, of bronze, was called "the decisive urn", for into it the judge dropped the disc which stood for his verdict. The other, of wood, was called "the inoperative urn", for into it the judge dropped the disc which he desired to discard. So at the end the jury dropped into the bronze urn either the disc that stood for acquittal or the one that stood for condemnation. To an onlooker they looked exactly alike and none could tell the verdict the judges gave. Then the discs were counted and the verdict given.

Even so some day we shall await the verdict of God. When we remember that, life becomes a tremendous and a thrilling thing, for in it we are making or marring a destiny, winning or losing a crown. Time becomes the testing ground of eternity.

THE NEW CREATION

2 Corinthians 5: 11–19

So then, it is because we know the fear of the Lord that we keep on trying to persuade men, but to God we are already known through and through, and I hope that in your conscience, too, we will come to be as completely known. We are not trying to give ourselves another testimonial, but we are giving you an opportunity to express your pride in us, so that you may be able to answer those who pride themselves on outward appearances but not in the things of the heart. For, if we have behaved like a madman, it is for the sake of God's work. If we behave like a sensible person, it is for your sake. For it is the love of Christ which controls us, because we have come to this conclusion that one died for all, and that the inevitable conclusion is that all died. And he did die for all in order that those who live should no longer live for their own sakes, but for the sake of him who died and was raised again. The result is that from now on we value no man on the world's standards. There was a time when we applied our human standards to Christ, but now that is no longer the way in which we know him. The result is that if a man is in Christ he has been created all over again. The old things have passed away, and lo! they have become new. And all things are from God who reconciled us to himself by means of Christ and who gave us the ministry of reconciliation, a ministry whose message is that God, through Christ, was reconciling the world to himself, not debiting their sins against them, and has given us the story of this reconciliation to tell.

THIS passage follows very directly on the one that has gone before. Paul had just spoken of standing at the judgment tribunal of Christ. All his life is lived with that kept in view. It is not so much the terror of Christ he really talks about It is rather awe and reverence that he means. The Old Testament is full of the thought of a cleansing fear. Job speaks of "the fear of the Lord that is wisdom." (*Job* 28: 28). "What does the Lord your God require of you?" asks the writer of Deuteronomy, and the first item on his answer is, "to fear the Lord your God." (*Deuteronomy* 10: 12). "The fear of the Lord," says Proverbs, "is the beginning of knowledge." (*Proverbs* 1: 7 cp. 9: 10). "By the fear of the Lord a man avoids evil." (*Proverbs* 16: 6). This does not describe the fear of a dog who waits for a whipping or of a cowed child. It is that which keeps even a thoughtless man from desecrating a holy place. It is that which keeps a man from doing things which would break the heart of someone whom he loves. "The fear of the Lord," said the psalmist, "is clean." (*Psalm* 19: 9). There is a cleansing fear without which a man cannot live the life he ought.

Paul is trying to persuade men of his own sincerity. He has no doubt whatever that in the sight of God his hands are clean and his motives pure, but his enemies have cast suspicion on them, and he wishes to demonstrate his sincerity to his Corinthian friends. This is not from any selfish desire to vindicate himself. It is from the knowledge that, if his sincerity is questioned, the impact of his message will be injured. A man's message will always be heard in the context of his character. That is why the preacher and the teacher must be beyond suspicion. We have to avoid, not only evil, but the very appearance of evil lest anything make others think less, not of us, but of the message which we bring.

In verse 13 Paul insists that behind all his conduct there has been one motive only—to serve God and to help the Corinthians. More than once Paul was thought to be crazy (*Acts* 26: 24). He was suffering the same misunderstanding as Jesus suffered (*Mark* 3: 21). The real enthusiast always runs the risk of seeming crazy to lukewarm people.

Kipling tells how, on a world tour, General Booth boarded the ship at a certain port. He was seen off by a horde of tambourine-beating Salvationists. The whole thing revolted Kipling's fastidious soul. Later he got to know the General and told him how much he disapproved of this kind of thing. "Young man," said Booth, "if I thought that I could win one more soul for Christ by standing on my hands and beating a tambourine with my feet I would learn to do it."

The real enthusiast does not care if others think he is a fool. If a man follows out the Christian way of generosity, forgiveness and utter loyalty, there will always be worldly-wise people who will bluntly call him crazy. Paul knew that there was a time for calm, sensible conduct, and he knew, too, that there was a time for the conduct which to the world looks mad. He was prepared to follow either for the sake of Christ and of men.

Paul goes on to the moving motive of the whole Christian life. Christ died for all. To Paul the Christian is, in his favourite phrase, *in Christ*, and therefore the old self of the Christian died in that death and he arose a new man, as new as if he had been freshly created by the hands of God. In this newness of life he has acquired a new set of standards. He no longer judges things by the standards the world uses. There was a time when Paul had judged Christ by human standards and had set out to eliminate the Christian faith from the world. But not now. Now his standards are different. Now the man whose name he had sought to obliterate is to him the most wonderful person in the world, because he had given to him that friendship of God which he had longed for all his life.

AMBASSADOR FOR CHRIST

2 Corinthians 5: 20—6: 2

> So then we are acting as ambassadors on Christ's behalf, for God is sending you his invitation through us. We beseech you on behalf of Christ, be reconciled to God. He made him who had no acquaintance with sin to be sin for us, that through him we might become the righteousness of God. Because we are trying to help him to win men, we urge you not to have received the offer of the grace of God all to no purpose. (For scripture says, "At an accepted time I heard you, and in the day of salvation I helped you." Lo! Now is the accepted time. Lo! Now is the day of salvation).

THE office that Paul claims as his one glory and his one task is that of ambassador for Christ. The Greek he uses (*presbeutes*) is a great word. It had two uses corresponding with the Latin word of which it is a translation (*legatus*).

(i) Roman provinces were divided into two types. One was under the direct control of the senate, the other under the direct control of the Emperor. The distinction was made on this basis—provinces which were peaceful and had no troops in them were senatorial provinces; provinces which were turbulent and had troops stationed in them were imperial provinces. In the imperial provinces, the man who administered the province on behalf of the Emperor, was the *legatus presbeutes*. So then, the word in the first place paints a picture of a man who has a direct commission from the Emperor; and Paul regarded himself as commissioned by Jesus Christ for the work of the Church.

(ii) But *presbeutes* and *legatus* have an even more interesting meaning. When the Roman senate decided that a country should become a province they sent to it ten *legati* or *presbeutai*, that is, *envoys*, of their own number, who, along with the victorious general, arranged the terms of peace with the vanquished people, determined the boundaries of the new province, drew up a constitution for its new administration, and then returned to submit what they had done for ratification by the senate. They were the men responsible for bringing others into the family of the Roman Empire. So Paul thinks of himself as the man who brings to others the terms of God, whereby they can become citizens of his empire and members of his family.

There is no more responsible position than that of ambassador.

(i) An ambassador of Britain is a Briton in a foreign land. His life is spent among people who usually speak a different language, who have a different tradition and who follow a different way of life. The Christian is always like that. He lives in the world; he takes part in all the life and work of the world; but he is a citizen of heaven. To that extent he is a stranger. The man who is not willing to be different cannot be a Christian at all.

(ii) An ambassador speaks for his own country. When a British ambassador speaks, his voice is the voice of Britain. There are times when the Christian has to speak for Christ. In the decisions and the counsels of the world his must be the voice which brings the message of Christ to the human situation.

(iii) The honour of a country is in its ambassador's hands. His country is judged by him. His words are listened to, his deeds are watched and people say, "That is the way such-and-such a country speaks and acts." Lightfoot, the great Bishop of Durham, said in an ordination address, "The ambassador, while acting, acts not only as an agent, but as a representative of his sovereign. . . . The ambassador's duty is not only to deliver a definite message, to carry out a definite policy; but he is obliged to watch opportunities, to study characters, to cast about for expedients, so that he may place it before his hearers in its most attractive form." It is the great responsibility of the ambassador to commend his country to the men amongst whom he is set.

Here is the Christian's proud privilege and almost terrifying responsibility. The honour of Christ and of the Church are in his hands. By his every word and action he can make men think more—or less—of his Church and of his Master.

We have to note Paul's message. "Be reconciled to God." The New Testament never speaks of God being reconciled to men, but always of men being reconciled to God. There is no question of pacifying an angry God. The whole process of salvation takes its beginning from him. It was because God so loved the world that he sent his son. It is not that God is estranged from man but that man is estranged from him. God's message, the message which Paul brought, is an appeal from a loving Father to wandering and estranged children to come home where love is waiting for them.

Paul beseeches them not to accept the offer of the grace of God all to no purpose. There is such a thing—and it is eternity's tragedy—as the frustration of grace. Let us think of the matter in human terms. Suppose that a father sacrifices and toils to give his son every chance, surrounds him with love, plans for his future with care, and does everything humanly possible to equip him for life. And suppose the son feels no debt of gratitude, never feels the obligation to repay by being worthy of all this; and suppose he fails, not because he has not the ability, but because he will not try, because he forgets the love that gave him so much. That is what breaks a father's heart. When God gives men all his grace and they take their own foolish way and frustrate that grace which might have recreated them, once again Christ is crucified and the heart of God is broken.

A BLIZZARD OF TROUBLES

2 Corinthians 6: 3–10

> We do our work, trying to put an obstacle in no man's way, for we do not wish the ministry to become a laughing stock for critics. But in everything we try to keep on commending ourselves as ministers of God must do—in much endurance, amidst the things which press sore upon us, in the inescapable pains of life, in anxieties, amidst stripes, in prisons, in tumults, in toils, in sleepless nights, in fastings, in purity, in knowledge, in patience, in kindness, in the Holy Spirit, in love unfeigned, in the declaration of the truth, in the power of God, with the weapons of righteousness for the right hand and for the left, in honour and in dishonour, in ill report and in good report; as deceivers, and yet true; as unknown, and yet well known; as dying, and lo! we live; as chastened, but not killed; as grieved, but always rejoicing; as poor, yet making many rich; as having nothing, yet possessing all things.

IN all the chances and changes of life Paul had only one concern—to show himself a sincere and profitable minister of Jesus Christ. Even as he made that claim, his mind's eye went back across what Chrysostom called "the blizzard of troubles" through which he had come and through which he was still struggling. Every word in this tremendous catalogue, which someone has called "the hymn of the herald of salvation," has its background in Paul's adventurous life.

He begins with one triumphant word of the Christian life— *endurance (hupomone)*. It is untranslatable. It does not describe the frame of mind which can sit down with folded hands and bowed head and let a torrent of troubles sweep over it in passive resignation. It describes the ability to bear things in such a triumphant way that it transfigures them. Chrysostom has a great panegyric on this *hupomone*. He calls it "the root of all goods, the mother of piety, the fruit that never withers, a fortress that is never taken, a harbour that knows no storms" and "the queen of virtues, the foundation of right actions, peace in war, calm in tempest, security in plots." It is the courageous and triumphant ability to pass the breaking-point and not to break and always to greet the unseen with a cheer. It is the alchemy which transmutes tribulation into strength and glory.

Paul goes on to speak of three groups, each of three things, in which this victorious endurance is practised.

(i) There are the internal conflicts of the Christian life.

(*a*) *The things which press sore upon us.* The word he uses is *thlipsis* which originally expressed sheer, physical pressure on a man. There are things which weigh down a man's spirit like the sorrows which are a burden on his heart and the disappointments which are like to crush the life out of him. The triumphant endurance can cope with them all.

(*b*) *The inescapable pains of life.* The Greek word (*anagke*) literally means *the necessities of life*. Certain burdens a man may escape, but others are inescapable. There are certain things which a man must bear. The greatest of these are sorrow, for only the life which has never known love will never know that, and death which is the lot of every man. The triumphant endurance enables a man to face all that is involved in being a man.

(*c*) *Anxieties.* The word Paul uses (*stenochoria*) literally means a too narrow place. It might be used of an army caught in a narrow, rocky defile with space neither to manoeuvre nor to escape. It might be used of a ship caught in a storm with no room either to ride it or to run before it. There are moments when a man seems to be in a situation in which the walls of life are closing round him. Even then the triumphant endurance makes him able to breathe the spaciousness of heaven.

(ii) There are the external tribulations of life.

(*a*) *Stripes*. For Paul the Christian life meant not only spiritual suffering, but also physical suffering. It is the simple fact that if there had not been those who were ready and able to bear the torture of the fire and the wild beasts we would not be Christian today. There are still some for whom it is physical agony to be a Christian; and it is always true that "the blood of the martyrs is the seed of the Church."

(*b*) *Prisons*. Clement of Rome tells us that Paul was in prison no fewer than seven times. From Acts we know that before he wrote to the Corinthians he was in prison in Philippi, and afterwards in Jerusalem, in Caesarea and in Rome. The pageant of Christians who were imprisoned stretches from the first to the twentieth century. There have always been those who would abandon their liberty sooner than abandon their faith.

(*c*) *Tumults*. Over and over again we have the picture of the Christian facing, not the sternness of the law, but the violence of the mob. John Wesley tells us of what happened to him in Wednesbury when the mob came "pouring down like a flood." "To attempt speaking was vain; for the noise on every side was like the roaring of the sea. So they dragged me along till we came to the town; when, seeing the door of a large house open, I attempted to go in; but a man, catching me by the hair, pulled me back into the middle of the crowd. They made no more stop till they had carried me through the main street, from one end of the town to the other." George Foxe tells us of what happened to him at Tickhill. "I found the priest and most of the chief of the parish together in the chancel. So I went up to them and began to speak, but immediately they fell upon me; the clerk took up the Bible as I was speaking, and struck me on the face with it, so that it gushed out with blood, and I bled exceedingly in the steeple-house. Then the people cried, 'Let us have him out of the Church'; and when they had got me out they beat me exceedingly, and threw me down, and over a hedge; and afterwards they dragged me through a house into the street, stoning an beating me as they drew me along, so that I was besmeared all over with blood and dirt. . . . Yet when I was got upon my legs again I declared to them the word of life and shewed them the fruits of their teachers, how they dishonoured Christianity." The mob has often been the enemy of Christianity; but nowadays it is not the violence but the mockery or the amused contempt of the crowd against which the Christian must stand fast.

(iii) There is the effort of the Christian life.

(*a*) *Toils.* The word Paul uses (*kopos*) is in the New Testament almost a technical term for the Christian life. It describes toil to the point of sheer exhaustion, the kind of toil which takes everything of body, mind and spirit that a man has to give. The Christian is the workman of God.

(*b*) *Sleepless nights.* Some would be spent in prayer, some in a situation of peril or discomfort where sleep was impossible. At all times Paul was ready to be the unsleeping sentinel of Christ.

(*c*) *Fastings.* No doubt what Paul means here is not deliberately chosen fastings, but times when he went hungry for the work's sake. We may well contrast with his spirit the spirit of the man who would not miss a meal to attend the worship of the house of God.

Now Paul turns away from the trials and the tribulations, which endurance enabled him to conquer, to his own God-given equipment for the Christian life. Once again he retains the same arrangement of three groups of three items.

(i) There are the God-given qualities of mind. (*a*) *Purity.* The word Paul uses (*hagnotes*) was defined by the Greeks as "the careful avoidance of all sins which are against the gods; the service of the honour of God as nature demands", as "prudence at its highest tension" and as "freedom from every stain of flesh and spirit." It is in fact the quality which enables a man to enter into the very presence of God.

(*b*) *Knowledge.* This kind of knowledge has been defined as "knowledge of the things that must be done." It was the knowledge which issued not in the theologian's fine-spun subtleties but in the actions of the Christian man.

(*c*) *Patience*. Usually in the New Testament this word (*makrothumia*) denotes patience *with people*, the ability to bear with them even when they are wrong, even when they are cruel and insulting. It is a great word. In First Maccabees it is said (8: 4) that the Romans conquered the world by "their policy and their *patience*" and there the word expresses that Roman unconquerableness which would never make peace under defeat. *Patience* is the quality of a man who may lose a battle but who will never admit defeat in a campaign.

(ii) There are the God-given qualities of heart. (*a*) *Kindness*. *Kindness* (*chrestotes*) is one of the great New Testament words. It is the very opposite of severity. One great commentator describes it as "the sympathetic kindliness or sweetness of temper which puts others at their ease and shrinks from giving pain." The great example is in *Genesis* 26: 17–22 which tells how Isaac would not fight or strive. It is the quality which thinks far more of others than of itself.

(*b*) *The Holy Spirit*. Paul knew well that no useful word could be spoken nor any good deed done without the help of the Holy Spirit. But the phrase may well mean not the Holy Spirit, but *a spirit of holiness*. It may mean that Paul's dominating motive was one which was holy, one which was directed solely towards the honour and service of God.

(*c*) *Unfeigned love*. The word Paul uses is *agape*, which is a characteristic New Testament word. It means unconquerable benevolence. It means that spirit which, no matter what anyone else does to it, will never seek anything but the other person's highest good, will never dream of revenge, but will meet all injuries and rebuffs with undefeatable good will.

(iii) There is the God-given equipment for the work of preaching the gospel.

(*a*) *The declaration of the truth*. Paul knew that Jesus had not only given him a gospel to proclaim but the strength and the ability to proclaim it. To God he owed both the word and the door of utterance that had been opened for it.

(*b*) *The power of God*. To Paul this was everything. It was the only power he had. It was said of Henry the Fifth after

the battle of Agincourt, "Neither would he suffer any ditties
to be made and sung by the minstrels of his glorious victory,
for that he would wholly have the praise and thanks
altogether given to God." Paul would never have said in pride,
"I did this," but always in humility, "God enabled me to do
it."

(c) *The weapons of righteousness for the right hand and for
the left.* This means the weapons for defence and for attack.
The sword or the spear was carried in the right hand and
the shield on the left arm; and Paul is saying that God
has given him the power to attack his task and to defend
himself from his temptations.

Paul completes this lyrical passage with a series of contrasts.
He begins with *in honour and in dishonour.* The word he
uses for *dishonour* is normally used in Greek for loss of rights
as a citizen (*atimia*). Paul says, "I may have lost all the rights
and privileges which the world can confer but I am still a
citizen of the Kingdom of God." In *ill-repute and in good-
repute.* There are those who criticize his every action and who
hate his very name, but his fame with God is sure.
Deceivers and yet true. The Greek word (*planos*) literally
means a wandering quack and impostor. That is what others
call him but he knows that his message is God's truth
Unknown yet well known. The Jews who slandered him said
he was a no-account nobody whom no one had ever heard of,
yet to those to whom he had brought Christ he was known
with gratitude. *Dying, and lo! we live.* Danger was his
companion and the prospect of death his comrade, and yet
by the grace of God he was triumphantly alive with a life
that death could never kill. *Chastened, but not killed.*
Things happened to him that might have chastened any man's
spirit but they could not kill the spirit of Paul. *Grieved, but
always rejoicing.* Things happened that might have broken any
man's heart but they could not destroy Paul's joy. *Poor, yet
making many rich.* He might seem to be penniless but he
brought with him that which would enrich the souls of men.
Having nothing, yet possessing all things. He might seem

to have nothing, but, having Christ, he had everything that mattered in this world and the next.

THE ACCENT OF LOVE

2 *Corinthians* 6: 11–13 and 7: 2–4

> My dear Corinthians, we have spoken to you without keeping anything back. Our heart lies wide open to you. If there is any constraint between us, it lies, not in us, but in your hearts. Give me fair exchange. I speak as to children. Do you, too, open wide your hearts to us. . . . Make room for us in your hearts. We have wronged no one. We have corrupted no one. We have taken advantage of no one. I am not speaking with any intention of condemnation. I have already told you that you are in our hearts, so that I am ready to die with you and to live with you. I have every confidence in you. I know that I can boast much about you. My comfort is complete. I am overflowing with joy amidst all the things that press sore upon me.

WE have here taken together 6: 11–13 and 7: 2–4, for the moment omitting 6: 14 to 7: 1. The reason will become clear when we deal with the latter passage.

Paul is speaking with the accents of purest love. The breaches are healed. The quarrels are all made up and love reigns supreme. The phrase that we have translated "Our heart lies wide open to you," literally means, "Our heart is enlarged." Chrysostom has a fine comment. He says that heat makes all things expand and the warmth of love will always expand a man's heart.

In the Authorised Version in verse 12 we note a translation which is very common in the New Testament and not very fortunate, "Ye are straitened in your own bowels." The word translated *bowels* is the Greek word *splagchna*. It literally means the upper viscera, the heart, the liver and the lungs. In these organs the seat of the emotions was supposed to lie. The form of expression sounds awkward but it is not really any more curious than our own English form.

We speak of a man being *melancholy* which literally means that he has a black liver. We put the seat of love in the heart, which, after all, is a physical organ. But in English idiom it is more natural to use the word *heart* than *bowels*.

Paul here makes a great series of claims. He has wronged no one, he has corrupted no one, he has taken advantage of no one. Towards the end of his life Sir Walter Scott made the great claim, "I have unsettled no man's faith, I have corrupted no man's principles." Thackeray, also towards the end of his life, wrote a prayer in which he prayed that he "might never write a word inconsistent with the love of God, or the love of man, might never propagate his own prejudices or pander to those of others, might always speak the truth with his pen, and might never be actuated by a love of greed."

Only one thing is worse than sinning oneself, and that is teaching another to sin. It is one of the grim truths of life that another must always present a person with his first temptation, must give him the first push into sin, and it is a terrible thing to introduce a younger or a weaker brother to the wrong thing.

Someone tells of an old man who on his death-bed seemed distressed by something. When asked what was the matter he said that, when he was a boy, he and some companions had been playing at a cross-roads in the middle of a common. There was a signpost there and it was loose in its socket. They turned it round so that its arms were facing in the wrong directions. And the old man said, "I cannot stop wondering how many people were sent on the wrong road by the thing we did that day."

There can be no regret like the regret of having sent another on the wrong way. It was Paul's proud claim that his guidance and his influence had always been towards the best.

He finishes this passage by telling the Corinthians how complete his comfort is and how overflowing his joy even although at the moment troubles are all around him. Surely there never was a clearer proof that human relationships are the most important thing in life. If a man is happy at home, he can face up to anything outside. If a man is in fellowship with his friends, he can withstand the slings and arrows of fortune with a smile. As the writer of the Proverbs has it, "Better is a dinner of herbs where love is, than a fatted ox and hatred with it." (*Proverbs* 15: 17).

GET YOU OUT

2 Corinthians 6: 14—7: 1

Do not allow yourselves to become joined in an alien yoke with unbelievers. What partnership can there be between righteousness and lawlessness? What fellowship can darkness have with light? What concord can there be with Christ and Belial? What share can the believer have with the unbeliever? What agreement can the temple of God have with idols? For you are the temple of the living God, even as God said, "I will dwell in them and I will walk in them, and I will be their God and they will be my people." Therefore, "Come out from among them and separate yourselves," the Lord says, "and, have no contact with impurity, and I will receive you, and I will be a father to you, and you will be sons and daughters to me," says the Lord, the ruler of all. So then, since we possess these promises, let us purify ourselves from every pollution of flesh and spirit, and let us thus make holiness complete in the fear of God.

WE come now to the passage which we omitted previously. There is no doubt that it comes in very awkwardly where it is. Its sternness is at odds with the glad and joyous love of the verses on either side of it.

In the introduction we saw that Paul wrote a letter prior to First Corinthians. In 1 *Corinthians* 5: 9 he says, "I wrote to you in my letter not to associate with immoral men." That letter may be altogether lost. Or it may be that this is a section of it. It could easily happen that, when Paul's letters were being collected, one sheet could get misplaced. It was not until A.D. 90 or thereby that the collection was made, and by that time there may well have been none who knew the proper order. Certainly, in substance, this well suits the letter referred to in 1 *Corinthians* 5: 9.

There are certain Old Testament pictures behind this. Paul begins by urging the Corinthians not to be joined to unbelievers in an alien yoke. Undoubtedly that goes back to the old commandment in *Deuteronomy* 22: 10, "You shall not plough with an ox and an ass together." (cp. *Leviticus* 19: 19). The idea is that there are certain things which are fundamentally incompatible and were never meant to be brought together. It is impossible for the purity of the Christian and the pollution of the pagan to run in double harness.

In the demand, "What has the temple of God to do with idols?" Paul's thought is going back to such incidents as Manasseh bringing a graven image into the temple of God (2 *Kings* 21: 1–9), and, in the later days, Josiah utterly destroying such things (2 *Kings* 23: 3 ff.). Or he is thinking of such abominations as are described in *Ezekiel* 8: 3–18. Men had sometimes tried to associate the temple of God with idol worship, and the consequences had been terrible.

The whole passage is a rousing summons not to hold any fellowship with unbelievers. It is a challenge to the Corinthians to keep themselves unspotted from the world. It has been well remarked that the very essence of the history of Israel is in the words, "Get thee out!" That was the word of God that came to Abraham as the Authorised Version has it. "Get thee out of thy country and from thy kindred and from thy father's house" (*Genesis* 12: 1). That was the warning that came to Lot before the destruction of Sodom and Gomorrah. (*Genesis* 19: 12–14). There are things in the world with which the Christian cannot and dare not associate himself.

It is difficult to realize just how many separations Christianity meant for the people who first accepted it.

(i) Often it meant that a man had to give up his *trade*. Suppose he was a stone mason. What was to happen if his firm received a contract to build a heathen shrine?

Suppose he was a tailor. What was to happen if he was instructed to cut and sew garments for priests of the heathen gods? Suppose he was a soldier. At the gate of every camp burned the light upon the altar sacred to the godhead of Caesar. What was to happen if he had to fling his pinch of incense on that altar in token of his worship? Time and time again in the early Church the choice came to a man between the security of his job and his loyalty to Jesus Christ. It is told that a man came to Tertullian. He told him his problem and then he said, "But after all I must live." "Must you?" said Tertullian.

In the early Church a man's Christianity often meant that he had to get out from his job. One of the most famous modern examples of this same thing was F. W. Charrington. He was the heir to a fortune made by brewing. He was passing a tavern one night. There was a woman waiting at the door. A man, obviously her husband, came out, and she was trying to keep him from going back in. With one blow of his fist the man felled her. Charrington started forward and then he looked up. The name above the tavern was his own, and Charrington said, "With that one blow that man did not only knock his wife out, he also knocked me clean out of that business forever." And he gave up the fortune he might have had, rather than touch money earned in such a way.

No man is keeper of another man's conscience. Every man must decide for himself if he can take his trade to Christ and Christ with him to his daily work.

(ii) Often it meant that a man had to give up *social life*. In the ancient world, as we saw when studying the section on meat offered to idols, many a heathen feast was held in the temple of a god. The invitation would run, "I invite you to dine with me at the table of our Lord Serapis." Even if that were not so, a heathen feast would begin and end with the pouring of a libation, a cup of wine, to the gods. Could a Christian share in that? Or must he get out and say good-bye to the social fellowship which used to mean so much to him?

(iii) Often it meant that a man had to give up *family ties.*
The pain of Christianity in the early years was the way it split
families. A wife became a Christian and her husband might
drive her from his house. A husband became a Christian and
his wife might leave him. Sons and daughters became
Christians and might find the door of the home shut and
barred in their faces. It was literally true that Christ came not
to send peace but a dividing sword upon earth and that men
and women had to be prepared to love him more than their
nearest and dearest. They had to be prepared to get out even
from their homes.

However hard it may be, it will always remain true that
there are certain things a man cannot do and be a Christian.
There are certain things from which every Christian must get
out.

Before we leave this passage, there is one point we may note.
In it Paul quotes scripture and his quotation is a mixture of
a variety of passages, none quoted accurately, from *Leviticus*
26: 11, 12, *Isaiah* 52: 11, *Ezekiel* 20: 34, 37: 27 and *2 Samuel*
7: 14. It is a fact that Paul seldom quotes accurately. Why?
We must remember that in his time books were written on
papyrus rolls. A book the size of Acts would require a roll
about thirty-five feet long, a very unwieldy thing. There were
no chapter divisions; they were inserted by Stephen Langton in
the thirteenth century. There were no verse divisions; they were
inserted by Stephanus, the Paris printer, in the sixteenth
century. Finally, there was no such thing as a concordance until
the sixteenth century. The result was that Paul did the only
sensible thing—he quoted from memory, and so long as he got
the substance right he did not worry about the actual
wording. It was not the letter of scripture but the message of
scripture which mattered to him.

GODLY SORROW AND GODLY JOY

2 Corinthians 7: 5–16

For when we arrived in Macedonia we could find no rest for our
body, but we were sore pressed on every side. There were wars

without and fears within. But he who comforts the lowly comforted us—I mean God—by the arrival of Titus. We found this comfort not only in his arrival, but in the comfort which he found amongst you, for he brought news of your longing to see me, of your grief for the past situation, of your zeal to show your loyalty to me. The consequence was that my gladness was greater than my troubles. For if I grieved you with the letter I sent you, I am not sorry that I sent it, although, to tell the truth I was sorry; for I see that that letter, if it was only for a time, did grieve you. Now I am glad, not that you were grieved, but that your grief was the way to repentance. It was a godly grief that came to you, so that you have lost nothing through our action, for godly grief produces repentance which leads to salvation and which no man ever regrets. But worldly grief produces death. Look now! This very thing, this godly grief—see what earnest longing it produced in you, what a desire to set yourselves right, what vexation at what you had done, what fear, what yearning, what zeal, what steps to inflict condign punishment on the man who deserved it! You have shown yourselves pure in this matter. If I did indeed write to you, it was not for the sake of him who committed the wrong, nor for the sake of him who was wronged; it was to make quite clear to you in the sight of God the earnestness you really possessed for us. Because of this we have been comforted. In addition to this comfort which came to us, we rejoiced with still more overflowing joy in the joy of Titus, because his spirit was refreshed by the way in which you all treated him. For if I did rather boast about him, I was not put to shame, but just as everything we have said to you was spoken with truth, so too our boast about Titus was proved to be the truth. And his heart goes out overflowingly to you when he remembers what obedience you showed, how you received him with fear and trembling. I am glad that in everything I am in good heart about you.

THE connection of this section really goes as far back as 2:12, 13, for it is there that Paul tells how in Troas he had no rest because he did not know how the Corinthian situation had developed and how he had set out to Macedonia to meet Titus to get the news as quickly as possible. Let us again remember the circumstances. Things had gone wrong in Corinth. In an attempt to mend them Paul had paid a flying visit which only made them worse and nearly broke his heart. After the failure of the visit he had despatched Titus with a letter of quite exceptional sternness and severity. He was so worried about the outcome of the whole unhappy business that he was quite unable to rest at Troas although there was much there that he might have done, so he set out to meet Titus to get the news as quickly as possible. He met Titus somewhere in Macedonia and learned to his overflowing joy that the trouble was over, the breach was healed and all was well. That is the background of events against which this passage must be read and it makes it very rich.

It tells us certain things about Paul's whole method and outlook on rebuke.

(i) He was quite clear that there came a time when rebuke was necessary. It often happens that the man who seeks an easy peace finds in the end nothing but trouble. The man who allows a perilous situation to develop because he shrinks from dealing with it, the parent who exercises no discipline because he fears unpleasantness, the man who will not grasp the nettle of danger because he wants to find the flower of safety, in the end simply piles up greater trouble for himself. Trouble is like disease. If it is dealt with at the right time, it can often easily be eradicated; if not, it can become an incurable growth.

(ii) Even admitting all that, the last thing Paul wished was to rebuke. He did it only under compulsion and took no pleasure whatever in inflicting pain. There are those who take a sadistic pleasure in seeing someone wince beneath the lash of their tongue, who pride themselves on being candid when they are only being rude and on being blunt when they are only being boorish. It is the simple fact that the rebuke which is given with a certain relish will never prove as effective as the rebuke which is obviously unwillingly dragged out and which a man gives only because he can do no other.

(iii) Further, Paul's sole object in giving rebuke was to enable people to be what they ought to be. By his rebuke he wished the Corinthians to see the real earnestness they possessed for him in spite of their disobedience and their trouble-making. Such a course might for the moment cause pain, but its ultimate object was not the pain; it was not to knock them down, but to lift them up; it was not to discourage them, but to encourage them; it was not simply to eradicate the evil, but to make the good grow.

This passage tells us also of three great human joys.

(i) There breathes through it all the joy of reconciliation, the healed breach and the mended quarrel. We all remember times in childhood when we had done something wrong and there was a barrier between us and our parents. We all know that can still happen between us and those we love. And we all know the flood of relief and the happiness when the barriers are gone and we are at one again with those we love. In the last analysis the man who cherishes bitterness hurts no one more than he hurts himself.

(ii) There is the joy of seeing someone in whom you believe justifying that belief. Paul had given Titus a good character and Titus had gone to meet a very difficult situation. Paul was overjoyed that Titus had justified his confidence in him and proved his words true. Nothing brings so deep a satisfaction as to know that our children in the flesh or in the faith do well. The deepest joy that a son or a daughter or a scholar or a student can bring to parent or teacher is to demonstrate that they are as good as the parent or the teacher believes them to be. Life's sorest tragedy is disappointed hopes and life's greatest joy is hopes come true.

(ii) There is the joy of seeing someone you love welcomed and well-treated. It is a fact of life that kindness shown to those we love moves us even more deeply than kindness shown to ourselves. What is true of us is true of God. That is why we can best show our love of God by loving our fellow men. The thing that delights the heart of God is to see one of his children kindly treated. Inasmuch as we do it to them we do it to him.

This passage also draws one of the most important distinctions in life. It draws the distinction between the *godly* and the *worldly* sorrow.

(i) A godly sorrow produces a true repentance, and a true repentance is one which demonstrates its sorrow by its deeds. The Corinthians proved their repentance by doing everything they could to mend the wretched situation that their thoughtless conduct had produced. Now they hated the sin they had committed, and even hated themselves for committing it, and they laboured to atone for it.

(ii) A worldly sorrow is not really sorrow at all in one sense but it is not sorrow for its sin or for the hurt it may have caused others; it is only resentment that it has been found out. If it got the chance to do the same thing again and thought it could escape the consequences, it would do it. A godly sorrow is a sorrow which has come to see the wrongness of the thing it did. It is not just the consequences of the thing it regrets; it hates the thing itself. We must be very careful that our sorrow for sin is not merely sorrow that we have been found out, but sorrow which, seeing the evil of the sinful thing is determined never to do it again and has dedicated the rest of its life to atone, by God's grace, for what it has done.

AN APPEAL FOR GENEROSITY

2 *Corinthians* 8: 1–15

Brothers, we want you to know about the grace of God which was given in the Churches of Macedonia. We want you to know that even when they were going through a severe test of their faith when things were pressing sorely on them, their overflowing happiness and their poverty which reached the very depths of destitution combined to overflow into the wealth of their generosity. For, I bear witness, they gave according to their ability, yes, beyond their ability, quite spontaneously, begging us and strongly urging us to give them the privilege of sharing in this service designed for the help of God's dedicated people. It was not only as we hoped that they gave, but, first, by God's will, they gave

themselves to the Lord and to us. We were so impressed by this
that we have invited Titus, as in your case he began it, so to
bring to its completion this act of generosity. But, just as you
excel in everything—in faith, in speech, in knowledge, and in all
earnestness and in the love which went out from you to come to
rest in us—I urge you to excel also in this act of generosity. This
is not an order that I am giving you, but I am using the example
of the earnestness of others to prove the genuineness of your love.
For you know the grace of our Lord Jesus Christ. You know that
it was for your sakes that, though he was rich, he became poor,
that you, by his poverty, might become rich. It is my opinion that
I give you in this matter. This is to your good, you, who as long
ago as last year, were the first not only to do this but to desire to
do it. Now complete the action, so that your readiness to set this
scheme in hand may be matched by your completing it according
to your means. For if readiness to give already exists, to make it
fully acceptable a man is called upon to give in proportion to
what he has and not in proportion to what he has not. You are
not called on to give so that others may have relief while you
yourselves are hard pressed. But things will even themselves up.
At the present time your abundance must be used to relieve their
lack, so that some day their abundance may be used to relieve
your lack, so that things may be evened up, just as it stands written,
"He who gathered his much had not too much, and he who gathered
his little had not too little."

ONE of the schemes that lay nearest to Paul's heart was the
collection that he was organizing for the Church of Jerusalem.
This was the Mother Church but she was poor, and it was
Paul's desire that all the Gentiles' Churches should remember
and help that Church which was their mother in the faith.
So here he reminds the Corinthians of their duty and urges
them to generosity.

He uses five arguments to appeal to them to give worthily.

(i) He cites the example of others. He tells them how
generous the Macedonian Churches had been. They were poor
and in trouble but they gave all they had, far more than
anyone could have expected. At the Jewish Feast of Purim
there is a regulation which says that, however poor a man is,
he must find someone poorer than himself and give him a

gift. It is not always those who are most wealthy who are most generous; often those who have least to give are the most ready to give. As the common saying has it, "It is the poor who help the poor," because they know what poverty is like.

(ii) He cites the example of Jesus Christ. For Paul the sacrifice of Jesus did not begin on the Cross. It did not even begin with his birth. It began in heaven, when he laid his glory by and consented to come to earth. Paul's challenge to the Christian is, "With that tremendous example of generosity before you, how can you hold back?"

(iii) He cites their own past record. They have been foremost in everything. Can they then lag behind in this? If men were only true to their own highest standards, if we all lived always at our best, what a difference it would make!

(iv) He stresses the necessity of putting fine feeling into fine action. The Corinthians had been the first to feel the appeal of this scheme. But a feeling which remains only a feeling, a pity which remains a pity only of the heart, a fine desire that never turns into a fine deed, is a sadly truncated and frustrated thing. The tragedy of life so often is, not that we have no high impulses, but that we fail to turn them into actions.

(v) He reminds them that life has a strange way of evening things up. Far more often than not we find that it is measured to us with the same measure as we measure to others. Life has a way of repaying bounty with bounty, and the sparing spirit with the sparing spirit.

Paul says a very fine thing about the Macedonians. He says that first of all they gave themselves—and so indeed they did. Two of them stand out above all the others. There was Aristarchus of Thessalonica. He was with Paul on the last journey to Rome (*Acts* 28: 2). Like Luke, he must have come to a great decision. Paul was under arrest and on his way to trial before the Emperor. There was only one way in which Aristarchus could have accompanied him, and that was by enrolling himself as Paul's slave. Aristarchus in the fullest

sense gave himself. There was Epaphroditus. When Paul was
in prison in the later days, he came to him with a gift from
Philippi, and there in prison he fell grievously ill. As Paul
said of him, "he nearly died for the work of Christ"
(*Philippians* 2: 26–30).

No gift can be in any real sense a gift unless the giver
gives with it a bit of himself. That is why personal giving
is always the highest kind, and that is the kind of giving of
which Jesus Christ is the supreme example.

The Old Testament quotation with which Paul concludes
this passage is from *Exodus* 16: 18, which tells how when the
Israelites gathered the manna in the wilderness, whether a
man gathered little or much, it was enough.

PRACTICAL ARRANGEMENTS

2 *Corinthians* 8: 16–24

> Thanks be to God who has put into the heart of Titus the same
> earnestness for you as there is in mine. His earnestness is proved
> by the fact that he not only welcomed my invitation, but that also,
> with characteristic earnestness, he is going to you of his own choice.
> Along with him we send the brother whose praise in the gospel
> is in all the Churches. Not only does he enjoy universal praise,
> but he has also been elected by the Churches to be our fellow-
> traveller in this act of charity which is being administered by us
> to promote the glory of God and to show your eagerness. We
> are making arrangements to ensure that no one will criticize us in
> our handling of the administration of this munificent gift. We aim
> to produce conduct which is fair not only in the sight of God
> but also in the sight of men. With them we send our brother
> whose earnestness we have often proved on many occasions, and
> who is now even more earnest in this work because of his great
> confidence in you. If any further questions are asked about Titus—
> he is my partner and my fellow-worker in all that concerns you.
> If any further questions are asked about our brothers—they are
> apostles of the Church, the glory of Christ. Give them un-
> answerable proof of your love and prove to them that our boasting

about you is true. You will be proving it in the face of the Churches.

THE great interest of this passage is its intensely practical character. Paul knew he had his enemies and his critics. He knew well that there would be those who would not hesitate to charge him with turning part of the collection to his own use, and so he takes steps to see that it would be impossible to level that charge against him, by ensuring that others will share with him the task of taking it to Jerusalem. Who the two unnamed brothers were no one knows. The first, the brother whose praise is in all the Churches, is usually identified with Luke. The Collect for St. Luke's Day assumes this identification. "Almighty God, who calledst Luke the Physician, whose praise is in the gospel, to be an Evangelist and Physician of the soul; may it please thee that by the wholesome medicines of the doctrine delivered by him, all the diseases of our souls may be healed." It was Paul's aim to make clear not only to God but also to men that he was above suspicion.

It is most interesting to note that this same Paul, who could write like a lyric poet and think like a theologian could, when it was necessary, act with the meticulous accuracy of a chartered accountant. He was a big enough man to do the little things and the practical things supremely well.

THE WILLING GIVER

2 Corinthians 9: 1–5

It is superfluous for me to write to you about this service designed to help God's dedicated people, for I know your eagerness, about which I have boasted for you to the Macedonians, for I have told them that Achaea has been ready since last year, and the story of your zeal has kindled the majority of them. But, all the same, I am sending the brothers, so that, in this particular matter, the boast I made of you may not be proved empty, so that you might be all ready, as I said you were. I do this in case the Macedonians should arrive with me and find you unprepared, and, in case, if that should happen, we—not to mention you yourselves—should be ashamed. I think it necessary to invite the brothers to go on ahead of us, and to get your promised bounty in order in good time, so that it should be ready as if you were eager to give and not as if I were forcing it out of you.

As many of the early fathers noted, there is a delightfully human touch in the background of this passage. Paul is dealing with the collection for the saints at Jerusalem. But now it becomes clear that he has been encouraging the Corinthians to generosity by quoting the example of the Macedonians (8: 1–5), and at the same time encouraging the Macedonians by quoting the Corinthians! And now he is just a little afraid that the Corinthians may let him down! It is typical of Paul and of the greatness of his heart. For the whole point is that he never criticized one Church to another; he praised one to another. No bad standard by which to test a man is whether he delights in retailing the best or the worst about others.

There are at least four ways in which a man may give a gift.

(i) He may give as a *duty*. He may discharge the claims of generosity but do so as one pays an account or sends a remittance to a tax-collector. It may be done as a grim duty and with such a bad grace that it would be almost better not to do it at all.

(ii) He may give simply to find *self-satisfaction*. He thinks far more of the pleasant feeling that he has when he makes the gift than of the feelings of the person who receives it. There are people who will give a penny to a beggar rather because of the glow of satisfaction they get than from any real desire to help. Such giving is in essence selfish; people who give like that give to themselves rather than to the recipient.

(iii) He may give from motives of *prestige*. The real source of such giving is not love but pride. The gift is given not to help but to glorify the giver. In fact the chances are that it would not be given at all if it were not seen and praised. It may even be that the giving is done in order to pile up credit with God—as if any man could put God in his debt.

(iv) None of these ways of giving are wholly bad, for at least the gift is made. But the real way to give is under *love's compulsion,* to give because one cannot help giving, to give because the sight of a soul in need wakens a desire that cannot be stilled. This is in fact to give in God's way; it was because he *so loved* the world that he gave his Son.

Paul's great desire is that the gift of the Corinthians should be ready and not have to be collected at the last moment. An old Latin proverb says, "He gives twice who gives quickly." That is always true. The finest gifts are those made, before they are requested. It was while we were yet enemies that Christ died for us. God hears our prayers even before we speak them. And we should be to our fellow men as God has been to us.

THE PRINCIPLES OF GENEROSITY

2 Corinthians 9: 6–15

Further, there is this He who sows sparingly will also reap sparingly, and he who sows bountifully will reap bountifully. Let each man give as he has decided in his heart. Let him not give as if it hurt him to give or as if it was being forced out of him, for it is the happy giver whom God loves. God can supply you with an overflowing measure of every grace, so that because in all things at all times you have all sufficiency, you may excel in every good work. As it stands written, "He scattered his seed, he gave to the poor; his righteousness remains for ever." And in every point you will be enriched for every kind of generosity, that generosity which, through you, produces thanksgiving to God. For the ministration of this act of voluntary service not only fills up the lacks of God's dedicated people, but it also does something special for God through the many thanksgivings it produces. Through your generosity the reality of your Christian service will be so signally proved that they will glorify God because of the way in which you obey your creed, which looks to the gospel of Christ, and because of the generous way in which you have shared with them and with all men; and they will pray for you and long for you because of the surpassing grace of God which is upon you. Thanks be to God for the free gift of God he gave to us, the story of which can never be fully told.

THIS passage gives us an outline of the principles of generous giving.

(i) Paul insists that no man was ever the loser because he was generous. Giving is like sowing seed. The man who sows with a sparing hand cannot hope for anything but a meagre harvest, but the man who sows with a generous hand will in due time reap a generous return. The New Testament is an extremely practical book and one of its great features is that it is never afraid of the reward motive. It never says that goodness is all to no purpose. It never forgets that something new and wonderful enters into the life of the man who accepts God's commands as his law.

But the rewards that the New Testament envisages are never material. It promises not the wealth of things, but the wealth of the heart and of the spirit. What then can a generous man expect?

(*a*) He will be *rich in love*. This is a point to which we will return. It is always true that no one likes the mean man and generosity can cover a multitude of other sins. Men will always prefer the warm heart, even though its very warmth may lead it into excesses, to the cold rectitude of the calculating spirit.

(*b*) He will be *rich in friends*. "A man that has friends must show himself friendly." An unlovable man can never expect to be loved. The man whose heart runs out to others will always find that the hearts of others run out to him.

(*c*) He will be *rich in help*. The day always comes when we need the help which others can give, and, if we have been sparing in our help to them, the likelihood is that they will be sparing in their help to us. The measure we have used to others will determine the measure which is given to us.

(*d*) He will be *rich towards God*. Jesus taught us that what we do to others we do for God, and the day will come when every time we opened our heart and hand will stand to our favour, and every time we closed them will be a witness against us.

(ii) Paul insists that it is the happy giver whom God loves. *Deuteronomy* 15: 7–11 lays down the duty of generosity to the poor brother, and verse 10 has it, "Your heart shall not be grudging when you give to him." There was a rabbinic saying which said that to receive a friend with a cheerful countenance and to give him nothing is better than to give him everything with a gloomy countenance. Seneca said that to give with doubt and delay is almost worse than not to give at all.

Paul then quotes from *Psalm* 112: 3, 9—verses which he takes to be a description of the good and generous man. He scatters his seed, that is he sows it not sparingly but generously; he gives to the poor; and his action is to his credit and joy forever. Carlyle tells how, when he was a boy, a beggar came to the door. His parents were out and he was alone in the house. On a boyish impulse he broke into his own savings-bank and gave the beggar all that was in it, and he tells us that never before or since did he know such sheer happiness as came to him in that moment. There is indeed a joy in giving.

(ii) Paul insists that God can give a man both the substance to give and the spirit in which to give it. In verse 8 he speaks of the all-sufficiency which God gives us. The word he uses is *autarkeia*. This was a favourite Stoic word. It does not describe the sufficiency of the man who possesses all kinds of things in abundance. It means independence. It describes the state of the man who has directed life not to amassing possessions but to eliminating needs. It describes the man who has taught himself to be content with very little. It is obvious that such a man will be able to give far more to others because he wants so little for himself. It is so often true that we want so much for ourselves that there is nothing left to give to others.

Not only that, it is God who can give us the spirit in which to give. Robert Louis Stevenson's native servants loved him. His boy used to waken him every morning with a cup of tea.

On one occasion his usual boy was off duty, and another had taken over. This boy woke him not only with a cup of tea but also with a beautifully cooked omelette. Stevenson thanked him and said, "Great is your forethought." "No, master," said the boy, "great is my love." It is God alone who can put into our hearts the love which is the essence of the generous spirit.

But in this passage Paul does more. If we read into its thought, we see that he holds that giving does wonderful things for three different persons.

(i) It does something *for others*. (*a*) It relieves their need. Many a time, when a man was at his wit's end, a gift from someone else has seemed nothing less than a gift from heaven. (*b*) It restores their faith in their fellow men. It often happens that, when a man is in need, he grows embittered and feels himself neglected. It is then that a gift shows him that love and kindness are not dead. (*c*) It makes them thank God. A gift in a time of need is something which brings not only our love but also God's love into the lives of others.

(ii) It does something *for ourselves*. (*a*) It guarantees our Christian profession. In the case of the Corinthians that was specially important. No doubt the Jerusalem Church, which was almost entirely Jewish, still regarded the Gentiles with suspicion and wondered in its heart of hearts if Christianity could be for them at all. The very fact of the gift of the Gentile Churches must have guaranteed to them the reality of Gentile Christianity. If a man is generous it enables others to see that he has turned his Christianity not only into words but into deeds as well. (*b*) It wins us both the love and the prayers of others. What is needed in this world more than anything else is something which will link a man to his fellow men. There is nothing so precious as fellowship, and generosity is an essential step on the way to real union between man and man.

(iii) It does something *for God*. It makes prayers of thanksgiving go up to him. Men see our good deeds and glorify not us but God. It is a tremendous thing that something we can

do can turn men's hearts to God, for that means that something
we can do can bring joy to him.

Finally, Paul turns the thoughts of the Corinthians to the
gift of God in Jesus Christ, a gift whose wonder can never be
exhausted and whose story can never be fully told; and, in so
doing, he says to them, "Can you, who have been so generously
treated by God, be anything else but generous to your fellow
men?"

Before we go on to study chapters 10 to 13 of our letter,
let us remember what we have already seen in the introduction.
There is a most surprising break between chapters 9 and 10.
Up to chapter 9 everything seems to be going well. The breach
is healed and the quarrel is over. Chapters 8 and 9 deal with
the collection for the Church at Jerusalem, and, now that that
practical matter is dealt with, we might expect Paul to draw
to a close. Instead, we find four chapters which are the saddest
and the sorest chapters Paul ever wrote. It makes us wonder
how they got there.

Twice in *2 Corinthians* Paul speaks of a severe letter that
he had written, a letter so stern that at one time he almost
regretted ever having written it (*2 Corinthians* 2: 4; 7: 8). That
description does not at all fit 1 *Corinthians*. So we are left with
two alternatives—either the severe letter is lost altogether or
at least part of it is contained in these chapters 10 to 13. All
the likelihood is that chapters 10 to 13 are the severe letter,
and that, when Paul's letters were being collected, it was
placed here by mistake. To get the right order of things we
really ought to read chapters 10 to 13 before we read chapters
1 to 9. We may well believe that we are reading here the letter
which it hurt Paul most of all to write, and which was written to
try to mend a situation which came near to breaking his heart.

PAUL BEGINS TO ANSWER HIS CRITICS

2 Corinthians 10: 1–6

It is I Paul who call upon you—and I am doing it in the gentleness and the sweet reasonableness of Christ—I, who, as you say, am a poor creature when I am with you, but a man of courage when I am absent. It is my prayer that, when I do come to you, I may not have to be bold with that confidence with which I reckon that I can boldly face some who reckon that we direct our conduct by purely human motives. It is true that we live in a human body, but for all that we do not carry on our campaign with human motives and resources (for the weapons of our campaign are not merely human weapons, but God has made them powerful to destroy fortresses). Our campaign is such that we can destroy plausible fallacies and all lofty-mindedness which raises itself up against the knowledge that God has given, such that we capture every intention and bring it into obedience to Christ, such that we are prepared to punish all disobedience, when your obedience has been fulfilled.

RIGHT at the beginning of this passage are two words which set the whole tone which Paul wishes to use. He speaks of the *gentleness* and the *sweet reasonableness* of Christ.

Prautes, gentleness, is an interesting word. Aristotle defined it as the correct mean between being too angry and being never angry at all. It is the quality of the man whose anger is so controlled that he is always angry at the right time and never at the wrong time. It describes the man who is never angry at any personal wrong he may receive, but who is capable of righteous anger when he sees others wronged. By using that word Paul is saying at the very beginning of his stern letter that he is not carried away by personal anger, but is speaking with the strong gentleness of Jesus himself.

The other word is even more illuminating. *Sweet reasonableness* is the Greek word *epieikeia.* The Greeks themselves defined *epieikeia* as "that which is just and even better than just." They described it as that quality which must enter in when justice, just because of its generality, is in danger of becoming unjust. There are times when strict justice can actually result in injustice. Sometimes real justice is not to insist on the letter of the law, but to let a higher quality enter into our decisions. The man who has *epieikeia* is the man who knows that, in the last analysis, the Christian standard is not justice, but love. By using this word Paul is saying that he is not out for his rights and to insist on the letter of the law; but is going to deal with this situation with that Christlike love which transcends even the purest of human justice.

Now we have come to a section of the letter which is very hard to understand—and for this reason, that we are hearing only one side of the argument. We are hearing only Paul's reply. We do not know accurately what the charges were which the Corinthians levelled against him; we have to deduce them from the answers which Paul gives. But we can at least try to make our deductions.

(i) It is clear that the Corinthians had charged Paul with being bold enough when he was not face to face with them but a pretty poor creature when actually there. They are saying that when he is absent he can write things that he has not the courage to say in their presence. Paul's reply is that he prays that he may not have occasion to deal with them personally as he knows he is quite capable of doing. Letters are dangerous things. A man will often write with a bitterness and peremptoriness which he would never use to another person's face. Exchange of letters can do a deal of harm which might well have been avoided by a face to face discussion. But Paul's claim is that he would never write anything which he was not prepared to say.

(ii) It is clear that they charged him with arranging his conduct on human motives. Paul's answer is that both his conduct and his power come from God. True, he is a man subject to all the limitations of manhood, but God is his guide and God is his strength. What makes this passage difficult to understand is that Paul uses the word *flesh* (*sarx*) in two different senses. (*a*) He uses it in the ordinary sense of the human body, flesh in its physical sense. "We walk," he says, "in the flesh." That simply means that he is, like anyone else, a human being. (*b*) But he also uses it in his own characteristic way for that part of human nature which gives a bridgehead to sin, that essential human weakness of life without God. So, he says, "We do not walk after, or according to, the flesh." It is as if he said, "I am a human being with a human body, but I never allow myself to be dominated by purely human motives. I never try to live without God." A man may live in the body and yet be guided by the Spirit of God.

Paul goes on to make two significant points.

(i) He says that he is equipped to deal with and to destroy all the plausible clevernesses of human wisdom and human pride. There is a simplicity which is a weightier argument than the most elaborate human cleverness. Once there was a house party at which Huxley, the great Victorian agnostic, was present. On the Sunday morning it was planned to go to church. Huxley said to a member of the party, "Suppose you don't go to church; suppose you stay at home and tell me why you believe in Jesus." The man said, "But you, with your cleverness, could demolish anything I might say." Huxley said, "I don't want you to argue. I want you just to tell me what this means to you." So the man, in the simplest terms, told from his heart what Christ meant to him. When he was finished, there were tears in the great agnostic's eyes. "I would give my right hand," he said, "if I could only believe that." It was not argument, but the utter simplicity of heartfelt sincerity which got home. In the last analysis it is not subtle cleverness which is most effective but simple sincerity.

(ii) Paul speaks of bringing every intention into captivity to Christ. Christ has an amazing way of capturing what was pagan and subduing it for his purposes. Max Warren tells of a custom of the natives in New Guinea. At certain times they have ritual songs and dances. They work themselves up into a frenzy and the ritual culminates in what are called "the murder songs," in which they shout before God the names of the people they wish to kill. When the natives became Christian, they retained these customs and that ritual, but in the murder songs, it was no longer the names of the people they hated, but the names of the *sins* they hated, that they shouted before God and called on him to destroy. An old pagan custom had been captured for Christ. Jesus never wishes to take from us our own qualities and abilities and characteristics. He wishes to take them and to use them for himself. His invitation is to come to him with just what we have to offer and he will enable us, to make a finer use of ourselves than ever before.

PAUL CONTINUES TO ANSWER HIS CRITICS

2 Corinthians 10: 7–18

Look at what lies in front of you. If anyone confidently believes that he belongs to Christ, let him examine his own case again, because, just as he belongs to Christ, so do we also. If I make what might look like excessive claims about our authority—that authority which the Lord gave us to upbuild you and not to destroy you—I will not be put to shame. And I am going to do just that very thing so that I may not seem, as it were, to be striking terror into you through a series of letters, because, to quote my opponents, "His letters are weighty and strong but his bodily presence is weak and his speech contemptible." Let the man who makes statements such as that consider that, such as we are in speech through letters when we are absent, that very thing we are in deed when we are present. Far be it from us to include ourselves among or compare ourselves with some people who commend themselves, but when their only standard of measurement is to measure themselves by themselves, and when their comparison does not go beyond comparing themselves with themselves, they are not sensible. As for us, we will not boast beyond our measure, but we will boast according to the measure of the sphere God has apportioned to us as our measure, a sphere which extends as far as you. For we are not overreaching ourselves, as if our sphere did not reach to you, for indeed we were the first to bring the gospel of Christ to you. We do not boast beyond our measure, but we do cherish the hope, that, as your faith increases, we will be given a greater share of honour among you, in a sphere which belongs to us, and which will enable us to preach the gospel to the regions beyond, and not to boast about things which have already been done in someone else's sphere. Let him who boasts boast in the Lord, for it is not the man who commends himself who is proved to be of sterling quality, but the man whom the Lord commends.

PAUL continues to answer his critics; and we are faced with the same problem that we are hearing only one side of the argument and can only deduce what the criticisms were from Paul's reply to them.

(i) It seems clear that at least some of Paul's opponents asserted that he did not belong to Christ in the same way as they did. Perhaps they were still casting up at him the fact that once he had been the arch-persecutor of the Church. Perhaps they claimed special knowledge. Perhaps they claimed a special holiness. In any event they looked down on Paul and glorified themselves and their own relationship to Christ.

Any religion which makes a man look down upon his fellow men and think himself better than they, is no true religion. When revival came to the East African Churches in recent years, one of its features was the public confession of sin. While the natives willingly took part in that confession, Europeans tended to stand aloof, and one of the missionaries wrote, "It is felt that to hold back from it is to refuse to be identified with the fellowship of forgiven sinners. Europeans are often accused of being proud and unwilling to share fellowship in this way." There can be no finer definition of the Church than *a fellowship of forgiven sinners*. When a man realizes that it is to such a fellowship he belongs there is no longer any room for pride. The trouble with the arrogant Christian is that he feels rather that Christ belongs to him than that he belongs to Christ.

(ii) It would seem that the Corinthians had actually sunk to taunting Paul about his personal appearance. His bodily presence, they jeered, was weak, and he was no speaker. It may well be that they were right. A description of Paul's personal appearance has come down to us from a very early book called *The Acts of Paul and Thecla*, which dates back to about A.D. 200. It is so unflattering that it may well be true. It describes Paul as "a man of little stature, thin-haired upon the head, crooked in the legs, of good state of body, with eyebrows meeting, and with nose somewhat hooked, full of grace, for sometimes he appeared like a man and sometimes he had the face of an angel." A little, balding, bandy-legged man, with a hooked nose and shaggy eyebrows—it is not a very impressive picture, and it may well be that the Corinthians made great play with it.

We might do well to remember that not seldom a great spirit has been lodged in a very humble body. William Wilberforce was responsible for the freeing of the slaves in the British Empire. He was so small and so frail that it seemed that even a strong wind might knock him down. But once Boswell heard him speak in public and afterwards said, "I saw what seemed to me a shrimp mount upon the table, but, as I listened, he grew and grew until the shrimp became a whale." The Corinthians had sunk nearly to the ultimate depths of discourtesy and of unwisdom when they taunted Paul upon his personal appearance.

(iii) It seems that they accused Paul of making boastful claims to authority in a sphere in which his writ did not run. No doubt they said that he might try to play the master in other Churches, but not in Corinth. His blunt answer is that Corinth is well within his sphere for he was the first man to bring them the good news of Jesus Christ. Paul was a Rabbi and it may be that he was thinking of a claim that the Rabbis often used to make. They claimed and received a very special respect. They claimed that respect for a teacher should exceed respect for a parent, for, they said, a parent brings a child into the life of this world, but a teacher brings a scholar into the life of the world to come. Surely no man had a greater claim to exercise authority in the Church of Corinth than the man who, under God, had been its founder.

(iv) Then Paul levels a charge at them. Ironically he says that he would never dream of comparing himself with those who are forever giving themselves testimonials, and then, with unerring precision, he puts his finger on the spot. They can give themselves testimonials only because their one standard of measurement is themselves and their one standard of comparison is with one another.

They had, as so many people have, the wrong standard of measurement. A girl may think herself a good pianist but let her go and compare herself with Solomon or Moiseiwitsch and she may change her mind. A man may think himself a good golfer but let him compare himself with Cotton or Hogan or Palmer or Nicklaus and he may change his mind. A man may think himself a good preacher but let him compare himself with one of the princes of the pulpit and he may feel that he never wishes to open his mouth in public again.

It is easy enough to say, "I am as good as the next man," and no doubt it is true. But the point is, are we as good as Jesus Christ? He is our true rod of measurement and our proper standard of comparison and when we measure ourselves by him there is no room left for pride. "Self-praise," says Paul, "is no honour." It is not his own but Christ's "Well done!" for which a man must seek.

Before we leave this passage we must look at a phrase which is characteristic of Paul's heart. He wishes to get things straightened out at Corinth because he longs to go on to *the regions beyond,* where no man has yet carried the story of Christ. W. M. Macgregor used to say that Paul was haunted by the regions beyond. He never saw a ship riding at anchor or moored to the quay but he wished to board her and carry the good news to the regions beyond. He never saw a range of hills blue in the distance but he wished to cross it and to carry the story of Christ to the regions beyond.

Kipling has a poem called "The Explorer" which tells the story of another man who was haunted by the regions beyond.

> " 'There's no sense in going further—it's the edge of
>   cultivation,'
>   So they said, and I believed it—broke my land and
>   sowed my crop—
>   Built my barns and strung my fences in the little
>   border station

> Tucked away below the foothills where the trails run
> out and stop.
>
> Till a voice, as bad as Conscience, rang interminable
> changes
> On one everlasting Whisper, day and night repeated—
> so:
> 'Something hidden. Go and find it. Go and look
> behind the ranges—
> Something lost behind the ranges. Lost and waiting
> for you. Go!'"

That is precisely how Paul felt. It was said of a great
evangelist that, as he walked the city streets, he was haunted
by the tramp, tramp, tramp of the Christless millions. The
man who loves Christ will always be haunted by the thought
of the millions who have never known the Christ who means
so much to him.

THE PERIL OF SEDUCTION

2 Corinthians 11: 1-6

> Would that you would bear with me in a little foolishness—but I
> know that you do bear with me. I am jealous for you with the
> jealousy of God, for I betrothed you to one husband, I wished to
> present a pure maiden to Christ. But I am afraid, that, as the
> serpent deceived Eve by his craftiness, your thoughts may be cor-
> rupted from the simplicity and the purity which look to Christ. For
> if he who comes preaches another Jesus, a Jesus whom we did not
> preach, if you take a different spirit, a spirit which you did not
> take, if you receive a different gospel, a gospel which you did not
> receive, you bear it excellently! Well, I reckon that I am in nothing
> inferior to these super-apostles. I may be quite untrained in speaking,
> but I am not untrained in knowledge, but, in fact, in everything and
> in all things we made the knowledge of God clear to you.

ALL through this section Paul has to adopt methods which
are completely distasteful to him. He has to stress his own
authority, to boast about himself and to keep comparing

himself with those who are seeking to seduce the Corinthian Church; and he does not like it. He apologizes every time he has to speak in such a way, for he was not a man to stand on his dignity. It was said of a great man, "He never remembered his dignity until others forgot it." But Paul knew that it was not really his dignity and honour that were at stake, but the dignity and the honour of Jesus Christ.

He begins by using a vivid picture from Jewish marriage customs. The idea of Israel as the bride of God is common in the Old Testament. "Your Maker," said Isaiah, "is your husband." (*Isaiah* 54: 5). "As the bridegroom rejoices over the bride, so shall your God rejoice over you." (*Isaiah* 62: 5). So it was natural for Paul to use the metaphor of marriage and to think of the Corinthian Church as the bride of Christ.

At a Jewish wedding there were two people called the friends of the bridegroom, one representing the bridegroom and one the bride. They had many duties. They acted as liaisons between the bride and the bridegroom; they carried the invitations to the guests; but they had one particular responsibility, that of guaranteeing the chastity of the bride. That is what is in Paul's thought here. In the marriage of Jesus Christ and the Corinthian Church he is the friend of the bridegroom. It is his responsibility to guarantee the chastity of the bride, and he will do all he can to keep the Corinthian Church pure and a fit bride for Jesus Christ.

There was a Jewish legend current in Paul's time that, in the Garden of Eden, Satan had actually seduced Eve and that Cain was the child of their union. Paul is thinking of that old legend when he fears that the Corinthian Church is being seduced from Christ.

It is clear that there were in Corinth men who were preaching their own version of Christianity and insisting that it was superior to Paul's. It is equally clear that they regarded themselves as very special people—super-apostles, Paul calls them. Ironically Paul says that the Corinthians listen splendidly to them. If they give them such an excellent hearing will they not listen to him?

Then he draws the contrast between these false apostles and himself. He is quite untrained in speaking. The word he uses is *idiotes*. This word began by meaning a private individual who took no part in public life. It went on to mean someone with no technical training, what we would call a *layman*. Paul says that these false but arrogant apostles may be far better equipped orators than he is; they may be the professionals and he the mere amateur in words; they may be the men with the academic qualifications and he the mere layman. But the fact remains, however unskilled he may be in technical oratory, he knows what he is talking about and they do not.

There is a famous story which tells how a company of people were dining together. After dinner it was agreed that each should recite something. A well-known actor rose and, with all the resources of elocution and dramatic art, he declaimed the twenty-third psalm and sat down to tremendous applause. A quiet man followed him. He too began to recite the twenty-third psalm and at first there was rather a titter. But before he had ended there was a stillness that was more eloquent than any applause. When he had spoken the last words there was silence, and then the actor leant across and said, "Sir, I know the psalm, *but you know the shepherd.*"

Paul's opponents might have all the resources of oratory and he might be unskilled in speech; but he knew what he was talking about because he knew the real Christ.

MASQUERADING AS CHRISTIANS

2 Corinthians 11: 7–15

Or did I commit a sin in humbling myself so that you should be exalted, because I preached the gospel of God to you for nothing? I plundered other Churches and took pay from them in order to render service to you. And when I was present with you and when I had been reduced to want I did not squeeze charity out of any man. The brothers who came from Macedonia again supplied my want. In everything I watched that I should not be a burden on you, and I will go on doing so. As Christ's truth is in me, as far as I am concerned this boast will not be silenced in the regions of Achaea. Why? Because I do not love you? God knows I love you. But I do this and I will continue to do it, in order to eliminate the opportunity of those who wish an opportunity to prove themselves the same as we are—and to boast about it. Such men are false apostles. They are crafty workers. They masquerade as apostles of Christ. And no wonder! For Satan himself masquerades as an angel of light. It is then no great wonder if his servants too masquerade as servants of righteousness. Their end will be what their deeds deserve.

HERE again Paul is meeting a charge that has been levelled against him. This time the charge is clear. It was rankling in the minds of the Corinthian Church that Paul had refused to accept any support from them whatsoever. When he was in want it was the Philippian Church who had supplied his needs (cp. *Philippians* 4: 10–18).

Before we go further with this passage, we must ask, how could Paul maintain this attitude of utter independence with regard to the Corinthian Church and yet accept gifts from the Philippian Church? He was not being inconsistent and the reason was a very practical and excellent one. As far as we know, Paul never accepted a gift from the Church at Philippi *when he was in Philippi*. He did so only after he had moved on. The reason is clear. So long as he was in any given place he had to be utterly independent, under obligation to no man. It is hardly possible to accept a man's bounty and then condemn him or preach against him. When he was in the middle of the Philippian community Paul could not be beholden to any man. It was different when he had moved on. He was then free to take what the love of the Philippians chose to give, for then it would commit him to no man or party. It would have been impossible for Paul, when in Corinth, to receive Corinthian support and at the same time maintain the independence which the situation demanded. He was not in the least inconsistent; he was only wise.

Why were the Corinthians so annoyed about his refusal? For one thing, according to the Greek way of thinking, it was beneath a free man's dignity to work with his hands. The dignity of honest toil was forgotten, and the Corinthians did not understand Paul's point of view. For another thing, in the Greek world, teachers were supposed to make money out of teaching. There never was an age in which a man who could talk could make so much money. Augustus, the Roman Emperor, paid Verrius Flaccus, the rhetorician, an annual salary of 100,000 sesterces, which, in present day purchasing power was the equivalent of a quarter of a million pounds. Every town was entitled to grant complete exemption from all civic burdens and taxes to a certain number of teachers of rhetoric and literature. Paul's independence was something that the Corinthians could not understand.

As for the false apostles, they, too, made Paul's independence a charge against him. They took support all right, and they claimed that the fact that they took it was a proof that they really were apostles. No doubt they maintained that Paul refused to take anything because his teaching was not worth anything. But in their heart of hearts they were afraid that people would see through them, and they wanted to drag Paul down to their own level of acquisitiveness so that his independence would no longer form a contrast to their greed.

Paul accused them of masquerading as apostles of Christ. The Jewish legend was that Satan had once masqueraded as one of the angels who sang praises to God and that it was then that Eve had seen him and been seduced.

It is still true that many masquerade as Christians, some consciously but still more unconsciously. Their Christianity is a superficial dress in which there is no reality. The Synod of the Church in Uganda drew up the following four tests by which a man may examine himself and test the reality of his Christianity.

(i) Do you know salvation through the Cross of Christ?

(ii) Are you growing in the power of the Holy Spirit, in prayer, meditation and the knowledge of God?

(iii) Is there a great desire to spread the Kingdom of God by example, and by preaching and teaching?

(iv) Are you bringing others to Christ by individual searching, by visiting, and by public witness?

With the conscience of others we have nothing to do, but we can test our own Christianity lest our faith also should be not a reality but a masquerade.

THE CREDENTIALS OF AN APOSTLE

2 Corinthians 11 : 16–33

Again I say, let no one think me a fool. But, even if you do, bear with me, even if it is as a fool that you do bear with me, so that I too may boast a little. I am not saying what I am saying as if talk like this was inspired by the Lord, but I am talking with boastful confidence as in foolishness. Since many boast about their human qualifications I too will boast, for you—because you are sensible people—suffer fools gladly. I know that this is true because you suffer it if someone reduces you to abject slavery, if someone devours you, if someone ensnares you, if someone behaves arrogantly to you, if someone strikes you on the face. It is in dishonour that I speak, because of course we are weak! All the same, if anyone makes daring claims—it is in foolishness I am speaking—I too can make them. Are they Hebrews? So am I. Are they Israelites? So am I. Are they the descendants of Abraham? So am I. Are they servants of Christ? This is madman's raving—I am more so. Here is my record—In toils more exceedingly, in prisons more exceedingly, in stripes beyond measure, in deaths often; at the hands of the Jews five times I have received the forty stripes less one; three times I have been beaten with rods; once I was stoned; three times I have been shipwrecked; a night and a day have I been adrift on the deep. I have lived in journeyings often, in perils of rivers, in perils of brigands, in perils which came from my own countrymen, in perils which came from the Gentiles, in perils in the city, in perils in the wilderness, in perils upon the sea, in perils among false brethren, in labour and toil, in many a sleepless night, in hunger and in thirst, in fastings often, in cold and nakedness. Apart altogether from the things I have omitted, there is the strain that is on me every day, my anxiety for all the Churches. Is there anyone's weakness which I do not share? Is there anyone who stumbles and I do not burn with shame? If I must boast, I will boast of the things of my weakness. The God and Father of our Lord Jesus Christ, he who is blessed forever, knows that I do not lie. In Damascus, Aretas, the king's governor, set a guard upon the city of the Damascenes to arrest me, and I was let down in a basket through an opening through the wall, and escaped out of his hands.

ALL against his will Paul is forced to produce his credentials as an apostle. He feels that the whole thing is folly, and, when it comes to comparing himself with other people, it seems to him like madness. Nevertheless, not for his own sake, but for the sake of the gospel that he preaches, it has to be done.

It is clear that his opponents were Jewish teachers who claimed to have a gospel and an authority far beyond his. He sketches them in a few lightning strokes, when he speaks about what the Corinthians are willing to endure at their hands. *They reduce the Corinthians to abject slavery.* This they do by trying to persuade them to submit to circumcision and the thousand and one petty rules and regulations of the Jewish law, and so to abandon the glorious liberty of the gospel of grace. *They devour them.* The Jewish rabbis at their worst could be shamelessly rapacious. Theoretically they held that a rabbi must take no money for teaching and must win his bread by the work of his hands, but they also taught that it was work of exceptional merit to support a rabbi and that he who did so made sure of a place in the heavenly academy. *They behaved arrogantly.* They lorded it over the Corinthians. In point of fact the rabbis demanded a respect greater than that given to parents, and actually claimed that, if a man's father and teacher were both captured by brigands, he must ransom his teacher first, and only then his father. *They struck them on the face.* This may describe insulting behaviour, or it may well be meant quite literally (cp. *Acts* 23: 2). The

Corinthians had come to the curious stage of seeing in the very insolence of the Jewish teachers a guarantee of their apostolic authority.

The false teachers have made three claims which Paul asserts that he can equal.

They claim to be *Hebrews*. This word was specially used of the Jews who still remembered and spoke their ancient Hebrew language in its Aramaic form, which was its form in the time of Paul. There were Jews scattered all over the world, for instance there were one million of them in Alexandria. Many of these Jews of the dispersion had forgotten their native tongue and spoke Greek; and the Jews of Palestine, who had preserved their native tongue, always looked down on them. Quite likely Paul's opponents had been saying, "This Paul is a citizen of Tarsus. He is not like us a pure-bred Palestinian but one of these Greekling Jews." Paul says, "No! I too am one who has never forgotten the purity of his ancestral tongue." They could not claim superiority on that score.

They claim to be *Israelites*. The word described a Jew as a man who was *a member of God's chosen people*. The basic sentence of the Jewish creed, the sentence with which every synagogue service opens, runs, "Hear, *O Israel,* the Lord our God is one Lord" (*Deuteronomy* 6: 4). No doubt these hostile Jews were saying, "This Paul never lived in Palestine. He has slipped away out of the chosen people, living in Greek surroundings in Cilicia." Paul says, "No! I am as pure an Israelite as any man. My lineage is the lineage of the people of God." They cannot claim superiority on that point.

They claim to be *descendants of Abraham*. By that they meant that they were Abraham's direct descendants and therefore heirs to the great promise that God had made to him (*Genesis* 12: 1–3). No doubt they claimed that this Paul was not of as pure descent as they. "No!" says Paul. "I am of as pure descent as any man" (*Philippians* 3: 5, 6). They had no claim to superiority here either.

Then Paul sets out his credentials as an apostle, and the

only claim he would put forward is the catalogue of his sufferings for Christ. When Mr. Valiant-for-truth was "taken with a summons" and knew that he must go to God, he said, "I am going to my Father's; and though with great difficulty I am got hither yet now I do not repent me of all the trouble I have been at to arrive where I am. My sword I give to him that shall succeed me in my pilgrimage, and my courage and skill to him that can get it. My marks and scars I carry with me, to be a witness for me, that I have fought his battles who will now be my rewarder." Like Mr. Valiant-for-truth, Paul found his only credentials in his scars.

When we read the catalogue of all that Paul had endured, the one thing that must strike us is how little we know about him. When he wrote this letter, he was in Ephesus. That is to say we have reached only as far as chapter 19 in the book of Acts; and if we try to check this catalogue of endurance against the narrative of that book, we find that not one quarter of it is there. We see that Paul was an even greater man than perhaps we thought, for Acts merely skims the surface of what he did and endured.

Out of this long catalogue we can take only three items.

(i) "Three times," says Paul, "I have been beaten with rods." This was a Roman punishment. The attendants of the magistrates were called the *lictors* and they were equipped with rods of birch wood with which the guilty criminal was chastised. Three times that had happened to Paul. It should never have happened to him at all, because, under Roman law, it was a crime to scourge a Roman citizen. But, when the mob was violent and the magistrate was weak, Paul, Roman citizen though he was, had suffered this.

(ii) "Five times," says Paul, "I received the forty stripes less one." This was a Jewish punishment. The Jewish law lays down the regulations for such scourging (*Deuteronomy* 25: 1–3). The normal penalty was forty stripes, and on no account must that number be exceeded, or the scourger himself was subject to scourging. Therefore they always stopped at thirty-nine. That is why scourging was known as "the forty less one."

The detailed regulations for scourging are in the Mishnah, which is the book in which the Jewish traditional law was codified. "They bind his two hands to a pillar on either side, and the minister of the synagogue lays hold on his garments—if they are torn, they are torn, if they are utterly rent, they are utterly rent—so that he bares his chest. A stone is set behind him on which the minister of the synagogue stands with a strap of calf-hide in his hand, doubled and re-doubled, and two other straps that rise and fall thereto. The handpiece of the strap is one handbreadth long and one handbreadth wide, and its end must reach to his navel (i.e. when the victim is struck on the shoulder the end of the strap must reach the navel). He gives him one third of the stripes in front and two thirds behind, and he may not strike him when he is standing or when he is sitting but only when he is bending down . . . and he that smites smites with one hand and with all his might. If he dies under his hand, the scourger is not culpable. But if he gives him one stripe too many, and he dies, he must escape into exile because of him." That is what Paul suffered *five times*, a scourging so severe that it was liable to kill a man.

(iii) Again and again Paul speaks of the dangers of his travels. It is true that in his time the roads and the sea were safer than they had ever been, but they were still dangerous. On the whole, the ancient peoples did not relish the sea. "How pleasant it is," says Lucretius, "to stand on the shore and watch the poor devils of sailors having a rough time." Seneca writes to a friend, "You can persuade me into almost anything now for I was recently persuaded to travel by sea." Men regarded a sea voyage as taking one's life in one's hands. As for the roads, the brigands were still here. "A man," says Epictetus, "has heard that the road is infested by robbers. He does not dare to venture on it alone, but waits for company—a legate, or a quaestor, or a proconsul—and joining him he passes safely on the road." But there would be no official company for Paul. "Think," said Seneca, "any day a robber might cut your throat." It was the commonest thing for a traveller to be caught and held to ransom. If ever a man was an adventurous soul, that man was Paul.

In addition to all this there was *his anxiety for all the Churches*. This includes the burden of the daily administration of the Christian communities; but it means more than that. Myers in his poem, *St. Paul,* makes Paul speak of,

"Desperate tides of the whole great world's anguish
Forced thro' the channels of a single heart."

Paul bore the sorrows and the troubles of his people on his heart.

This passage comes to a strange ending. On the face of it, it would seem that the escape from Damascus was an anticlimax. The incident is referred to in *Acts* 9: 23–25. The wall of Damascus was wide enough to drive a carriage along it. Many of the houses overhung it and it must have been from one of these that Paul was let down. Why does he so directly and definitely mention this incident? It is most likely because it rankled. Paul was the kind of man who would find this clandestine exit from Damascus worse than a scourging. He must have hated with all his great heart to run away as a fugitive in the night. His bitterest humiliation was to fail to look his enemies in the face.

THE THORN AND THE GRACE

2 Corinthians 12: 1–10

> I must continue to boast. It is not good for me to do so, all the same I will come to visions and revelations given to me by the Lord. I know a man in Christ, who, fourteen years ago—whether it was in the body I do not know; whether it was out of the body I do not know; God knows—was caught up to the third heaven. And I know that this man about whom I am speaking—whether it was with the body or without the body, I do not know; God knows—was caught up to Paradise and heard words which can never be uttered, which it is not lawful for a man to speak. It is about such a man that I will boast. About myself I will not

boast, for, if I wish to boast, I will not be such a fool, for I will speak the truth. But I forbear to boast in case anyone forms a judgment about me beyond what he sees in me and hears from me. And because of the surpassing nature of the revelation granted to me—the reason was that I might not become exalted with pride—there was given to me a stake in the flesh, a messenger of Satan to buffet me, that I might not be exalted with pride. Three times I prayed urgently to the Lord about this, beseeching him that it might depart from me. And he said to me, "My grace is enough for you, for power is perfected in weakness." So it is with the greatest gladness that I boast in my weaknesses so that the power of Christ may pitch its tent upon me. Therefore I rejoice in weaknesses, in insults, in inescapable things, in persecutions, in straitened circumstances, for whenever I am weak, then I am strong.

IF we have any sensitiveness, we should read this passage with a certain reverence, for in it Paul lays bare his heart and shows us at one and the same time his glory and his pain.

All against his will he is still setting out his credentials, and he tells of an experience at which we can only wonder and which we cannot even try to probe. In the strangest way he seems to stand outside himself and look at himself. "I know a man," he says. The man is himself and yet Paul can look at the man who had this amazing experience with a kind of wondering detachment. For the mystic, the great aim of all religious experience is the vision of God and union with him.

The mystic always has aimed at that moment of wonder when "the seer and the Seen are one." In their traditions the Jews said that four rabbis had had this vision of God. Ben Azai had seen the glory and had died. Ben Soma beheld it and went mad. Acher saw it and "cut up the young plants," that is, in spite of the vision he became a heretic and ruined the garden of truth. Akiba alone ascended in peace and in peace came back. We cannot even guess what happened to Paul. We need not form theories about the number of heavens because of the fact that he speaks of the third heaven. He simply means that his spirit rose to an unsurpassable ecstasy in its nearness to God.

One lovely thing we may note, for it will help a little. The word *Paradise* comes from a Persian word which means *a walled-garden*. When a Persian king wished to confer a very special honour on someone specially dear to him, he made him *a companion of the garden* and gave him the right to walk in the royal gardens with him in intimate companionship. In this experience, as never before and never again, Paul had been the companion of God.

After the glory came the pain. The Authorised Version and the Revised Standard Versions speak of *the thorn* in the flesh. The word (*skolops*) can mean thorn but more likely it means *stake*. Sometimes criminals were impaled upon a sharp stake. It was a stake like that that Paul felt was twisting in his body. What was it? Many answers have been given. First we look at those which great men have held but which, in face of the evidence, we must discard.

(i) The thorn has been taken to mean *spiritual temptations;* the temptation to doubt and to shirk the duties of the apostolic life, and the sting of conscience when temptation conquered. That was Calvin's view.

(ii) It has been taken to mean *the opposition and persecution* which he had to face, the constant battle with those who tried to undo his work. That was Luther's view.

(iii) It has been taken to mean *carnal temptations*. When the monks and the hermits shut themselves up in their monasteries and their cells they found that the last instinct that could be tamed was that of sex. They wished to eliminate it but it haunted them. They held that Paul was like that; and this is the common Roman Catholic view to this day.

None of these solutions can be right, for three reasons. (*a*) The very word "stake" indicates an almost savage pain. (*b*) The whole picture before us is one of physical suffering. (*c*) Whatever the thorn was, it was intermittent, for, although it sometimes prostrated Paul, it never kept him wholly from his work. So then let us look at the other suggestions.

(iv) It has been suggested that the thorn was Paul's *physical appearance*. "His bodily presence is weak" (2 *Corinthians* 10:

10). It has been suggested that he suffered from some disfigurement which made him ugly and hindered his work. But that does not account for the sheer pain that must have been there.

(v) One of the commonest solutions is *epilepsy*. It is painful and recurrent, and between attacks the sufferer can go about his business. It produced visions and trances such as Paul experienced. It can be repellent; in the ancient world it was attributed to demons. In the ancient world when people saw an epileptic they spat to ward off the evil demon. In *Galatians* 4: 14 Paul says that when the Galatians saw his infirmity they did not *reject* him. The Greek word literally means *you did not spit at me*. But this theory has consequences which are hard to accept. It would mean that Paul's visions were epileptic trances, and it is hard to believe that the visions which changed the world were due to epileptic attacks.

(vi) The oldest of all theories is that Paul suffered from *severe and prostrating headaches*. Both Tertullian and Jerome believed that.

(vii) That may well lead us to the truth, for still another theory is that Paul suffered from *eye trouble* and this would explain the headaches. After the glory on the Damascus Road passed, he was blind (*Acts* 9: 9). It may be that his eyes never recovered again. Paul said of the Galatians that they would have plucked out their eyes and would have given them to him (*Galatians* 4: 15). At the end of Galatians he writes, "See in what large letters I am writing to you" (*Galatians* 6: 11), as if he was describing the great sprawling characters of a man who could hardly see.

(viii) By far the most likely thing is that Paul suffered from chronically recurrent attacks of a certain virulent malarial fever which haunted the coasts of the eastern Mediterranean. The natives of the country, when they wished to harm an enemy, prayed to their gods that he should be "burnt up" with this fever. One who has suffered from it describes the headache that accompanies it as being like "a red-hot bar thrust through the forehead." Another speaks of "the grinding, boring pain in one temple, like the dentist's drill—the phantom wedge driven in between the jaws," and says that when the thing became acute it "reached the extreme point of human endurance." That in truth deserves the description of a thorn in the flesh, and even of a stake in the flesh. The man who endured so many other sufferings had this agony to contend with all the time.

Paul prayed that it might be taken from him, but God answered that prayer as he answers so many prayers—he did not take the thing away but gave Paul strength to bear it. That is how God works. He does not spare us things, but makes us able to conquer them.

To Paul came the promise and the reality of the all-sufficient grace. Now let us see from his life some few of the things for which that grace was sufficient.

(i) It was sufficient for *physical weariness*. It made him able to go on. John Wesley preached 42,000 sermons. He averaged 4,500 miles a year. He rode 60 to 70 miles a day and preached three sermons a day on an average. When he was 83 he wrote in his diary, "I am a wonder to myself. I am never tired, either with preaching, writing, or travelling." That was the work of the all-sufficient grace.

(ii) It was sufficient for *physical pain*. It made him able to bear the cruel stake. Once a man went to visit a girl who was in bed dying of an incurable and a most painful disease. He took with him a little book of cheer for those in trouble, a sunny book, a happy book, a laughing book. "Thank you very much," she said, "but I know this book." "Have you read it already?" asked the visitor. The girl answered, "*I wrote it.*" That was the work of the all-sufficient grace.

(iii) It was sufficient for *opposition*. All his life Paul was up against it and all his life he never gave in. No amount of opposition could break him or make him turn back. That was the work of the all-sufficient grace.

(iv) It made him able, as all this letter shows, to face *slander*. There is nothing so hard to face as misinterpretation and cruel misjudgment. Once a man flung a pail of water over Archelaus the Macedonian. He said nothing at all. And when a friend asked him how he could bear it so serenely, he said, "He threw the water not on me, but on the man he thought I was." The all-sufficient grace made Paul care not what men thought him to be but what God knew him to be.

It is the glory of the gospel that in our weakness we may find this wondrous grace, for always man's extremity is God's opportunity.

THE DEFENCE DRAWS TO AN END

2 Corinthians 12: 11–18

> I have become a fool—you forced me to it. I ought to have been commended by you, not by myself. I am in no way inferior to the super-apostles, even if I am nothing. The signs of an apostle have been wrought among you in all endurance, with signs and wonders and deeds of power. In what have you been surpassed by the rest of the churches, except that I have not squeezed charity out of you? Forgive me for this sin. Look you! I am ready to come to you for the third time, and I still will take no charity from you. It is not your money I want, it is you. Children should not have to accumulate money for their parents, but parents for children. Most gladly I will spend and be spent to the uttermost for your lives. If I love you to excess, am I to be loved the less for that? But, suppose you say that I myself was not a burden to you, but that, because I was a crafty character, I snared you by guile. Of those I sent to you, did I through any of them take advantage of you? I exhorted Titus to go to you, and with him I despatched our brother. Did Titus take any advantage of you? Did we not walk in the same spirit? In the same steps?

THIS passage, in which Paul is coming near to the end of his defence, reads like the words of a man who has put out some tremendous effort and is now weary. It almost seems that Paul is limp with the effort that he has made.

Once again he speaks with distaste of this whole wretched business of self-justification; but the thing has got to be gone through. That he should be discredited might be a small thing, but that his gospel should be rendered ineffective is something that cannot be allowed.

(i) First of all, he claims that he is every bit as good an apostle as his opponents with their claims to be super-apostles. And his claim is based on one thing—*the effectiveness of his ministry*. When John the Baptist sent his messengers to ask Jesus if he really was the promised one or if they must look for another, Jesus's answer was, "Go back and tell John what is happening" (*Luke* 7: 18–22). When Paul wants to guarantee the reality of the gospel which he preached in Corinth, he makes a list of sins and sinners and then adds the flashing sentence, "And such were some of you" (1 *Corinthians* 6: 9–11). Once Dr. Chalmers was congratulated on a great speech to a crowded assembly. "Yes," he said, "*but what did it do?*" Effectiveness is the proof of reality. The reality of a Church is not seen in the splendour of its buildings or the elaborateness of its worship or the wealth of its givings or even the size of its congregations; it is seen in *changed lives,* and, if there are no changed lives, the essential element of reality is missing. The one standard by which Paul would have his apostleship judged was its ability to bring the life-changing grace of Jesus Christ to men.

(ii) It must have sorely rankled with the Corinthians that Paul would accept nothing from them, for again and again he returns to that charge. Here he lays down again one of the supreme principles of Christian giving. "It is not your money I want," he says, "it is *you*." The giving which does not give itself is always a poor thing. There are debts that we can discharge by paying money, but there are others in which money is the least of it.

H. L. Gee somewhere tells of a tramp who came begging to a good woman's door. She went to get something to give him and found that she had no change in the house. She went to him and said, "I have not a penny of small change. I need a loaf of bread. Here is a pound note. Go and buy the loaf and bring me back the change and I will give you something." The man executed the commission and returned and she gave him a small coin. He took it with tears in his eyes. "It's not the money," he said, "it's the way you trusted me. No one ever trusted me like that before, and I can't thank you enough." It is easy to say that the woman took a risk that only a soft-hearted fool would take, but she had given that man more than money, she had given him something of herself by giving her trust.

Turgeniev tells how one day he was stopped on the street by a beggar. He felt in his pocket; he had absolutely no money with him. Impulsively he stretched out his hand, "My brother," he said, "I can give you nothing but this." The beggar said, "You called me brother; you took my hand; that too is a gift." The comfortable way to discharge one's duty to the Church, to the charities which help our fellow men, to the poor and the needy, is to give a sum of money and have done with it. It is not nothing, but it is far from everything, for in all true giving the giver must give not only his substance but himself.

(iii) It seems that the Corinthians had had one last charge against Paul. They could not say that he had ever taken any advantage of them; not even their malignancy could find any grounds for that. But they seem to have hinted that quite possibly some of the money collected for the poor of Jerusalem had stuck to the fingers of Titus and of Paul's other emissary and that Paul had got his share that way. The really malicious mind will stick at nothing to find a ground of criticism. Paul's loyalty to his friends leaps to defend them. It is not always safe to be the friend of a great man; It is easy to become involved in his troubles. Happy is the man who has supporters whom he can trust as he would trust his own soul. Paul had followers like that. Christ needs them, too.

THE MARKS OF AN UNCHRISTIAN CHURCH

2 *Corinthians* 12: 19–21

You have been thinking for a long time that it is to you that we have been making our defence. It is before God, in Christ, that we speak. All that we have said, beloved, is for your upbuilding, for I am afraid, in case, when I come, I may find you not such as I wish that you should be, and that I should be found by you not such as you wish me to be. I am afraid that, when I come, there may be amongst you strife, envy, outbursts of anger, the factious spirit, slanderings, whisperings, all kinds of conceit and disorder. I am afraid that, when I come, God may humiliate me again in your presence and that I may have to mourn for many of those who sinned before and who have not repented of the impurity and fornication and uncleanness which they committed.

As he comes near the end of his defence one thing strikes Paul. All this citing of his qualifications and all this self apology may look as if he cared a great deal for what men thought of him. Nothing could be further from the truth. So long as Paul knew himself to be right with God, he did not greatly care what men thought, and what he has said must not be misconstrued as an attempt to win their approval. On one occasion Abraham Lincoln and his counsellors had taken an important decision. One of the counsellors said, "Well, Mr. President, I hope that God is on our side." Lincoln answered, "What I am worried about is, not if God is on our side, but if we are on God's side." Paul's supreme aim was to stand right with God no matter what men thought or said.

So he moves on to the visit which he intends to pay to Corinth. Rather grimly he says that he hopes that he will not find them as he would not wish them to be, for, if that happens, they will assuredly find him what they would not wish him to be. There is a certain threat there. He does not want to take stern measures, but, if necessary, he will not shrink from them. Then Paul goes on to list what might be called the marks of the unchristian Church.

There is *strife* (*eris*). This is a word of battles. It denotes rivalry and competition, discord about place and prestige. It is the characteristic of the man who has forgotten that only he who humbles himself can be exalted.

There is *envy* (*zelos*). This is a great word which has come down in the world. Originally it described a great emotion, that of the man who sees a fine life or a fine action and is moved to emulation. But emulation can so easily become envy, the desire to have what is not ours to have, the spirit which grudges others the possession of anything denied to us. Emulation in fine things is a noble quality; but envy is the characteristic of a mean and little mind.

There are *outbursts of anger* (*thumoi*). This does not denote a settled and prolonged wrath. It denotes sudden explosions of passionate anger. It is the kind of anger which Basil described as *the intoxication of the soul,* that sweeps a man into doing things for which afterwards he is bitterly sorry. The ancients said themselves that such outbursts were more characteristic of beasts than men. The beast cannot control itself; man ought to be able to do so; and when passion runs away with him he is more kin to the unreasoning and undisciplined beast than he is to thinking man.

There is *the factious spirit* (*eritheia*). Originally this word simply described *work which is done for pay,* the work of the day labourer. It went on to describe the work which is done for no other motives than for pay. It describes that utterly selfish and self-centred ambition which has no idea of service and which is in everything for what it can get out of it for itself.

There are *slanderings* and *whisperings* (*katalaliai* and *psithurismoi*). The first word describes the open, loud-mouthed attack, the insults flung out in public, the public vilification of some person whose views are different. The second is a much nastier word. It describes the whispering campaign of malicious gossip, the slanderous story murmured in someone's ear, the discreditable tale passed on as a spicy secret. With the first kind of slander a man can at least deal because it is a frontal attack. With the second kind he is often helpless to deal because it is an underground movement which will not face him, and an insidious poisoning of the atmosphere whose source he cannot attack because he does not know it.

There is *conceit* (*phusioseis*). Within the Church a man

should certainly magnify his office, but, equally certainly, he should never magnify himself. When men see our good deeds, it is not we whom they should glorify but the Father in heaven whom we serve and who has enabled us to do them. There is *disorder* (*akatastasiai*). This is the word for tumults, disorders, anarchy. There is one danger which ever besets a Church. A Church is a democracy, but it may become a democracy run mad. A democracy is not a place where every man has a right to do what he likes; it is a place where people enter into a fellowship in which the watchword is not independent isolation but interdependent togetherness.

Finally there are the sins of which even yet some of the recalcitrant Corinthians may not have repented. There is *uncleanness* (*akatharsia*). The word means everything which would unfit a man to enter into God's presence. It describes the life muddied with wallowing in the world's ways. Kipling prayed,

> "Teach us to rule ourselves alway,
> Controlled and cleanly night and day."

Akatharsia is the very opposite of that clean purity.

There is *fornication* (*porneia*). The Corinthians lived in a society which did not regard adultery as a sin and expected a man to take his pleasures where he could. It was so easy to be infected and to relapse into what appealed so much to the lower side of human nature. They must lay hold on that hope which can,

> "Purge the soul from sense and sin,
> As Christ himself is pure."

There was *uncleanness* (*aselgeia*). Here is an untranslatable word. It does not solely mean sexual uncleanness; it is sheer wanton insolence. As Basil defined it, "It is that attitude of the soul which has never borne and never will bear the pain of discipline." It is the insolence that knows no restraint, that has no sense of the decencies of things, that will dare anything that wanton caprice demands, that is careless of public opinion and its own good name so long as it gets what it wants. Josephus ascribes it to Jezebel who built a temple to Baal in the very city of God itself. The basic Greek sin was *hubris,* and *hubris* is that proud insolence which gives neither God nor man his place. *Aselgeia* is the insolently selfish spirit, which is lost to honour, and which will take what it wants, where it wants, in shameless disregard of God and man.

A WARNING, A WISH, A HOPE AND A BLESSING

2 Corinthians 13

> For the third time I am coming to you. Everything will be established in the mouth of two or three witnesses. To those who have already sinned and to all others I have already said, and I now say, just as I said it when I was with you on my second visit, now I say it while I am absent, that if I come to you again, I will not spare you. I will take decisive action because you are looking for a proof that Christ really is speaking in me, Christ who is not weak where you are concerned, but who is powerful among you. True, he was crucified in weakness, but he is alive by the power of God. Keep testing yourselves to see if you are in the faith. Keep proving yourselves. Or do you not recognize that Jesus Christ is in you—unless in any way you are rejected? But we pray to God that you should do no evil. It is not that we want a chance to prove our authority. What we do want is that you should do the fine thing even if that means that there will be no opportunity for us to prove our authority. For we cannot do anything against the truth, but we must do everything for the truth. For we rejoice when we are weak while you are strong. For this too we pray—your complete perfecting. The reason why I write these things when I am absent is so that when I am present I may not have to deal sternly with you according to the authority which the Lord gave me to use to build up and not to destroy.
>
> Finally, brothers, farewell! Work your way onwards towards perfection. Accept the exhortation we have offered you. Live in agreement with each other. Be at peace. And the God of love and peace will be with you. Greet each other with a holy kiss.
>
> All God's dedicated people send you their greetings.

The grace of our Lord Jesus Christ, and the love of God and the fellowship of the Holy Spirit be with you all.

IN this last chapter of the severe letter Paul finishes with four things.

(i) He finishes with *a warning*. He is coming again to Corinth and this time there will be no more loose talk and reckless statements. Whatever is said will be witnessed and proved once and for all. To put it in our modern idiom, Paul insists that there must be a show down. The ill situation must drag on no longer. He knew that there comes a time when trouble must be faced.

(ii) He finishes with *a wish*. It is his wish that they should do the fine thing. If they do, he will never need to exert his authority, and that will be no disappointment to him but a deep and real joy. Paul never wanted to show his authority for the sake of showing it. Everything he did was to build up and not to destroy. Discipline must always be aimed to lift a man up and not to knock him down.

(iii) He finishes with *a hope*. He has three hopes for the Corinthians. (*a*) He hopes that they will go onwards to perfection. There can be no standing still in the Christian life. The man who is not advancing is slipping back. The Christian is a man who is ever on the way to God, and therefore each day, by the grace of Christ, he must be a little more fit to stand God's scrutiny. (*b*) He hopes that they will listen to the exhortation he has given them. It takes a big man to listen to hard advice. We would often be a great deal better off if we would stop talking about what we want and begin listening to the voices of the wise, and especially to the voice of Jesus Christ. (*c*) He hopes that they will live in agreement and in peace. No congregation can worship the God of peace in the spirit of bitterness. Men must love each other before their love for God has any reality.

(iv) Finally, he finishes with *a blessing*. After the severity, the struggle and the debate, there comes the serenity of the benediction. One of the best ways of making peace with our enemies is to pray for them, for no one can hate a man and pray for him at the same time. And so we leave the troubled story of Paul and the Church of Corinth with the benediction ringing in our ears. The way has been hard, but the last word is peace.

THE DAILY STUDY BIBLE

Published in 17 Volumes

FURTHER READING

1 Corinthians

F. F. Bruce, *1 and 2 Corinthians* (NCB; *E*)
J. Hering, *The First Epistle of Paul to the Corinthians* (translated by A. W. Heathcote and P. J. Allcock)
J. Moffatt, *1 Corinthians* (MC; *E*)
A. Robertson and A. Plummer, *1 Corinthians* (ICC; *G*)

2 Corinthians

F. F. Bruce, *1 and 2 Corinthians* (NCB; *E*)
J. Hering, *The Second Epistle of Paul to the Corinthians* (translated by A. W. Heathcote and P. J. Allcock)
A. Plummer, *2 Corinthians* (ICC; *G*)
R. V. G. Tasker, *The Second Epistle of Paul to the Corinthians* (TC; *E*)

Abbreviations

ICC : International Critical Commentary
MC : Moffatt Commentary
NCB: New Century Bible
TC : Tyndale Commentary

E : English Text
G : Greek Text